OUTDOOR LEADERSHIP

—— The Noble Gift ——

A Practical Guide for Outdoor Leaders

T. Scott Cook, Ph.D.

Deeper Vision Publishers

Outdoor Leadership: The Noble Gift
Copyright © 2007 T. Scott Cook, Ph.D.
Published by Deeper Vision Publishers

All rights reserved. No part of this book may be reproduced (except for inclusion in reviews), disseminated or utilized in any form or by any means, electronic or mechanical, including photocopying, recording, or in any information storage and retrieval system, or the Internet/World Wide Web without written permission from the author or publisher.

This book is intended for a general audience, does not purport to give legal advice and is not intended as a substitute for professional assistance and therefore no individual should undertake the recommendations contained herein without careful study and critical consideration. The author and publisher make no warranties or representation as to the effectiveness of the suggestions contained herein for specific readers and their specific situations. Because no two situations may be the same, and it is recommended to always consult with professionals. The publisher and author disclaim any responsibility for adverse affects resulting directly or indirectly from information contained herein.

For further information, please contact:
taylor.cook@comcast.net

Book design by:
Arbor Books Inc.
www.arborbooks.com

Printed in the United States

Outdoor Leadership: The Noble Gift
T. Scott Cook, Ph.D.

1. Title 2. Author 3. Leadership/Outdoor recreation

Library of Congress Control Number: 2007902227

ISBN 10: 0-9794794-0-1
ISBN 13: 978-0-9794794-0-3

TABLE OF CONTENTS

Acknowledgments ix
Preface–The Making of a Waukabiashi xi
Introduction–Why we need good Leaders. xv

1. **Leadership from within** 1
    a. Personal Core Competencies 3
        i. Respect 3
        ii. Circle. 3
        iii. Sharing 3
        iv. Silence 3
    b. The Leadership practices inventory 4
        i. Challenging the process 4
        ii. Inspiring a shared vision 4
        iii. Enabling others to act 4
        iv. Modeling the way 5
        v. Encouraging the heart 5
        vi. Getting things done. 5
    c. Core competencies for outdoor leaders 6
        i. Organizational skills. 6
        ii. Technical skills. 6
        iii. Environmental philosophy. 7
        iv. Safety sense and Risk management 7
        v. Instructional strategies 7
        vi. Group development. 7
        vii. Decision making 7
        viii. Problem solving 7
        ix. Effective communication 7
        x. Experience based judgment skills. 8
        xi. Leadership ethics 8
        xii. Sharing vision 8

2. **Leadership Style**. 9
    a. Five typical patterns of leadership behavior 11
        i. Telling 11
        ii. Selling 11
        iii. Testing 11
        iv. Consulting. 11
        v. Joining. 11

- b. 3 Styles of leadership ... 11
  - i. Authoritarian ... 12
  - ii. Participative ... 12
  - iii. Delegative ... 12
  - iv. How do we use leadership styles? ... 12
  - v. 30 vital Leadership actions ... 14

3. Working with groups ... 17
- a. The Circle of Group Growth ... 17
  - i. Illumination—East ... 18
  - ii. The Big Winds ... 18
  - iii. Innocence and Trust—South ... 18
  - iv. Gentle Breezes ... 18
  - v. Introspection—West ... 19
  - vi. Harvest Winds ... 19
  - vii. Wisdom—North ... 19
  - viii. Dawn Winds ... 19
- b. Five Stages of Group Development ... 20
  - i. Forming ... 20
  - ii. Storming ... 20
  - iii. Norming ... 21
  - iv. Performing ... 21
  - v. Adjourning ... 21
- c. The seven relationships of expedition behavior ... 22
  - i. Individual to individual ... 22
  - ii. Individual to group ... 23
  - iii. Group to individual ... 23
  - iv. Group to group ... 23
  - v. Individual and group to multiple users ... 23
  - vi. Individual and group to administration agencies ... 24
  - vii. Individual and group to local populace ... 24
  - viii. Expedition behavior—The finer points ... 24

4. Working with Individuals ... 27
- a. Fear ... 32
- b. Screening of participants ... 36

5. Learning Styles ... 45
- a. Learnership ... 45
- b. Traditional views about how people learn ... 48
- c. Cognitive style ... 49
- d. Extraversion ... 49
- e. Introversion ... 49
- f. Sensing ... 50
- g. Intuition ... 50
- h. Thinking ... 50
- i. Feeling ... 51
- j. Judging ... 51
- k. Perceiving ... 51
- l. The Doer ... 52

    m. The Thinker.. 53
    n. The Watcher/Seer 53
    o. The Feeler... 53
    p. The Struggler 53
    q. The Achiever 53

6. Ethics 55
    a. Ethical issues in Outdoor settings... 56
    b. Sample Code of Ethics 59
    c. Ethical Reasoning 60

7. Setting Goals 63
    a. SMART Goals 64
    b. Steps in Setting Goals 67

8. PREPARE to Lead 69
    a. Trip Goals and Objectives (G.O.)... 70
    b. Participants.. 71
    c. Resources 72
    d. Equipment and Clothing 73
    e. Plan 74
    f. Access 75
    g. Rationing 76
    h. Emergency Plan 77
    i. Logistics 81
    j. Leave No Trace 83
    k. Wilderness Education Association 18 point Curriculum 83
    l. Participant Screening 83
    m. Medical Screening. 84
    n. Skill Screening 86

9. Equipment lists 89
    a. Essential gear- Common Sense... 89
    b. The ten Essentials... 89
    c. Ultra light Backpacking Equipment List 91
    d. All Day Hikes.. 91
    e. All Overnight Trips.. 93
    f. Mountain Bike Day Trips.. 99
    g. Multi-day Kayaking and Rafting 100
    h. Overnight Ski or Snowshoe Trips 104
    i. Do-it-Yourself Survival Kit 108

10. Risk Management 111
    a. Definitions 111
    b. Philosophy of Risk Management 113
    c. Liability and Insurance 114
    d. Commercial General Liability.. 116
    e. Types of Liability 116
    f. What to do in the event of an accident 121
    g. Emergency Procedures 124

    h. Policy and Forms Pre Program defense 125
        i. Communication regarding trip, equipment,
           physical demands, nature of risks. Group policies and procedures 126
    i. Outdoor Safety Management 126
    j. Standards and Standards of Care 126
        i. Theory of Accidents. 127
        ii. Environmental Hazards 127
        iii. Human Hazards. 128
    k. Special Concerns about working with Children 131
    l. All Leaders get Old. 132

11. Emergency Readiness **135**
    a. First Aid and Accident Scene Management 135
    b. Wilderness First Aid Kits 136
    c. Prevention, Self Sufficiency and Accident Scene Management 141
    d. Leadership 143
    e. Ten Commandments of Wilderness First Aid Management. 144
    f. Weather 144
    g. Wind Chill 146
    h. Lightning Guidelines 147
    i. General First Aid Procedures 149

12. Experiential Facilitation **159**
    a. Using your Noble Gift 161
    b. Varieties of Facilitation 163
    c. Choosing a Facilitation Style 166

13. Conclusion or a Beginning? **169**

Appendices **177**
    a. Health Forms 177
    b. Accident Forms. 181
    c. Pro-forma: Analysis of activities for risk and safety management 183
    d. Lessons of Leadership from Geese 185
    e. Leadership Secrets from Penguins. 186
    f. Team Building Quotes 188
    g. Big Dog's Leadership Quotes 189
    h. Trends, Change & Future in Outdoor Education 197

Credits and Sources **199**

ACKNOWLEDGEMENTS

This book is dedicated to the scores of people who have helped shape my adventurous attitude. Countless people and various helping hands have assisted me in creating a lifestyle and a career that encourages people to take risks, while staying within limits. Adventure education has become my passion as well as my profession. This group of people at some point believed in the magic of my dreams. I hope you know who you are because you are everything to me.

I would like to thank my Dad Taylor "Chief" Cook for his visions, inspiration and his attitude! I remember as a child looking up above my Dad's desk at a canoe paddle mounted on the wall. It was signed by a lot of people, and it had a map on it. I thought it was pretty cool! What's that? I asked, "That's Old Faithful" he replied. Now definitely intrigued, a paddle enshrined in my house. I had to find out more. This was the paddle my Dad used as a teenager to paddle the Delaware River. The pictures started to form, of a teenager braving the wilds- the image remained clear- I grew up to be like that! Thanks Dad.

My Mom June Cook "Cookie" a leader for thousands and a role model for everyone. She was a gardener of the human spirit and ability. She is missed by all who knew the gentle touch of her compassion, talent and leadership.

I have been lucky to have terrific "in-laws" who have supported, yet worried about some of my exploits. My mother in law Elaine who has served as the editor for this work has helped me complete this dream, thank-you, Ken & Elaine

My life would not be complete without Laura my wife in it. She is amazing and truly understands me and my need to play hard. She never questions me and often encourages me to go out and paddle for the day. Laura, I love you with every seed in the wind, and with every drop of rain. Together we make life beautiful.

To Aubrey my Daughter, my paddling, climbing and cycling partner. I have enjoyed watching you grow up in my circle of friends and experience the value of purposeful play. You are amazing in all respects of human personality and ability.

To all the circle members and Waukabiashi. Thanks for sharing the dream and walking with the vision. The challenge remains, we all must make a difference.

This book is intended to serve as a source, so that you too, may find the inner peace and tranquility that nature has to offer. But you must look for it. Perhaps in a small way this book can help you look deeper within yourself and deeper within our world.

Using this book (or any other) cannot complete any picture. Important if not vital, are the components of each experience. Please make sure you are prepared. Hopefully this book will help you prepare to lead others as you develop your "Noble Gift."

As you lead, please remember to walk with respect, paddle with perspective and love the life that surrounds you with each step or each stroke you take!

Respectfully,
T. Scott Cook, Ph.D.—The builder of Castles.

PREFACE

THE MAKING OF A WAUKABIASHI

Photo By Ryan Crockett

It was the summer of 1975. After attending a summer camp for most of my childhood, watching my parents as the camp directors and my sister as a counselor, it was finally going to be my turn, "I'd finally have my own group." Was it my destiny to lead these six and seven year olds to greatness? Not likely! I was 18 and I barely knew how to balance a checkbook.

I showed up for the staff training with my long hair and faded jeans. Greeted by the rest of the staff, I did not know then that these people would soon become my dearest and most trusted friends. I was introduced to the young man who would be my Junior Counselor. His name was Reginald Sanders a newcomer from the city! We hit it off, and started to come up with some crazy ideas on what we could do with our little munchkins. The idea of failure never entered into our young minds. We hit the woods on Monday morning with our six and seven year old boys in tow. Never looking back, we bushwhacked, hiked, played games, swam in streams, and then dammed those streams, to create a bigger swimming area. When it was time to go home those kids were dirty and dog-tired. The parents loved it! Reggie and I looked at each other and collapsed. In that moment we knew, we were an unstoppable team.

TAYLOR SCOTT COOK, PH.D.

The summer progressed I was training for an Appalachian Trail hike after camp. We did some serious trekking with those little men. The rest of the camp took notice when we failed to show up for our scheduled activities, sometimes even missing our free swim! We were just too busy having fun to stop and do something else. It became apparent to the parents, staff and kids that the Reg and Scott combo was a winning mix. That summer we did so many things and shared so many memories, we look back now and laugh. The kids we had that first summer still stay in touch with us.

Our groups for the next four years together were known simply as the "Waukabiashi Men." A name made up by one of our campers. Like our first summer together, Reggie and I always had the best group in camp. The kids loved what we did. We loved what we did! We were leaders and we got paid for having fun and bringing kids along with us. As the campers got older, they asked what about next year? What are we going to do? Reggie and I would ask to be moved up to the next age level, and we would have our Waukabiashi Men back for another summer of adventures in the camp woods. I was now in school majoring in Recreation and Environmental Leadership, a career goal, made that first summer. My ideas grew as my ability to plan grew. Soon we were canoeing, rock climbing, backpacking and doing other things the camp had never thought of doing, and we did those activities with kids maybe 10—11 years old by now. My Waukabiashi Men were in a quandary, because camp stopped serving kids at age 11. "What now"? They would ask. I went to the Camp Director and begged him to let me start a wilderness group. I had to promise that it would pay for itself the first summer. I made the promise, because the idea of failure was never in my young mind.

That first summer for the new wilderness group, all of our original Waukabiashi's came back. We did amazing things. In the following two years this group became the largest part of camp. Reggie and I worked together until I was asked to become the Camp Director. I was now finishing my undergraduate degree in Outdoor & Adventure Education so I was ready. It was hard not to be with Reggie daily, as I watched him become a legend in the Waukabiashi Woods. My pride in my campers grew as I watched those I loved grow into respected and talented leaders in their own right.

How did these two young leaders pull this off? Simple. Leadership! As you read in following chapters you will see we had it, that and a burning desire to share our vision! We were also lucky to have leadership above us who allowed us to think outside the box (thanks Dad). We know our kids personally benefited from our enthusiasm, knowledge and our leadership. Their parents supported our ideas, because all the pieces were there! The Waukabiashi's grew in ways that Reggie and I still shake our heads and say wow, what amazing kids.

Over the years to become a Waukabiashi was every campers dream! To be the leader of a Waukabiashi group meant your leadership was solid and now you had to live up to the challenge. Since those early years there have been thousands of Waukabiashi campers and if you were to meet one and ask what it meant, they would simply say, "Those were the best times of my life."

But, this is not a story about great or amazing leaders doing great and amazing things with awesome kids in the woods. It is a story about a couple of average leaders, meeting some average kids and because of their confidence and convictions did amazing things.

In the process they all grew. Isn't that what education is intended to do?

When the administrator who replaced my Dad, said no to an idea about expanding the Waukabiahi program. Captain Cook as I was called in those early days, went on to start my own Wilderness Camp, Instructional/Program and retail facility. We now serve thousands of kids every year in all types of programs, having fun every day, just like that first day when Reggie and I knew we were an unstoppable team. Reggie has gone on to become a Colonel in the Army, and the leader of a very large part of the Chrysler

THE NOBLE GIFT

Company. Captain Cook and Colonel Sanders have continued to make our mark, with the strength of leadership.

As you read this book, I hope you envision a path illuminated by true leadership. That as you become a leader you continually look inward, clarifying your personal vision and looking for ways to share it with others. As you grow may you lead with the innocence of a child and the trust of all you touch. May your wisdom grow and like your leadership, may you look for ways to teach the lessons you have been fortunate enough to learn.

When you have put yourself on this path, and you like the shoes you are wearing, take a group on a hike and have some fun. Who cares if you're late for Arts & Crafts!

Safe Adventures,
T. Scott Cook, Ph.D.
T. Scott Cook, Ph.D.

A note to Reggie I am so glad we walked next to each other for such a great adventure. Our lifelong friendship is the best part. Thanks for sharing, believing and dreaming with me! We are the great big, hairy chested, Waukabiashi Men! We are the greatest in all the Camp! How How!

INTRODUCTION

WHY WE NEED LEADERS

Photo by Ryan Crockett

We all had super heroes as children. You know that bigger than life figure who would save the world when things would go crazy and some villain had created a scheme to take over the world. As I grew older, I saw things that needed fixing. I saw life forms whose existence was threatened every day. I learned things were not as they seemed in a young child's mind! There were no super heroes! Or perhaps there were!

Who comes to the aid of a dying population of birds? Or who will save the river from the villains dumping toxic waste into it for their convenience? Who will put their life on the line to stop the slaughter of fur bearings seals, so our elite class can complete their vain self image. Who speaks for those who cannot speak for themselves? Who fights for the defenseless? Our super heroes! Those people who can see with their extra senses that things need help. They feel with their extra dose of compassion. They act with the conviction, courage and confidence of a nobleman. They are our leaders! They reach out and help when things are wrong. Their voice is not easily lost in the mire of politics. Their spirit never wanders from the mission. This is a noble gift.

If our children could learn the lessons of these unsung, quiet heroes and rise to each challenge, seeking nothing but the satisfaction of making a difference then we could all walk with the confidence knowing full well that if some creature were in need, a hero would rise to the solution.

We as educators must learn to teach ways to bring about this change. A level of ownership, we need all people to stake claim to a part of the problem and to fight that quest with the vigor of our childhood super heroes.

As creatures that can't defend themselves perish from our greed, ignorance and plundering will our super heroes, those with the "Noble Gift of Leadership" step up and make a difference? I believe the biggest pressing problem in our society is how we teach. Teaching to conform only teaches us to accept what is! When "what is" has broken, how is anything ever going to get fixed? LEADERSHIP! Effective outdoor leadership is just one venue, and that is what this book is intended to address. It would be just grand if my students had the gift to lead others, and help others whenever and wherever needed.

We should teach people about their super powers. When our education system has accomplished this goal then there is hope for the future. We must also hasten to remember one thing with leadership can come corruption of power. As you will read, leadership is diverse. It sparkles with insight into the unfolding of the human spirit. Yet we need to be vigilant against those who would abuse this gift.

As leaders, our greatest accomplishment is to allow people to become better leaders than you. So how do we as leaders take on the world's problems? Simple, find passion, not the kind of passion you read about in romance novels. The kind that burns deep inside you, lighting the way for your spirit to follow. If you can not claim something you are passionate about, you are missing your mark. You are missing your chance to share your super powers, or put differently your noble gift! Search the world or your backyard. There are plenty of things, people, critters and situations that need a leader. Then make your voice heard. When you speak, follow the wisdom of your heart and lead. You will be amazed how good it feels to make a difference. To me leadership goes like this;

We understand what we can touch and feel,

We respect what we understand,

We love what we respect. T.S.Cook

The value of Experiential /Adventure Education is so rich that once you open your spirit to the power of learning by doing, your heart will lead the way to amazing lessons and great memories.

Passion is fire burning within you, but as a leader you have the ethical chance to plant passion in those who are on your trail. A poem I wrote when my Mom passed away summarizes how she was a leader and how she planted in me a seed that burns with such vigor, I hope the depth of her vision can be reached by my attempts to make a difference.

I include it as a tribute to her great leadership.

THE NOBLE GIFT

"The Gardener"

By T. Scott Cook

April 9, 2002
It has been said,
Those who invest in the human spirit…
are truly blessed!
"The Gardener"
The Gardener knows
where to plant the seed,
The Gardener knows
when to plant each seed,
She also knows
how to plant each seed,
Most importantly she knows
Why she is planting that particular seed and
what it will look like in the grand scheme of things to come,
With love, nourishment and some luck,
New growth is inevitable.
Now,
The real Gardener knows…
The secret…
She will watch, support and encourage, (careful to never to get in the way)
Soon,
The gardens flourish, each individual plant sharing her quest…
To make this place just a little more beautiful,
Each small miracle
Looks toward the sun for its next challenge.
"The next life to enrich",
I stand strong, mature and able to face the future,
Yet, I look for my guiding light,
and she is gone.
Thou, in me lives the knowledge,
That I am part of her Garden!
The Garden,
She began creating years ago…
Nourished by Kindness, Love, Tenacity, Patience, Unfaltering support,
and a special vision…
To make this place just a little more beautiful!
You and I are her Garden…
With but one Challenge…
To work in harmony with nature and beautify everyone's life we come in contact with. When we have done this…
Then we will be…
As blessed as my MOM!
With Love,
Your son… The builder of castles.
T. Scott Cook, Ph.D.

CHAPTER 1

LEADERSHIP FROM WITHIN

T. Scott & Aubrey Cook—Costa Rica

One can never consent to creep when one feels an impulse to soar.
—Helen Keller

My camp counselor said to me at the end of the season "You have great leadership skills, Thank-you for your help this summer." Those words will stay with me like no other in my life! "Leadership," she saw it in me, I didn't know it was there. I am special, I am a leader! What now? I decided to sign up for the leadership training program the next summer, instead of the awesome camp program I had been a part of for most of my childhood.

The next summer I discover how hard it is to lead. But by the same token I felt the value of my personality reaching out to others. I have to work hard, so what, I say. I love this!

Was leadership planted in me? Was my counselor a gardener, knowing the seed of leadership would grow in my fertile mind and spirit? Did I really have "leadership"? Did it just need a place and time to come out? Did I discover my passion? Did my passion discover me? What will I do with this gift? How will I use it?

In any case I felt the burning desire to explore, create, lead and help others.

You too can begin a journey that will create a spark so bright others will follow. Your gift will grow and become a noble gift, but the gift of leadership is a two edge sword. One blade soft, kind, compassionate, caring and ethically balanced. The other side lays sharp to the touch, cold, hard, morally corruptible and painfully dangerous. It is up to you how you will lead! This chapter deals with the building blocks of leadership, you and specifically the challenges of taking others into your outdoor classroom.

Before you can begin leading others you need to get to know yourself. You need a time of personal reflection so that you can look at:
What are your passions?
What do you value?
Who are you? Not what you do.
What are your visions?
Do you have written goal statements?
What makes you happy, sad, mad?

A would-be leader needs to self assess before a leaders influence can be felt. The questions above are just a few of the questions that must have concrete answers.

A great tool to learn about yourself is the Solo experience. This tool has been used in adventure programming as an experience used to teach people about themselves and their special place in the world. I suggest that a leader spends some time on what I would call a "Leadership Quest" weekend. A solo that addresses the key personal issues a leader must get their head and heart around.

The quest for leadership begins within.

During this solo experience you will define:
1. **Your ten critical choices.** These are the ahhh moments in your life when you look back and say "ahhhh I am glad I made that choice." What were the benefits and/ or consequences of these choices?
2. **Your seven defining moments.** These are the moments now realized as moments that went on to shape who you were to become. They are the times of remarkable clarity now, but at the time may not have been such.
3. **Your five pivotal people.** Who were these people and why? Do they know how important they are How did this person help shape and define who you were to become?
4. **State three personal values** that guide your life and form the substance of your existence.
5. **Define your Leadership goal.** (source unknown)

At the conclusion, you the new leader should emerge with profound answers and clearer vision. Your mission, passions, ethics, and abilities should show themselves to you. Soon these same qualities will influence the people you will be leading.

Next begins the hard work of building your leadership skills, or what we will call your core competencies. These competencies build the structure of your leadership castle, the place from which your "Noble Gift" can shine! These blocks serve as your foundation. Hard work on your foundation will be rewarded for years to come. Soon your mission and the value of your vision will reward those who travel with you.

THE NOBLE GIFT

It is critical for a leader to thoroughly explore all facets of their personality, value system, beliefs, morals, ethics and emotions so that the sacred responsibility of leading others can not be corrupted. A problem we see all too often when leadership gets mistaken for power. We will explore this dilemma when we learn about ethics of leadership.

Let's look at the personal core competencies. I define them as, Respect, Circle, Sharing and Silence.

1. **Respect**—If you have respect for all living things, others and yourself you would never do anything to disrespect, harm, embarrass, destroy, take advantage of, or in any way set yourself to be anything but an equal with all things living and non living in the great scheme of things. When you show respect you earn respect, you needn't be coercive, mean or flex your power. Those who see the wisdom of your vision will find you easy to follow. This one quality is the greatest of all the Noble Gifts, because with this one quality taken to its deepest meaning, the problems facing mankind, and all species would be solved.

2. **Circle**—It is important for you to remember that we are all in this together. What we do affects all things! We are all part of a circle, the circle of life. Around each of us are other circles, circles, of family, friends, colleagues, peers, and those following your vision. When we understand our place in this circle, we develop our niche adding structure and strength to those around us. A circle has no beginning and no end therefore the journey is never over. Learning remains exciting and teaching continues to be rewarding. Helping others in our circle becomes a force to drive you forward in the face of adversity.

3. **Sharing**—There are so many things to be shared, feelings, beliefs, ideas, knowledge, experiences, the list goes on. In the rush to share with others we must hasten to remember that others have a great deal to share with us. When we are open to learning from others our circle stays balanced, and we bond with each other with respect. As outdoor leaders another form of sharing must be remembered, we need to thank the outdoors for sharing with us! Mother Earth will share regardless of who you are or your readiness to learn. Recognize the fact that there is much to be learned from all parts of our circle, especially nature. This places us in a position of great responsibility. We must be respectful of the lessons nature will share with us, as well as prepared for them. To take people outside and share with them the beauty, strength, exhilaration and fun of being in the outdoors puts us as leaders in a delicate place. We will explore this in later chapters.

4. **Silence**—This seems like a strange leadership quality! Aren't leaders supposed to be heard? Yes, but sometimes leaders learn best by listening to those around them. Without getting too political here, wouldn't it be nice if our leaders really listened to us and not their own agenda? In addition to listening to others, let's talk about listening to what nature is saying to us, how we can interpret that and teach from it. When you go into the woods do the trees scream to you a story about their life and their contributions to the circle? If so you have much to share! Those who can't speak for themselves need people to speak up for them, but you will not hear the message to share if you don't take the time to listen. Another part of silence that should be explored is leaders need to take the time to listen to themselves, to the things that are going on in their heart, head and body. By taking the time to do this simple self check you can be surer of your results when leading others.

<u>Personal Core Competencies</u>
1. Respect
2. Circle
3. Sharing
4. Silence

From these Core Competencies others grow, but I believe these are the foundation of effective leadership of others in the outdoors. When practiced participants will follow the wisdom of your actions and see the purpose of your vision. They will be willing to begin a journey with you and along the way be willing to look deeper within themselves, others and the world around them. They will trust you with the innocence of a child and you will respect them as would your own child.

In the work <u>The Leadership Practices Inventory: A Self-Assessment and Analysis</u> by James M. Kouzes and Barry Z. Posner, Ph.D. (1993). Kouzes & Posner identify the following general leadership competencies for aspiring outdoor leaders. These need to be adapted to our situation.

1. Challenging the Process
"Leaders are pioneers—people who seek out new opportunities and are willing to change the status quo. They innovate, experiment, and explore ways to improve the organization. They treat mistakes as learning experiences. Leaders also stay prepared to meet whatever challenges may confront them. Challenging the Process involves searching for opportunities, experimenting and taking risks."

   a. Creates a prudent risk-taking environment
   b. Seeks innovation
   c. Embraces life-long learning for oneself and opportunities for others
   d. Accepts mistakes and turns them into learning opportunities
   e. Identifies alternatives to status quo *and* advocates for system changes as defects are identified

2. Inspiring a Shared Vision
"Leaders look toward and beyond the horizon. They envision the future with a positive and hopeful outlook. Leaders are expressive and attract followers through their genuineness and skillful communications. They show others how mutual interests can be met through commitment to a common purpose. Inspiring a Shared Vision involves envisioning the future and enlisting the support of others."

   a. Communicates well
   b. Envisions an uplifting and ennobling future
   c. Enlists others in a common vision
   d. Values people's contributions to the mission and the desired results

3. Enabling Others to Act
"Leaders infuse people with spirit and develop relationships based on mutual trust. They stress collaborative goals. They actively involve others in planning, giving them discretion to make their own decisions. Leaders ensure that people feel strong and capable. Enabling Others to Act involves fostering collaboration and strengthening others."

   a. Builds trusting relationships
   b. Provides resources to remove obstacles to achieve desired results
   c. Works system to enable others to act effectively within the bureaucracy
   d. Encourages others to move up in the leadership ranks
   e. Creates an environment for collaboration and cooperation

THE NOBLE GIFT

    f. Provides independence and does not micro-manage
    g. Shares authority, power and information

4. Modeling the Way

"Leaders are clear about their business values and beliefs. They keep people and projects on course by behaving consistently with these values and modeling how they expect others to act. Leaders also plan projects and break them down into achievable steps, creating opportunities for small wins. By focusing on key priorities, they make it easier for others to achieve goals. Modeling the Way involves setting an example and planning small wins."

    a. Sets the example
    b. Keeps it simple (KISS)
    c. Stands up for his or her beliefs
    d. Sets the values for clients and models them
    e. Is consistent between word and deed—behaves with credibility
    f. Acknowledges own mistakes
    g. Is approachable
    h. Employs leadership style appropriate to the situation
    i. Models successful problem solving skills
    j. Models honest and ethical behavior
    k. Demonstrates and promotes civic responsibility

5. Encouraging the Heart

"By linking recognition with accomplishments, thereby visibly recognizing contributions to the common vision, leaders encourage people to persist in their efforts. Leaders express pride in the team's accomplishments, letting people know that their efforts are appreciated. Leaders also find ways to celebrate achievements. They nurture a team spirit, which enables people to sustain continued efforts. Encouraging the Heart involves recognizing contributions and celebrating accomplishments."

    a. Shows appreciation
    b. Recognizes individual contributions
    c. Celebrates team accomplishments
    d. Creates a friendly and challenging environment
    e. Encourages persistence
    f. Connects individual strengths with organizational needs and requirements
    g. Displays an optimistic and positive demeanor
    h. Inspires others with courage and hope
    i. Encourages and nurtures teamwork
    j. Treats people with dignity
    k. Conveys pride in the organization
    l. Encourages the aspirations of others

6. Getting Things Done

Leadership is often the difference between getting the work done and not meeting schedules. Leaders take pride in their performance, their reputation, and their commitment to make their organization a world-class provider of services and products. Well-developed management skills are the background for pulling together and providing support for all the other leadership skills. Getting Things Done involves developing and perfecting management skills.

a. Establishes plans and milestones
b. Organizes (self and organization)
c. Manages core processes (personnel, procurement, budgeting, information technology)
d. Manages time efficiently
e. Mentors and coaches others
f. Resolves conflicts
g. Manages team relations
h. Negotiates and facilitates
i. Ensures accountability
j. Promotes cultural competence and diversity
k. Manages political aspects
l. Gathers, applies, and analyzes key information for fact-based decision making.
m. Improves quality continuously
n. Measures and evaluates program outcomes and results
o. Manages participant satisfaction
p. Utilizes effective marketing and public relations skills, including media relations
q. Understands legal and regulatory aspects of the job
r. Enhances personal and organizational performance thru continual process improvement
s. Manages change and welcomes it as a growing opportunity
t. Accomplishes the task

<u>The Leadership Practices Inventory: A Self-Assessment and Analysis</u> by James M. Kouzes and Barry Z. Posner, Ph.D. (1993). Kouzes & Posner

Core Competencies for Outdoor Leaders

This list adapted from a paper by Marni Goldenberg, University of Minnesota entitled "Outdoor and Risk Educational Practices" represents 12 core competencies that emerge from all research. Several outdoor leadership researchers e.g., Cousineua 1977, Swiderski 1981, Buell 1983, Hattie 1997, Shiner 1970, Mendence 1979, Simmons 1982, Priest 1988, have examined the competencies required for an outdoor leader.

These Core Competencies guide an outdoor leader allowing you to share the outdoors in a safe manner. While also encouraging your participants to develop their leadership skills and personal strengths while gaining a respect for the environment.

   1. Organizational skills—The leader must be able to plan, prepare, execute and assess successful outdoor experiences. Attention to detail can make or break someone's whole experience. How would you feel when your leader forgot the toilet paper, car keys or fuel for the camp stoves?
   2. Technical skills—An Outdoor leader must be a "Jack of all Trades and the Master of a Few." Today's leaders must know the practical, hands-on skills required for the type of outdoor activity in which the group will be participating, yet needs to be able to set a tent and cook a meal. Better yet a leader should be able to teach the clients how to do it.

THE NOBLE GIFT

3. Environmental philosophy—Simply stated we have no business going into the nature centered environment without an environmental morality. We must share what is right, what is wrong, with the future users of the environment. Perhaps as they become policy makers, parents and leaders will know and respect the environment and would not do anything to harm it. Being a life student and role model of this competency is extremely important. As we teach environmental stewardship we can limit or prevent damage to the natural surroundings in all outdoor activities.

4. Safety sense and risk management—I am a believer in the "Hair on the Neck theory." If something makes your hair stand up, pay attention because something is wrong! By developing a six sense—A safety sense- you are constantly aware of all aspects of your surroundings. This sounds daunting and it is! You need to be aware of your participants, their needs, physical, spiritual, emotional and social. You have these same needs, so be aware of these. Often ignoring your needs can get you and hence the group in bigger trouble. Your surroundings include the immediate environment, weather, sun, rain, snow, avalanche, water levels, time of day, nutrition, hydration, medical needs, temperatures and temperature extremes. Assess and safely manage risks in a way that promotes the clients' understanding, but does not detract from the satisfaction of the experience.

5. Instructional strategies—We have all had the teacher who was brilliant, really knew his/ her stuff, but could not teach. We have all seen the teacher lose it when something went differently than planned. As an outdoor leader you need to be flexible and skilled in a wide variety of styles of teaching. We will explore these in other chapters. Your skills must allow you to teach clients technical, safety and environmental skills related to outdoor activities at an age-appropriate level, in a wide range of conditions and levels of readiness to learn.

6. Group Development—There are many ways to help a group grow, we will learn about these in the section on Group Process. Your leadership will foster relationships within the group that optimize the experience as the group works together toward the goals of the activity.

7. Decision-making—Some leaders feel they need to make all the decisions. Others feel they should involve the participants. Your leadership style will allow you flexibility and your experience will help you to discover and assess multiple options and selecting the best choice either individually or by accord.

8. Problem-solving—Not all things go smoothly! You have just hiked 12 miles in the pouring rain; one member of your group forgot the rainfly to their four person tent in their fathers car. While tying up the bear bag the group came up with a better solution. They put it on top of the outhouse, at four in the morning you hear a crash, the outhouse is knocked over and you find out your whole food bag is gone! Leadership is recognizing and solving problems. In fact some leaders enjoy the challenge of having to solve complex problems. You need to recognize and define situations whether they are personal, physical, social, medical or emotional. Anticipate possible outcomes, identify and evaluate possible solutions.

9. Effective communication—As we saw in Our Personal Core Competencies- Silence is a key skill. By being silent we are able to be better listeners. By being better listeners we learn to communicate more effectively. A leader needs to speak up and be heard. A leader should be prepared to speak from the heart, share the wisdom of his / her thoughts, verbalize their vision, motivate and congratulate. A leader needs to exchange information in a manner that results in all participants having a positive experience in the activity. (Goldenberg) I think Thomas Jefferson summed it up rather well when he said:

In matters of style, swim with the current; In matters of principle, stand like a rock.
—T. Jefferson

Here is a list of important words for leaders:
- The six most important words: "I admit I made a mistake."
- The five most important words: "You did a good job."
- The four most important words: "What is your opinion."
- The three most important words: "If you please."
- The two most important words: "Thank you,"
- The one most important word: "We"
- The least most important word: "I" (Author unknown)

10. Experience-based judgment skills—Outdoor leaders are always considering their past experiences and evaluating each in terms of successes, failures and apply the learning to future situations.

11. Leadership ethics—Leading using the moral standards and values that are demanded of adults working with youth. This is a subject we will devote a complete chapter to.

12. Sharing valuesg—Role modeling the behaviors and attitudes that are expressed in your Mission, Principles, Promise and Law and a role model that encourages participants to do the same. *(Goldenberg M., pg 133. Outdoor and Risk Educational Practices)*

When looking at the work required of an aspiring Outdoor Leader one might feel a bit overwhelmed. But the work we do with clients is rewarding, fulfilling, and leads to greater self confidence. It also gives a better sense of purpose this allows greater ability to do the job using the professional standards we self-impose, or perhaps standards, certification or the law impose.

When you have begun to build these competencies, you will have laid the foundation for your castle. Strong walls welcome participants from every walk of life and accept new creative ways of reaching out into the kingdom. Your noble gift grows from within.

Quality leadership in action

CHAPTER 2

LEADERSHIP STYLE

The leader has to be practical and a realist, yet must talk
the language of the visionary and the idealist.
—Eric Hoffer

In the previous chapter we essentially built our castle. We laid the foundation that is our core personal skills. We constructed the walls, known as Leadership Competencies adding form to our abilities. We installed the doors and windows that allow our participants to see and follow our vision. Our leadership now has form. You have or will work hard on these competencies. You will be rewarded, as will those you will be privileged to lead.

Now, it is time to build the inner workings, the true guts of your castle. ***Your leadership styles.*** Like any complex operation your leadership style senses change, remains sensitive, and is flexible. At any given moment your style may shift from one end of the scale to the complete opposite. Your ability to learn the different styles of leading others will be a necessary part or your "Noble Gift." Good luck.

You are a staff person working at an outdoor adventure center. The group scheduled to show up for a day of top rope rock climbing will be arriving any minute. You have gone to great lengths to gather and inspect the equipment required for your day on the rocks. The group has eight female members. They have basic climbing experience from the local climbing gym. Your co-leader can't wait to get going. The bus pulls in and out comes your next favorite group.

Wait, something is different. The group members are all limb deficient! Your day and climbing as you know it, has just changed drastically. You have no experience with this. Regardless, you are a leader, and there are people waiting for you to teach and lead. You go for it. Along the way, you change your goals slightly. You restate your objectives your group lets you know how you can help them accomplish their goals.

The day is amazing. Your perceptions of ability and determination are shattered. You feel as if you learned more that day than your new friends did. You can't stop thinking about what happened. When one member comes up to you and says thank-you, you can see from the glow in her eyes, how her perceptions of ability and determination have also changed! You see her climb into the bus a different person. You sit down with your co-leader to debrief. To reflect, the best part of the day was the thank-you and the glow of confidence present throughout the day. You confess, you will never look at anybody the same! No matter who, what or where, you will see ability instead of disability.

This amazing learning experience was made possible because you were flexible and your leadership style was able to change. While you had the technical skills, you were able to adapt and meet the participants in a place of mutual respect and learning. WOW! If all teachers could be so flexible. The day was safe and organized. But not anything like the day you envisioned before the bus pulled in. You think back at a decision you made, and you now realize that was a pivotal moment in your life. It has guided you throughout your career! What was that decision? To treat all people as equals, and to treat them with respect. To share with them your gift, so they could share theirs with you. In your mind you have gone over that day countless times and it balances your life. From it you draw strength and determination. You are a better person, your noble gift has made a difference.

Early in your career you decided you were going to make a difference. Now ready to retire, a look at your adventure center, amazing pride is the emotion to describe the 10,000 limb deficient people you have led around the world. A look at your co-leader who will take over for you. Your last hug is a big one, you with two arms, her with one arm! This time you say "thank-you" and get into your car and drive away with the knowledge that your leadership has changed the world's perception of ability and determination.

Could all of this have turned out differently? Yes. Let's go back to the bus. The girls get off and you realize they are limb deficient. You go to your boss, and say you can't do this. Story closed because you were not willing or able to adapt your leadership style. You never grew.

> "Don't be afraid to take a big step when one is indicated.
> You can't cross a chasm in two small steps."
> —David Loyd George

Leadership style is something that has been written and explored for centuries. The military is truly concerned about the nature of its leaders. Our political system has leaders some good, some not so good. Our educational system recognizes its leaders.

Work places have leaders some talented, some not. The outdoor industry has recently been very involved in its ability to create consistent, caring and compassionate leaders. For the most part we are doing an adequate job, but like most things, a great deal of work needs to be done. We will explore some of that work in this chapter and in future chapters about ethics, skills and risk management.

Is leadership something we are born with? Where does it come from? How do we teach it? We will look at some of the classic theories of leadership and compare their applications into different outdoor setting.

THE NOBLE GIFT

What are the classic theories? There are a number of different approaches, or styles to leadership that are based on different theory and principles. The leadership style that any individual will use will be based on a combination of their core beliefs, their value system and preferences, as well as the society and the norms which will encourage some styles and discourage others.

FIVE TYPICAL PATTERNS OF LEADERSHIP BEHAVIOR

In the article entitled <u>Leaders: The Strategies for Taking Charge</u> by Warren Bennis and Burt Nanus. They state "an experienced leader uses many complex and subtle means to exercise his/her influence and stimulate those he/she leads to creative and productive efforts." From the complex range of leader behavior, they selected five of the most typical patterns, ranging from highly leader-centered to highly group-centered:

Telling–The leader identifies a problem, considers alternative solutions, chooses one of them, and then tells others what they are to do. The leader may or may not consider what the group members will think or feel about the decision, but group members clearly do not participate directly in the decision making. Coercion may or may not be used or implied.

Selling–The leader, as before, makes the decision without consulting the group. However, instead of simply announcing the decision, he/she tries to persuade the group members to accept it. The leader points out how he/she has considered organization goals and the interest of group members and states how the member will benefit from carrying out the decision.

Testing–The leader identifies a problem and proposes a tentative solution. Before finalizing it, however, he/she gets the reactions of those who will implement it. The leader says, in effect, "I'd like your frank reactions to this proposal, and I will then make the final decision."

Consulting–The leader here gives the group members a chance to influence the decision from the beginning. Problems and relevant background information are presented, then the members are asked for their ideas. In effect, the group is invited to increase the number of alternative actions to be considered. The leader then selects the solution he/she regards as most promising.

Joining–The leader here participates in the discussion as "just another member"—and agrees in advance to carry out whatever decision the group makes. The only limits placed on the group are those given to the leader by his superiors. (Many research and development teams make decisions this way.)

<u>Source</u>: <u>Leaders: The Strategies for Taking Charge</u> by Warren Bennis and Burt Nanus.

Another popular view of Leadership style breaks leadership down to three styles. The following descriptions are taken from a web site created by Donald Clark May 11, 1997

- **Authoritarian or autocratic**
- **Participative or democratic**
- **Delegate or Free Reign**

Authoritarian (autocratic)

This style is used when the leader tells her participants what she wants done and how she wants it done, without getting the advice of her followers. Some of the appropriate conditions to use it is when you have all the information to solve the problem, you are short on time, and your participants are well motivated.

Some people tend to think of this style as a vehicle for yelling, using demeaning language, and leading by threats and abusing their power. This is not the authoritarian style…rather it is an abusive, unprofessional style called **bossing people around**. it has no place in a leaders repertoire.

The authoritarian style should normally only be used on rare occasions. If you have the time and want to gain more commitment and motivation from your employees, then you should use the participative style.

Participative (democratic)

This type of style involves the leader including one or more participants in on the decision making process (determining what to do and how to do it). However, the leader maintains the final decision making authority. Using this style is not a sign of weakness, rather it is a sign of strength that your participants will respect.

This is normally used when you have part of the information, and your employees have other parts. Note that a leader is not expected to know everything—this is why you work with *knowledgeable* and *skillful* participants. Using this style is of mutual benefit—it allows them to become part of the team and allows you to make better decisions.

Delegative (free reign)

In this style, the leader allows the participants to make the decision. However, the leader is still responsible for the decisions that are made. This is used when participants are able to analyze the situation and determine what needs to be done and how to do it. You cannot do everything! You must set priorities and delegate certain tasks.

This is not a style to use so that you can blame others when things go wrong. Rather this is a style to be used when you have the full trust and confidence in the people around you. Do not be afraid to use it, however, use it wisely.

Note: Also known as laissez faire which is the noninterference in the affairs of others. (Clark)

How do we use these Leadership Styles?

In the following pages you will find different "leadership scenarios." Each scenario can be met with a wide variety of style choices. You will be asked to make a choice and defend your choice.

Scenario # 1

While on a day long canoe trip on a local river, you clearly tell all participants "not to tip their canoe." You see a canoe tip over and you suspect it was done on purpose. Your trip now needs to be shortened, because the wet participants are getting cold. The rest of the group is angry and looking for you to make some decisions.

What do you do?
What leadership style will work well in this situation?

What are the benefits and consequences of using different styles?
How do you deal with the wet participants? The rest of the group?

Scenario #2
While briefing a group for the upcoming caving trip, you go over the equipment list that participants should have brought with them. You discover well over half the group is under prepared. The van is ready to leave.

What do you do?
What leadership style will work well in this situation?
What are the benefits and consequences of using different styles?
How do you deal with the unprepared participants? The rest of the group?

Scenario #3
You are at a trail junction, with your backpacking group. All have been taught about route finding, map and compass. The group is in disagreement about which trail to take. You know the answer (obviously).

What do you do?
What leadership style will work well in this situation?
What are the benefits and consequences of using different styles?
How do you deal with this decision making process?

Scenario # 4
You are helping the group load the kayaks for a four day Island to Island trip. You notice a participant is going to forget the special dessert for the 4th of July dinner.

What do you do?
What leadership style will work well in this situation?
What are the benefits and consequences of using different styles?

Scenario #5
While rafting in Maine, you are scouting a rapid, when you smell marijuana? This is clearly a violation of a non-use agreement with your group.

What do you do?
What leadership style will work well in this situation?
What are the benefits and consequences of using different styles?
How do you deal with the offending participants? The rest of the group?

Scenario # 6
You wake up on the 2nd morning of a 7 day backpack trip. One member is not present! The tent mate of the missing tent mate stated that "on the first night he talked about taking off." You need to find this missing camper ASAP.

What do you do?
What leadership style will work well in this situation?
What are the benefits and consequences of using different styles?
How do you deal with the missing camper when you find him? The rest of the group?

Scenario # 7
You are facilitating a ropes course program for the incoming freshman of your local college. The group has been together for two days and are moving to high elements with a high degree of skill.

What do you do?
What leadership style will work well in this situation?
What are the benefits and consequences of using different styles?
When processing this experience what learning do you want to highlight?

Scenario # 8
One member of your rock climbing group makes all the decisions, bosses the other participants around, and is somewhat demeaning to the opposite sex. You see members willing to share ideas with you but unable to.
What do you do?
What leadership style will work well in this situation?
What are the benefits and consequences of using different styles?
How do you deal with the offending participant? The rest of the group?

The following are 30 Vital Leadership Actions
Reprinted with permission from William A. Cohen, PhD—President, The Institute of Leader Arts

7 WAYS TO ATTRACT FOLLOWSHIP

1. **Make others feel important.** People will follow you when you make them feel important, not when you make yourself feel important.
2. **Promote your vision.** No one will follow you simply because you decide you want to lead. You must have a clear idea where you want to take the group you lead - then you must promote it and convince those you lead that the goal is worthwhile.
3. **Treat others as you would be treated yourself.** You wouldn't want to follow a leader who treated you poorly, and neither would anyone else.
4. **Take responsibility for your actions and the actions of those you lead.** If you don't, you are no longer the leader.
5. **Praise in public, criticize in private.** If someone has earned your praise, let everyone know about it. If someone has earned your ire, let only that person know about it.
6. **See and be seen.** You've got to get around to really know what's going on, to fix what's wrong, and to capitalize on what's right. It's also the only way those you lead can be sure you're for real.
7. **Use competition to make striving a game.** People love to compete. It is the secret of successful products from professional sports to video games. It is the secret of unbelievable achievements in all activities. Use competition as a positive force to reach your objectives.

THE NOBLE GIFT

7 METHODS OF TAKING CHARGE IN CRISIS OR HIGH RISK SITUATIONS
1. **Establish your objective at once.** You can't lead anywhere until you know where you want to go.
2. **Communicate what you want done.** Do this in a way likely to get the attention of those you lead.
3. **Act boldly.** This isn't the time to be cautious. This is the time to take risks.
4. **Be decisive.** Don't put off making decisions. Do it now!
5. **Dominate the situation.** Do this by taking the initiative. If you don't, the situation will dominate you.
6. **Lead by example.** Make your credo "follow me." Live by it.
7. **Dump people who can't do the job.** Hire replacements fast…but do a thorough job of interviewing to minimize risk.

7 ACTIONS TO DEVELOP YOUR CHARISMA
1. **Show your commitment.** Charismatic leaders are committed to their missions.
2. **Look the part of your vision.** If you don't, you start out with a disadvantage. If you do, it reinforces your commitment.
3. **Dream big.** Important leaders have important dreams.
4. **Keep moving toward your goals.** He who hesitates is lost…and so is the group he or she leads.
5. **Do your homework.** You keep ahead by working while others rest.
6. **Build a mystique.** Magicians have power because of the mystery they create. Charismatic leaders.
7. **Use the indirect approach.** Direct assault produces resistance. An indirect approach produces agreement.

4 MEANS OF BUILDING LEADER SELF-CONFIDENCE
1. **Become an "uncrowned" leader.** Become the leader in situations where others don't want to lead.
2. **Be an unselfish teacher and helper of others.** Help and teach others whenever they need your help and are ready to accept it.
3. **Develop your expertise.** Leaders don't know everything, but they need to know something, and expertise is a source of leadership power.
4. **Use positive imagery.** Simulations in the mind are rehearsals for success.

5 STEPS TO MOTIVATE THOSE YOU LEAD
1. **Work on the important things first.** High pay, top benefits and ironclad security are nice, but they are not the most important.
2. **Treat others with respect.** They won't respect you if you don't respect them.
3. **Make the work interesting.** No one wants to get bored to death while working.
4. **Always give recognition for good work.** It's more than the right thing to do - it is a leader's duty.
5. **Give those you lead an opportunity to develop their skills.** Skill builds pride. More importantly others have dreams. A leader helps followers to achieve their dreams.

Source: (Cohen, W. 2003—www.stuffofheroes.com—30 Vital Leadership Actions)

CHAPTER 3

WORKING WITH GROUPS

To lead people, walk beside them…
As for the best leaders, the people do not notice their existence.
The next best, the people honor and praise.
The next, the people fear;
and the next, the people hate…
When the best leader's work is done the people say,
"We did it ourselves!"
—Lao-tsu

Your group has been working together for one day, they have accomplished all the low elements and have gone into the high elements. There appears to be a fair amount of tension as members prepare to climb and belay in teams. Going back over the previous activities, you have an "ahhh moment"! Trust, the group had difficulty showing it, feeling it and sharing it. They are stuck in the Big Winds, the winds of change that brings the group to wide acceptance and understanding of each other and their purpose. What can be done at this stage? Your co-leader suggests "we do nothing" letting the emotions play out!

Knowing the nature of this group, you suggest "we have a refocus meeting" and see if the group is in touch with these feelings. It works! The members talk about the level of trust they need to feel comfortable progressing into the high elements. They assure each other that trust is one consideration they will all focus on. The day progresses and the group is amazing!

Now it is time to go. Some members are sharing their feelings, while thanking others for "being there." There are statements of uneasiness, a feeling of regret about the group's time being over. The group members depart with new wisdom, a sense of growth. Your group has come full circle.

When you understand how groups work and the stages they go through, you will better be able to lead. Your gift of leadership allows you to reach participants at their present level and help them progress full circle. As we will see, there is a great deal of research and generally agreeing theories about group growth. In this chapter you will learn some of the widely accepted ideas and some new ones.

One of our guiding core Competencies was **"Circle"** I present here a circle theory. This Circle idea is not new. It represents a compilation of leading ideas about group growth. Starting in the East, the group travels around the circle. Between each primary direction is the **"winds of change"** that carry the group to the next part of their journey. Not all groups will complete the circle.

Illumination—East

This is the place for beginning. The point in our circle of life where the sun comes up. It is the compass direction that all creatures face at the beginning of their day. Characteristics of this stage of group growth would be uncertainty, nervousness, casual discussions, searching for common ground, exploring purpose and the beginning of vying for power. Group members will want to know why they have been brought together. The specific agenda for each group is usually communicated by the leader. They are not yet a group but a set of individuals. This juncture is depicted by talk about the reason for the group, its makeup, leadership model, and life-span. In this stage, each individual tends to want to establish an identity within the group and make an impression.

The Big Winds—East to South

As the group begins to travel around the circle toward the south, following the natural circle of life, nature like life will throw some turbulence toward the group experience, Individuals articulate their positions. Unfavorable comments are frequent. Bids for power begin between group members in an effort to convince each other that their position on an issue is correct. Often the field of candidates vying for leadership narrows, as fewer members try to establish power. Some of those who contributed freely to the group discussion in earlier stages now remain silent, wishing not to engage in a power struggle. It is noted that interactions arising out of this phase do not usually result in optimum solutions. Hence, there is a great need for structure and patience in this stage.

Divergence of attitudes can occur. You can expect a reaction to the evolving roles. In this phase an individual's need for approval begins to diminish as members examine their group's purpose and begin to set goals. Often social cliques will begin to form as members begin to feel as though they fit in.

Innocence and Trust—South

As the sun continues its arc thru the southern sky, it helps things grow. This stage of group growth I call "IT" Innocence and Trust. These qualities will help any friendship, relationship and group grow. You will know "IT" when your group has arrived. This stage is marked by the sharing of sincere interactions. It is the best direction for solving problems, where animosity is nominal. Balance has occurred within the group. Individual roles are accepted by the group. Members begin to accept that others have an opinion worth expressing. The team spirit replaces selfish interests. Often new levels of creativity are achieved and the group's productivity soars. If new individuals are introduced into the group at this point they will be viewed as outsiders and the group will have to evolve again, by going back a step or two in the circle.

Gentle Breezes—Toward the West

Here the group moves about its purpose with ease showing harmony, and support of effort. It is during this shift of development (assuming the group gets this far) that the participants experience a feeling of belonging to the group. This allows the group to focus on the task. Different points of view enrich the group process. The facilitator can relax and watch the group work very effectively. Leadership styles frequently change at this point as more control is given to the group and its members.

During the gentle breezes there is sometimes a brief desertion of the task, when a period of play, an enjoyment of the unity that is being experienced takes place.

Introspection—West

In the West we take the time to look within ourselves, our task, the environment, generally taking a deeper look at all things. In this part of our circle there can be amazing clarity, fog, and sometimes despair. As we look within, we realize our time and purpose as a group is drawing to maturity. The effort of our task can now be seen, felt or experienced. This direction is not achieved by many groups, and is characterized by interdependence in personal relations. This means that members have the ability to work individually, in any subgroup, or as a total unit.

A reflective, thoughtful silence coexists. Members are still playful with each other. The task seems completed or near its conclusion and there is a need for closure, relax, and quiet.

If the group develops the understanding that this position offers the possibility for a new beginning, the group may begin at this new starting point and work through the circle in a different fashion. There will be renewed enthusiasm and the new problems and purpose for staying together will be explored.

Harvest Winds, Toward the North

This part of the journey is one of reaping the fruits of our hard work. While putting to use our labors, deeper meaning has been sought and now must be put to use. Approval and a general high spirit are the trail markers of this part of the trek around our circle of group growth.

Wisdom—North

North is the place of ending, of resting and internalizing our experience. Nature sleeps. It is a time of renewal. We say good-bye in a number of ways. In the North we finish the task behaviors and disengage from the relationships formed within the group. Yet as we rest in North, some group's reform, plan a new task and begin all over again.

A planned conclusion usually includes recognition for participation or achievement and an opportunity for members to say goodbyes.

Concluding a group can create some trepidation - in effect, a minor crisis. Termination of the group is a form of giving up control, to give up inclusion in the group. The most effective leadership styles in this stage are those that assist termination and the release of members to greet their world with new power and growth.

Dawn Winds–Toward the East

These winds bring us back to new beginnings with feelings of excitement, nervousness, and a sense of purpose.

Cook, T. Scott. "The Winds of Change": Working with Groups, 2004

Other classic theories of group growth can be found in Tuckmans widely accepted 5 stage theroy.

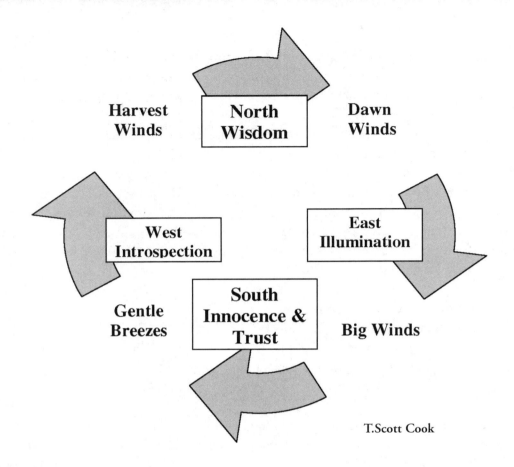

5 Stages of Group Development

Stage 1: Forming
In the *Forming* stage, personal relations are characterized by dependence. Group members rely on safe, patterned behavior and look to the group leader for guidance and direction. Group members have a desire for acceptance by the group and a need to be know that the group is safe. They set about gathering impressions and data about the similarities and differences among them and forming preferences for future sub grouping. Rules of behavior seem to be to keep things simple and to avoid controversy. Serious topics and feelings are avoided.

The major task functions also concern orientation. Members attempt to become oriented to the tasks as well as to one another. Discussion centers around defining the scope of the task, how to approach it, and similar concerns. To grow from this stage to the next, each member must relinquish the comfort of non-threatening topics and risk the possibility of conflict.

Stage 2: Storming
The next stage, which Tuckman calls *Storming*, is characterized by competition and conflict in the personal-relations dimension, an organization in the task-functions dimension. As the group members attempt to organize for the task, conflict inevitably results in their personal relations. Individuals have to bend and mold their feelings, ideas, attitudes, and beliefs to suit the group organization. Because of "fear of exposure" or "fear of failure," there will be an increased desire for structural clarification and

commitment. Although conflicts may or may not surface as group issues, they do exist. Questions will arise about who is going to be responsible for what, what the rules are, what the reward system is, and what criteria for evaluation are. These reflect conflicts over leadership, structure, power, and authority. There may be wide swings in members' behavior based on emerging issues of competition and hostilities. Because of the discomfort generated during this stage, some members may remain completely silent while others attempt to dominate.

In order to progress to the next stage, group members must move from a "testing and proving" mentality to a problem-solving mentality. The most important trait in helping groups to move on to the next stage seems to be the ability to listen.

Stage 3: Norming

In Tuckman's *Norming* stage, interpersonal relations are characterized by cohesion. Group members are engaged in active acknowledgment of all members' contributions, community building and maintenance, and solving of group issues. Members are willing to change their preconceived ideas or opinions on the basis of facts presented by other members, and they actively ask questions of one another. Leadership is shared, and cliques dissolve. When members begin to know-and identify with-one another, the level of trust in their personal relations contributes to the development of group cohesion. It is during this stage of development (assuming the group gets this far) that people begin to experience a sense of group belonging and a feeling of relief as a result of resolving interpersonal conflicts.

The major task function of stage three is the data flow between group members: They share feelings and ideas, solicit and give feedback to one another, and explore actions related to the task. Creativity is high. If this stage of data flow and cohesion is attained by the group members, their interactions are characterized by openness and sharing of information on both a personal and task level. They feel good about being part of an effective group.

The major drawback of the norming stage is that members may begin to fear the inevitable future breakup of the group; they may resist change of any sort.

Stage 4: Performing

The *Performing* stage is not reached by all groups. If group members are able to evolve to stage four, their capacity, range, and depth of personal relations expand to true interdependence. In this stage, people can work independently, in subgroups, or as a total unit with equal facility. Their roles and authorities dynamically adjust to the changing needs of the group and individuals. Stage four is marked by interdependence in personal relations and problem solving in the realm of task functions. By now, the group should be most productive. Individual members have become self-assuring, and the need for group approval is past. Members are both highly task oriented and highly people oriented. There is unity: group identity is complete, group morale is high, and group loyalty is intense. The task function becomes genuine problem solving, leading toward optimal solutions and optimum group development. There is support for experimentation in solving problems and an emphasis on achievement. The overall goal is productivity through problem solving and work.

Stage 5: Adjourning

Tuckman's final stage, *Adjourning,* involves the termination of task behaviors and disengagement from relationships. A planned conclusion usually includes recognition for participation and achievement and an opportunity for members to say personal goodbyes. Concluding a group can create some apprehension—in effect, a minor crisis. The termination of the group is a regressive movement from giving up control to giving up inclusion in the group. The most effective interventions in this stage are those that facilitate task termination and the disengagement process.

Adapted from:

Tuckman, B. (1965) Developmental Sequence in Small Groups. Psychological Bulletin, 63, 384-399.

Tuckman, B. & Jensen, M. (1977) Stages of Small Group Development. Group and Organizational Studies, 2, 419-427.

Expedition Leadership

In the book *The Backcountry Classroom-* published by the Wilderness Education Association, an article about expedition leadership points out some interesting traits about the process of living, playing, eating, working and challenging ourselves. As well as how this can bring out some interesting behaviors. The leader should know these expected behaviors in an effort to be prepared to deal with them when they appear.

Expedition behavior on the positive side could easily be the envy of any parent, educator or manager. Some of these behaviors are respectfulness, flexibility, open-mindedness toward others and their opinions, courtesy, effective communication / problem solving, self-awareness, resilience in the face of stress and teamwork.

To develop these and other skills needed to lead groups both on extended trips the professional outdoor leader needs to develop strategies to implement a plan. Their leadership style needs to adapt and their awareness of the group cycle helps fine tune the group toward accomplishment of the leaders vision.

On the negative side Expedition members can easily slide into behaviors such as neurotic, blaming, not productive, selfish behaviors. All of the qualities that represent a positive group can turn opposite. How do we deal with these? Awareness, preparation, details and encouragement of open honest/ non hurting communication. Be conscious of your role and your state of mind. Chances are if you are feeling something is wrong so are the group members, (remember the hair on the neck theory).

The Seven Relationships of Expedition Behavior

"Poor expedition behavior is a breakdown in human relations caused by selfishness, rationalization, ignorance of personal faults, dodging blame or responsibility, physical weakness, and in extreme cases, not being able to risk one's own survival to insure that of a companion." Paul Petzoldt

One–Individual to individual:

This relationship is personified by tent partners but exists between every individual in the group. Getting along with individuals can be accomplished by using the guidelines below. As individuals, we contribute to good expedition behavior by keeping the following in mind:

    a. Be tolerant and considerate of others.
    b. Manage conflict effectively.
    c. Maintain good personal hygiene practices. This is important for:
       (1) Good health

THE NOBLE GIFT

        (2) Aesthetics (who wants to look at someone with granola and raisins between their teeth?)
           This makes it more gender neutral compared to the beard statement
    d. Don't take offense
    e. Maintain a "cow-like" attitude—"be laid back", have fun, don't let things become a hassle, . there is no crisis.
    f. Switch tent partners if there is no way to get along.

Two–Individual to group:
The responsibility the individual has to be part of the group:
    a. Be organized.
    b. Be reasonably clean and neat.
    c. Be conscious of offensive and annoying habits.
    d. Be cooperative.
    e. Avoid dangerous activities.
    f. Take part in group activities.
    g. Be honest about personal needs (e.g., stop the group to take care of a blister).

Three–Group to individual:
The responsibility the group has to each individual. The group must accept the individual as a member of the group and keep from either ganging up on the individual or holding grudges against the individual.
    a. Be aware of click formation
    b. Be careful not to scapegoat a member
    c. If individual has special needs (e.g. diet) be sensitive

Four–Group to group:
The responsibility of groups to respect each other. (Intra group dynamics (small groups within your larger group—example—tent groups, cook groups, canoe pairs, rope teams, etc.) Be courteous of other groups within your group. Examples—share food and equipment among cook groups; share the ideal tent sites rather than always being first into camp and scurrying to claim the perfect site; Split up boat use from day to day rather than "hogging" the new, expensive demo brought on the trip. (Inter group examples - When encountering other groups who are engaged in the same activity. It is best to be courteous but leave the group to its own privacy. Except in an emergency, it is best not to impose on other groups (e.g., borrowing or using food or equipment).
    a. When encountering uneducated campers who are doing unsafe or harmful things to the environment, one must use tact. If an approach of assertiveness or arrogance is used, the objective of changing their behavior may be negated; they may resent being told what to do by strangers.

Five–Individual and group to multiple users:
Understanding that everyone has a right to use the out-of-doors within the limitations of the law is an important concept. Just because the group does not like a certain outdoor activity does not mean that the activity shouldn't be allowed. Respect of the multiple user will contribute to a better understanding of outdoor users and promote good public relations between groups.

Six–Individual and Group to administrative agencies:
Understanding and respecting administrative agencies and their representatives contributes to good relations. Administrative representatives are generally hard-working professionals working for under-funded agencies. Their job is made easier when groups cooperate and work with them.
   a. Obey rules and regulations. Don't ask for special favors which must be denied.
   b. Be courteous and cooperative when encountering rangers and other administrative representatives in the field.
   c. Sign in and out at registration locations as appropriate.
   d. Do not expect field representatives to know everything about the out-of-doors or the area they are responsible for. Employees of administrative agencies may not be trained in the outdoors and are frequently transferred providing little time to become experts in their areas.

Seven–Individual and group to the local populace:
Local residents of popular outdoor recreation areas often see visiting outdoor users as overeducated urban intruders. They are sometimes politically threatened by these outsiders. Every effort should be made by outdoor users to understand their point of view and try to be cooperative and respectful.

Drury, J & Bonner B.–(1992), *The Backcountry Classroom*–Wilderness Education Association.

Expedition Behavior–The Finer Points By ; Howard Tomb
   A good expedition team is like a powerful, well-oiled, finely tuned machine. Members cook meals together, carry burdens together, face challenges together and finally go to bed together.
   A bad expedition on the other hand is an awkward, ugly, embarrassing thing characterized by bickering, filth, frustration and crispy macaroni.
   Nearly all bad expeditions have one thing in common- poor expedition behavior (EB). This is true even if team members follow the stated rules, such as Don't Step on the Rope, Kerosene and Food, No Soap in the River, No Raccoons in the Tent, Keep your Ice Axe Out of My Eye, etc.
   Unfortunately, too many rules of expedition behavior remain unspoken. Some leaders seem to assume that their team members already have strong and generous characters like their own. But judging from a few of the campers we've encountered, more rules ought to be spelled out. Here are ten of them.

   RULE #1 <u>Get the hell out of bed.</u>
Suppose your tent mates get up early to fetch water and fire up the stove while you lie comatose in your sleeping bag. As they run an extensive equipment check, coil ropes and fix your breakfast, they hear you start to snore. Last night you were their buddy; now they're drawing up list of things about you that make them want to spit. They will devise cruel punishments for you. You have earned them. The team concept is now defunct. Had you gotten out of bed, nobody would have had to suffer.

   RULE #2 <u>Do not be cheerful before breakfast.</u>
Some people wake up perky and happy as fluffy bunny rabbits. They put stress on those who wake up mean as rabid wolverines. Exhortations such as "Rise and shine, sugar!" and "Greet the dawn, pumpkin!" have been known to provoke pungent expletives from rabid wolverine types. These curses in turn may

THE NOBLE GIFT

offend fluffy bunny types. Indeed, they are issued with the sincere intent to offend. Thus, the day begins with flying fur and hurt feelings. The best early morning behavior is simple: Be quiet.

RULE #3 <u>Do not complain.</u>
About anything. Ever. It's ten below zero, visibility is four inches and wind driven hailstones are embedding themselves in your face like shotgun pellets. Must you mention it? Do you think your friends haven't noticed the weather? Make a suggestion. Tell a joke. Lead a prayer. Do NOT lodge a complaint! Your pack weighs 87 pounds and your cheap backpack straps are—surprise! surprise! - cutting into your flesh. Were you promised a personal sherpa? Did somebody cheat you out of a mule team? If you can't carry your weight, get a motor home.

RULE #4 <u>Learn to cook at least one thing right.</u>
One expedition trick is so old that it is no longer amusing: on the first cooking assignment, the clever cook prepares a dish that resembles, say, burnt socks in toxic waste sauce. The cook hopes to be relieved permanently from cooking duties. This is the childish approach to a problem that's been with us since people first started throwing dead lizards on the fire. Tricks are not a part of a team spirit. If you don't like to cook, say so. Offer to wash dishes and prepare the one thing you do know how to cook. Even if it's only tea. Remember that talented camp cooks sometimes get invited to join major expeditions in Nepal all expenses paid.

RULE #5 <u>Either A) Shampoo, or B) Do not remove your hat for any reason.</u>
After a week or so on the trail, without shampooing, hair forms angry little clumps and wads. These leave the person beneath looking like an escapee from a mental ward. Such an appearance could shake a team's confidence in your judgment. If you can't shampoo, pull a wool hat down over your ears and leave it there, night and day, for the entire expedition.

RULE #6 <u>Do not ask if anybody's seen your stuff.</u>
Experienced adventurers have systems for organizing their gear. They very rarely leave it strewn around camp or laying back on the trail. One of the most damning things you can do is ask your teammate if they've seen the tent poles you thought you packed 20 miles ago. Even in the unlikely event you get home alive, you will not be invited on the next trip. Should you ever leave the tent poles 20 miles away, do not ask if anybody's seem them. Simply announce with a good-natured chuckle, that you are about to set off in the dark on a 40 mile hike to retrieve them and that you are sorry. It's unprofessional to lose your spoon or your toothbrush. If something like that happens, don't mention it to anyone.

RULE #7 <u>Never ask where you are.</u>
If you want to know where you are, look at the map. Try to figure it out yourself. If you're still confused, feel free to discuss the identity of landmarks around you and how they correspond to the cartography. If you A) suspect that a mistake has been made; and B) have experience in interpreting topographical maps, and C) are certain that your group leader is a novice or on drugs, speak up. Otherwise, follow the group like a sheep.

RULE #8 <u>Always carry more than your fair share.</u>
When the trip is over, would you rather be remembered as a rock or a sissy? Keep in mind that a pound or two of extra weight in your pack won't make your back hurt any more than it already does. In any

given group of flatlanders, somebody is bound to bicker about the weight. When an argument begins, take the extra weight yourself. Then shake your head and gaze with pity upon the slothful one. This is the mature response to childish behavior. On the trail that day, during a break, load the tenderfoot's pack with 20 pounds of gravel.

    RULE # 9 <u>Do not get sunburned.</u>
Sunburn is not only painful and unattractive, it's also an obvious sign of inexperience. Most green horns wait too long before applying sunscreen. Once you've burned on an expedition, you may not have a chance to get out of the sun. Then the burn gets burned, skin peels away, blisters sprout on the already swollen lips. Anyway, you get the idea. Wear zinc oxide. You can see exactly where and how thickly it's applied and it gives you just about 100% protection. It does get on your sunglasses, all over your clothes and in your mouth. But that's OK. Unlike sunshine, zinc oxide is non-toxic.

    RULE #10 <u>Do not get killed.</u>
Suppose you make the summit of K2 solo, chain-smoking camels and carrying the complete works of Hemingway in hardcover. Pretty macho, huh? Suppose now that you take a vertical detour down a crevasse and never make it back to camp. Would you still qualify as a hero? And would it matter? Nobody's going to run any fingers through your new chest hair. The worst thing to have on your outdoor resume is the list of the possible locations of your body.

    All expedition behavior really flows from this one principle: Think of your team, the beautiful machine, first. You are merely a cog in that machine. If you have something to prove, forget about joining an expedition. Your team will never have more than one member. (Tomb)

CHAPTER 4

WORKING WITH INDIVIDUALS

*Earn your success based on service to others,
not at the expense of others.*
—H. Jackson Brown, Jr.

There is much to learn about leadership, the environment, activities and the people we will lead. In this chapter we will study the effects of the individual on our groups. We will also explore the roles of the members, the effects of fitness, fear, risk taking and adapting your leadership style.

In chapter 5 we will look at how all this comes together and as a skilled leader we can create in our participants a sense of "learnership." This is where we pass on our "Noble Gift" in the form of a hunger to learn, and explore to all options.

When we build in wood, it will rot before the onslaught of weather.
When we build in stone, it is crumble with the passing of time.
When we build in human personality, the future will rise to call us blessed.

Adapted—Author unknown

Leaders and Groups
*It's one thing to be proficient at an outdoor activity and quite another to
lead a group of people proficiently on an outdoor activity.*

In the Appalachian Mountain Clubs Leadership guide the authors present the following ideas about leading others. Leadership is an elusive concept. What makes people follow a leader? And why do some people follow while others do not? Are people born with the ability to lead or can it be developed? Exactly what is leadership?

The Situation: There must exist a situation where leadership is required. This can be a crisis, a planned event, a group of people learning to interact with each other, or a situation in which something needs to happen. Leadership is a response to a need.

The Followers: The individual members of a group must be willing to be led, and they must agree to follow a course of action to meet the group's goals. Group members must view their acceptance of the leader's guidance as the way to achieve their own goals. Leadership fails when the group no longer accepts the leader.

The Leader: Simply defined, *leadership* is the association between an individual—the leader—and a group of people sharing a common interest or goal, with the leader directing the group to behave in a certain way. The leader accepts responsibility for the needs of the group and influences its members to work together for the benefit of all.

No single personality type is preferable for leadership, though a person who is comfortable making decisions and who enjoys responsibility and the dependence of others will find more enjoyment in serving as a leader. Shy, retiring people may not enjoy being in the leadership role, but they can be very effective leaders. Good leadership traits may be found in all personality types.

Some people seem to be *born leaders*. But most become good leaders through hard work and many years of experience. In the outdoors, a leader must be prepared to face physiological, psychological, and environmental challenges. Experience will generally reduce the leader's anxiety about the situations that may confront him or her, and make the leader more confident and skillful than someone who lacks experience. An experienced leader will also have a better idea of how their personality will affect others and will have more skill in selecting appropriate approaches to his or her followers, depending on the situation.

Participant Roles

As we saw in the preceding section, leadership is not isolated in the leader but is very strongly linked to the participants. Just as there are models for leadership styles, there are also models for participant roles. Below is a partial list of negative blocking roles. When a participant assumes one of these roles, it blocks the group from achieving its potential, or worse. Some of these blocking roles appear in the *Peanuts* comic strip.

1. The **AGREER** (Marci) goes along with anything. Marci just "yeses" Charlie Brown to death. This can get the individual in trouble and can prevent the group from reaching the best possible decision.

2. The **OPPOSER/CRITICIZER** (Lucy) tends to criticize, challenge, and either overtly or covertly undermine the leader. This can be very subtle such as someone in the back of the line muttering and complaining under his/her breath or very obvious such as someone who is constantly questioning the leader's decisions in front of the whole group. Some leaders are intimidated, but you need to recognize this as an almost universal occurrence in a group. Study group life cycles to understand when this behavior is most likely to surface.

3. The **SILENT OBSERVER** (Snoopy) has important contributions to make but doesn't make them. A leader needs to solicit and encourage these members to speak out.

4. The **NON-LISTENER** (Schroeder) cannot possibly be helping the group. Members need to be good listeners just as does the leader. At the most basic level, a leader needs to be sure that anything said can be heard by the entire group.

5. The **CLOWN** (Peppermint Patty) in the group must not become a blocker. Humor has its appropriate time and place but should not be allowed to get in the way.

6. The **DOMINATOR** asserts authority or superiority through manipulating the group or certain members. This may take the form of flattery, asserting a superior status or right to attention, or giving directions. The leader may need to recruit their co-leader to assist in mitigating this role.

7. The **INTERRUPTER** may or may not be the dominator. A group needs rules, and all should be allowed to speak without being interrupted.

Participants can also interact with the leader and the group in more positive ways. Below are two roles that will not usually block the group from achieving its potential.

1. The **FOLLOWER** respects authority and is usually very supportive of the leader. This participant may develop a real dependence on the leader or may just have a need to accept someone else's guidance. The leader's reaction to this person is usually one of appreciation. This is the follower who confirms the leader's role.

2. The **BYSTANDER** tends to be somewhat aloof, going along with the program, whatever it may be. If there is a conflict in the group, the bystander will not become involved or take sides. The leader's reaction to this person is bland or neutral as contrasted with the negative reaction to the opposer and the positive reaction to the follower.

Just as with leadership style, participant roles are flexible. A person, who is by nature a follower, may suddenly become an opposer if he or she is put into a position that is threatening or uncomfortable. Conversely, an opposer might decide to be a follower if he or she is impressed with the actions of the group leader and gains sufficient respect for him or her.

Adapting Leadership Styles to Participant Roles

How does the leader's style mesh with the participants' roles and abilities? When do you use what style? What situation calls for what style? These are difficult questions to answer but can be the key to excellent, flexible leadership. We can make a few suggestions based on examples of different situations and different types of groups. You will notice that safety and risk are critical—the greater the risk, the more forceful or decisive your leadership style will most likely need to be. However, because each group is different, any style may work in any situation.

<u>Situation and Followers Possible Leadership Styles</u>

The objective dangers are high and the participant's skill level is low.	Authoritarian
The objective dangers are low and the participant's skill level is low.	Selling Consulting
The objective dangers are high and the participant's skill level is high.	Consulting Selling
The objective dangers are low and the participant's skill level is high.	Engaging Laissez Faire

There are no rules and regulations governing the choice of leadership style. The leader must approach each situation and each follower as a new and unexplored adventure. A leader's experience in previous situations will help get him or her get started, but flexibility and the ability to recognize the need for flexibility are the keys to success. Leaders need the ability to switch from one style to another as the situation changes and as they get to know their followers.

This is also an important factor to consider when selecting or working with a co-leader. If there is a particular leadership style that is most challenging for you, you may want to seek out co-leaders who are able to take over when that style is needed. For example, in working with a co-leader, you should discuss your strengths and weaknesses in terms of leadership style so that you can give each other support as well as opportunities to practice different roles. (AMC)

Stages of Social-Emotional Development.

In this section you will be presented an overview of the developmental tasks involved in the social and emotional development of children and teenagers which continues into adulthood. The presentation is based on the Eight Stages of Development developed by psychiatrist, Erik Erikson in 1956. Relative to leaders it is imperative that you understand these so you may design, plan and conduct age appropriate activities. It also helps to realize that the teenager who is acting out is "normal." This section is adapted from a web based article by the Child Development Institute 2005

According to Erikson, the socialization process consists of eight phases - the "eight stages of man." His eight stages of man were formulated, not through experimental work, but through wide - ranging experience in psychotherapy, including extensive experience with children and adolescents from low - as well as upper - and middle - social classes. Each stage is regarded by Erikson as a "psychosocial crisis," which arises and demands resolution before the next stage can be satisfactorily negotiated. These stages are conceived in an almost architectural sense: satisfactory learning and resolution of each crisis is necessary if the child is to manage the next and subsequent ones satisfactorily, just as the foundation of a house is essential to the first floor, which in turn must be structurally sound to support the second story, and so on.

Erikson's Eight Stages of Development

1. Learning Basic Trust Versus Basic Mistrust (Hope)

Chronologically, this is the period of infancy through the first one or two years of life. The child, well - handled, nurtured, and loved, develops trust and security and a basic optimism. Badly handled, he becomes insecure and mistrustful.

2. Learning Autonomy Versus Shame (Will)

The second psychosocial crisis, Erikson believes, occurs during early childhood, probably between about 18 months or 2 years and 3½ to 4 years of age. The "well - parented" child emerges from this stage sure of himself, elated with his new found control, and proud rather than ashamed. Autonomy is not, however, entirely synonymous with assured self - possession, initiative, and independence but, at least for children in the early part of this psychosocial crisis, includes stormy self - will, tantrums, stubbornness, and negativism. For example, one sees many 2 year olds resolutely folding their arms to prevent their mothers from holding their hands as they cross the street. Also, the sound of "NO" rings through the house or the grocery store.

3. Learning Initiative Versus Guilt (Purpose)

Erikson believes that this third psychosocial crisis occurs during what he calls the "play age," or the later preschool years (from about 3½ to, in the United States culture, entry into formal school). During it, the healthily developing child learns: (1) to imagine, to broaden his skills through active play of all sorts, including fantasy (2) to cooperate with others (3) to lead as well as to follow. Immobilized by guilt, he is: (1) fearful (2) hangs on the fringes of groups (3) continues to depend unduly on adults and (4) is restricted both in the development of play skills and in imagination.

4. Industry Versus Inferiority (Competence)

Erikson believes that the fourth psychosocial crisis is handled, for better or worse, during what he calls the "school age," presumably up to and possibly including some of junior high school. Here the child learns to master the more formal skills of life: (1) relating with peers according to rules (2) progressing from free play to play that may be elaborately structured by rules and may demand formal teamwork, such as baseball and (3) mastering social studies, reading, arithmetic. Homework is a necessity, and the need for self-discipline increases yearly. The child who, because of his successive and successful resolutions of earlier psychosocial crisis, is trusting, autonomous, and full of initiative will learn easily enough to be industrious. However, the mistrusting child will doubt the future. The shame - and guilt-filled child will experience defeat and inferiority.

5. Learning Identity Versus Identity Diffusion (Fidelity)

During the fifth psychosocial crisis (adolescence, from about 13 or 14 to about 20) the child, now an adolescent, learns how to answer satisfactorily and happily the question of "Who am I?" But even the best - adjusted of adolescents experiences some role identity diffusion: most boys and probably most girls experiment with minor delinquency; rebellion flourishes; self - doubts flood the youngster, and so on.

Erikson believes that during successful early adolescence, mature time perspective is developed; the young person acquires self-certainty as opposed to self-consciousness and self-doubt. He comes to experiment with different - usually constructive - roles rather than adopting a "negative identity" (such as delinquency). He actually anticipates achievement, and <u>achieves</u>, rather than being "paralyzed" by feelings of inferiority or by an inadequate time perspective. In later adolescence, clear sexual identity - manhood or womanhood - is established. The adolescent seeks leadership (someone to inspire him), and gradually develops a set of ideals (socially congruent and desirable, in the case of the successful adolescent). Erikson believes that, in our culture, adolescence affords a "psychosocial moratorium," particularly for middle - and upper-class American children. They do not yet have to "play for keeps," but can experiment, trying various roles, and thus hopefully find the one most suitable for them.

6. Learning Intimacy Versus Isolation (Love)

The successful young adult, for the first time, can experience true intimacy - the sort of intimacy that makes possible good marriage or a genuine and enduring friendship.

7. Learning Generativity Versus Self-Absorption (Care)

In adulthood, the psychosocial crisis demands generativity, both in the sense of marriage and parenthood, and in the sense of working productively and creatively.

8. Integrity Versus Despair (Wisdom)

If the other seven psychosocial crisis have been successfully resolved, the mature adult develops the peak of adjustment; integrity. He trusts, he is independent and dares the new. He works hard, has found a well - defined role in life, and has developed a self-concept with which he is happy. He can be intimate without strain, guilt, regret, or lack of realism; and he is proud of what he creates - his children, his work, or his hobbies. If one or more of the earlier psychosocial crises have not been resolved, he may view himself and his life with disgust and despair.

These eight stages of man, or the psychosocial crises, are plausible and insightful descriptions of how personality develops but at present they are descriptions only. We possess at best rudimentary and tentative knowledge of just what sort of environment will result, for example, in traits of trust versus distrust, or clear personal identity versus diffusion. Helping the child through the various stages and the positive learning that should accompany them is a complex and difficult task, as any worried parent or teacher knows. The best ways of accomplishing this task accounts for much of the research in the field of child development.

Socialization, then is a learning - teaching process that, when successful, results in the human organism's moving from its infant state of helpless but total egocentricity to its ideal adult state of sensible conformity coupled with independent creativity. **(Child Development Institute)**

> "Fear makes the wolf bigger than he is."
> —German Proverb

Fear

We should have some discussion about fear and its effects on group and individual behavior. All people carry different fears with them. These fears can manifest themselves in varying and sometimes debilitating ways. As an outdoor leader you should have a general sense of these and how to deal with them effectively.

On a caving trip in January you are responsible for eight participants, a co-leader and a shadow (Leader in training). The group consists of four Father and Son pairings. The equipment check and pre trip talk have all gone well. It is felt by the co-leaders and yourself that you can do the easy section of the cave and end with a fairly tight crawl.

The trip begins, you place yourself at the first tight, hard spot- the entrance way. You do this for safety reasons, but to also gauge your participant's reactions to the new environment and their fear level. All goes well, but one father on his way past you is breathing heavy, seems uncoordinated and appears to have a high level of anxiety. This is a great opportunity to interject, "Is everything OK?" The answer received is the one expected. "I'm fine." In your head the phrase "Denial is a big river, but a bigger emotion," you know everything is not OK.

The group meets for a debriefing of the planned route and a detailed review of the safety procedures and techniques used in this cave. Your co-leader covers this talk and demonstration. In the background you are the observer, the training you have received over the years has led you to be an astute student of student behavior. While talking about the planned route for the day, you leave off the harder crawl at the end of the day. Your co-leader looks at you in wonder? The three leaders sneak a moment while the group explores the room you are in. Your co-leader questions you about the route—the answer back is "Did you see Dan, he's terrified?" He replies back "No" they now watch his actions during this free time. It's obvious now! As a group of leaders you decide if he works through this you might do the crawl or give him other options. Positioned in the back of the group, carrying one of the safety kits you ask Dan to help you pull up the rear. The kids charge off to the front of the line. As the group moves forward, you ask Dan if he is up to carrying the safety kit for a while, you share your energy bar with him and grab a quick drink of water. You share with Dan you first reaction to caving, which in this case is exactly Dan's reaction. You explain how you worked through your fears, and now with some training caving is one of the favorite activities you get to lead. There are mutual thanks for the snack, the assistance and off you go.

The day goes without a hitch! Dan is amazing, he does the crawl on the way out as a special bonus challenge, and says "This is the coolest thing I've ever done." For you as the leader, hanging out at the back with Dan has been rather boring. But there is nothing that should have been changed about this trip. You helped Dan across his chasm of fears, your co-leaders got a chance to lead, and you did what any leader should do best—You led quietly, compassionately and conservatively. Your integrity allowed someone to grow. The day is one of a hundred such days for you, but it is one in a million for Dan and the participants. In the parking lot at the outdoor center the "shadow" and Dan are having a conversation. Later, after the group leaves you ask the co-leader what was the nature of that conversation? Not because you are nosey, but because you forecasted that moment, when you asked Dan to carry the safety kit! Dan asked her "what was necessary to become a shadow" her reply surprised you! She said "nothing more than care, about others, the environment and herself." In your entire body you feel your pride well up and you want to cry. You tell her "Great job today. Thanks for your help." But when you walk away, you feel as though your leadership has been tested on all levels, and despite your own fears, you had risen to every challenge!

Dealing with fear will not always be this easy or for that matter obvious. A well seasoned leader who is leading with their Noble Gift (for the right reasons) will find it second nature most times, but remember we all have our own fears and as a leader you need to know these intimately. You need to know what triggers situations, conditions and what affects these have on you. You can not afford a trip on the Nile River (denial). That is simply not a good place to be leading from.

What is fear?

Fear is defined by Wikipedia dictionary as; an unpleasant feeling of perceived risk or danger, whether it be real or imagined. Fear also can be described as a feeling of extreme dislike to some objects/ conditions such as; fear of darkness, fear of ghosts, etc..

Fear is one of our primary emotions.

In the work <u>Overcoming Fears</u> written by; James J. Messina, Ph.D. & Constance M. Messina, Ph.D. 2005 They define fear and fears as;

Fears are the:
- Irrational beliefs about how an object, event, happening, or feeling will result in negative, disastrous, life threatening, disturbing, or unsettling consequences for you.
- Result of giving power to your objects of irrational belief, letting them rule you rather than you ruling them.
- Underlying motive behind many of your actions and lack of action that block your thinking, problem solving and decision making abilities.
- Negative self-scripts you have either given yourself or that were given to you about how you will suffer dire consequences if you involve yourself in certain activities, behavior, or events.
- Disabling beliefs you carry in yourself that prevent you from living a productive, healthy, and growth-enhancing life.
- Underlying foundation of a weak self-image and self-concept; they keep you from fully asserting yourself, and that hinders your quest for self-actualization.
- Inhibitors, emotional blocks, unconscious messages, and uncovered elements of your psychological make up. They result in your being resistant, hesitant, or unwilling to participate in nurturing, healing activities such as counseling, support groups, or therapy.
- Beliefs about not only the known elements of life, but also of the nebulous, transient, and unknown elements of life that result in your inability to feel comfortable in ill-defined situations.
- "Comfortable" ways of acting and responding. Because of their habitual and well established

nature, fears can become second nature; therefore, being extremely resistant to change or alteration.
- Basis of your negative belief system. If you were no longer the recipient of the negative consequences that the fears predicted, you would have to take off your "mask" and become authentic.
- Excuses behind which people hide to avoid change or growth. To rid yourself of your fears is to rid yourself of the lifelong reasons for avoiding personal growth.

The implications of these characteristics can be overwhelming and one can begin to see even in ourselves why we do some of the things we do. Their exhaustive research on fears by, James J. Messina, Ph.D. and Constance M. Messina, Ph.D. go on to explain the forms fear take.

What forms do fears take?
Fears come in a variety of packages for people who have low self-esteem, such as the fear of:
- *places:* school, church, crowds, planes or enclosed places, heights above or below ground
- *animals:* snakes, rats, mice, others
- *objects:* guns, knives, computers
- *people:* men or women, strangers, homosexuals, making problems or trouble for others, feeling over-responsible, not doing enough for others, losing others,
- *events:* nuclear holocaust, war, crime
- *atmosphere:* dark, shadowy, gloomy, foreboding, being alone, strange or unknown setting
- *family member:* getting ill, being lost, running away
- *disaster:* fire, hurricane, tornado, lightening, losing job or being fired, injury or pain (self or others), death (self or others), losing security and financial stability
- *reactions or responses to self:* rejection, disapproval, not being liked, being made fun of, disappointing others, being ignored, being the ``real'' you
- *results of taking a risk to do something:* failure, success, making a mistake, being judged, repeating mistakes from the past
- *public speaking:* taking a leadership role, getting nervous in front of others, making a fool of yourself
- *feelings about oneself:* feeling guilty, ``not being good enough'', being unstable or crazy, being held accountable, being pressured to produce, explaining your behavior, being exposed for the weaknesses or failures in your past, being useless or unwanted
- *the unknown:* new things, e.g., technology, change, making a decision, growing old alone, retirement, inactivity
- *authority figures:* being told what to do, being embarrassed

What are some negative consequences of fear?
Fear can:
- Immobilize decision making.
- Prevent you from overcoming your insecurity, prevent you from trusting in others, and prevent you from being willing to become vulnerable in order to grow.
- Prevent you from being willing to let go of old habits or ways of thinking in order to change.
- Make you resistant to all offers of help from others.

- Terrify you and make you unwilling to venture out into the world, making you a prisoner in your home.
- Stifle your motivation to pursue an education or a career.
- Keep you locked in self-destructive behavior.
- Prevent you from believing in your chances to become a fully functioning, healthy individual.
- Be the reason why you find yourself stuck in old ways of acting and believing.
- Be the roadblock to change and growth; if not overcome fear becomes the patterned way of living an unhealthy life-style.

What new behaviors are needed to overcome fear?

To overcome fear people need to:

- Refute irrational beliefs
- Affirm themselves
- "Let go" of fear
- Identify the fear, label it, visualize it, and deal with it as if it were an object or entity to be remolded, changed, or altered.
- Make an honest assessment of their fear and create a consistent, systematic plan of action to overcome it.
- Relax physically, reduce anxiety and tension, be able to call themselves into a relaxed state.
- Establish a sense of confidence in their ability to overcome and deal with the feared objects or events.
- Be sensitized to the stimuli of the feared object or event.
- Let go of insecurity, develop trust in themselves and others, and permit themselves to be vulnerable to change and growth.
- Be persistent in their efforts, recognizing that it may take a lifelong effort to eliminate some fears.
- Stop or "turn off" obsessing thoughts about the feared objects or events.
- Put it into a realistic perspective, so that it is not seen as the major focal point of their energy, efforts, and attention.
- Allow for discomfort, pain, hurt, and the disquieting emotions of the fear recurring in greater intensity as they initially address the treatment of fear.
- Accept their human qualities and lack of omnipotence. They will probably be confronting fear for their entire life. It is OK to know this and to accept it as a normal part of the human condition.
- Maintain the motivation to change and grow.
- Allow for relapses and set backs without undue discouragement.

What beliefs do people with an active fear-led life share?

- No matter what I do, I'll never be able to overcome that fear.
- Things are always going to be this way, so there is no use in trying.
- I'll never change. It is just a waste of time to try.
- Everyone in my family had the same fears. Why should I be different?
- I'm so scared of these things. It is impossible to feel differently.
- There are so many reasons why I should feel the way I do. It is useless to believe I could feel differently.
- I am a useless specimen who deserves no better than this.

- These fears are a part of me. I've felt this way forever. It is too much work and too difficult to let go of them.
- I have no idea what it is I'm afraid of. I only know I feel fear, anxiety, and tension.
- It takes too much work to overcome all of these fears, so just forget it.
- Most of the methods used to relax fear are silly and childish. They can't possibly work.
- I've never been able to get rid of these fears, and I can't do it now.
- It is impossible for me to picture anything in my mind. The visualization techniques are use less for me.
- No one can help me with this.
- Why try? I'll only end up regretting the waste of time and energy in the end.
- If fear is a fact of life I need to accept, why do I need to learn to overcome it? Wouldn't it be better to just accept it and go on?
- It is impossible not to think about these fears.
- I have no way of having a happy life with these fears.
- If a fear regains strength it is close to impossible to get rid of it a second time.
- Fear is an unacceptable feeling or behavior; anyone who has fear must be crazy. (Messina)

Photo Ryan Crockett

Screening Participants

You have looked forward to leading this Five day backpacking trip to your favorite spot in the Adirondack Mountains ever since you were there as a college student. Now you will be leading a group of freshman from college. You look at the list, send out the required equipment lists and necessary logistics. Just like clockwork the group arrives, all group gear is packed, all things are go!

The trailhead is just as you remembered it. You sign in your group of Six who are performing well. Tomorrow you will led the group over the pass and into a remote lake between two majestic mountains. The first day is fine, camp is set, meals prepared after some discussion it's time for bed.

Today the weather looks OK. It should be in the low 60's. The hike begins fine the climb up to the pass and into the valley. Where you will camp is hard but reasonable. The group looks fit, but then a group member slips dislocates his knee and smashes his elbow. You get to the person at that point he is angry and saying "not again." Did you miss something? Yes this is his fifth dislocated knee! Your trip has just changed. Could screening have changed this outcome? Perhaps.

As a leader you have the responsibility to know who is on your trip and what their health, fitness and motivation levels are. You should also know their experience level. As you will see in this next section, you have a sacred responsibility to bring everyone home safe. If you can prevent an accident, then you have done your job.

Screening Participants

The AMC in the "Mountain Leadership Manual" recommends the following approach to participant screening. An essential part of trip planning and leadership as well as risk management is determining who is qualified to participate in your trip. As mentioned before, the broad range of trips one might consider has a direct effect on the level and depth of screening—from no screening (show and go) to extensive questioning of participants and possible reference checking. The goals, location, and time of year of the trip also affect the requirements of the trip and consequently the screening. Likewise, screening will vary depending on whether the trip is intended for children, adults, or both.

Although good screening will not eliminate all problems that might occur during the trip, it can go a long way to limiting risk proactively before a trip. The main goal of screening is to match a participant with the physical and equipment requirements of the trip. You want the trip to be enjoyable for all (remember that the goals of all trips are: safety, fun, and reaching the final planned outcome.) During the initial contact with a prospective participant, you have the opportunity to explain the trip's expectations and requirements (equipment, clothing, cost, goals). Sometimes people will screen themselves from a trip after they hear additional details and requirements. This is certainly preferred over your having to screen them off the trip by indicating that it is too difficult. Alternatively, you can list or point them to easier trips.

Another purpose in screening is to limit group size. Certain locations have regulations on the maximum number of people traveling and/or camping together. Note that if neither you nor your co-leader has done the trip before it will be more difficult to screen since the physical requirements will be less clear. In this case you may need to set a higher experience level and requirements.

If your trip is advertised in publications or a newsletter here are some important points to keep in mind:

• Be prepared for a phone call anytime—did you state when to call? Avoid screening via email unless you know the person and their abilities. A direct conversation is preferred since it is more interactive and allows you to get a better sense of a person's true abilities and experience.

• Have a list handy of questions to ask (see below). The conversation should not be an exercise in wearing each other out. You may need to explain why you are asking these questions (as the leader you are responsible for the group and want everyone to have a good time). Develop your own style. A relaxed conversation that encourages the potential participant to volunteer information about themselves is better than just hitting them with a battery of questions.

• If they qualify for the trip, provide initial information (follow-up later with email or printed information sheet).

• Remember that screening does not end until the trip actually begins—be sure to check equipment/clothing at the trailhead or starting location.

The following questions can be used to screen participants for outdoor trips. The difficulty level of the trip will determine which questions to ask.

QUESTIONS:
1. What is your name? (spell if necessary)
2. What is your address?

3. What is your telephone number?
4. Are you a member of any club or group?
5. Who is coming with you? (that person needs to call the leader). Do not allow the caller to "register" another person unless you already know that person and their experience level.
6. What is your experience level? Explain the trip rating system if necessary and one exists.
7. What is the longest trip you have been on?
8. Have you gone with a group before?
9. What other trips have you been on and who led them? What trips have you done in the past Six months? What kind of exercise do you do regularly? How often?
10. What kind of equipment do you have?
11. What is the worst problem you have ever had on a trip?
12. Do you have any special medical problems or are you taking any medication? Allergies?
13. Do you have any medical training?
14. Do you have any questions?

YOUR RESPONSES: After obtaining answers, you may then decide whether the trip will be beyond their level of skill, within it, or too elementary. If they wish to participate in too-easy a trip, that is their decision, but if they wish to go on a trip that is beyond their ability that is your decision.

For an advanced trip it is best not to accept someone that you do not know until you have a chance to check their references—others they have gone with and leaders. As a leader it will be your responsibility to recommend that they do not participate. If they persist, you may have to refuse to take them. Explain that the trip includes certain risks (mention them) and that an inexperienced participant could create a possible burden on the leader and other participants. Encourage them to try another easier trip so they can build up their skills.

If their equipment is incomplete or inadequate, you may require them to obtain the proper gear, for their own comfort and safety and that of the group.

If they qualify for the trip, mention the requirements, such as deadline for deposit, cancellation policy, length of trip, where and when to meet and what type of snack or food to bring. Explain how long after the set meeting time you will wait for all to appear. Say that you will start the trip promptly. Note that a goal of outdoor trip is to make them comfortable, inviting and accessible for people of any age, gender, race, religion, ethnicity, ability, sexual orientation, or socioeconomic status. Some programs are designed for a certain age range of members or for a special activity or topic. However, any person who meets the minimum qualifications (skills, experience, fitness) established by the trip leader(s) for an activity is eligible to attend, if space is available. Remember that a well-planned trip and well-prepared participants make for an enjoyable and safe experience for all. Good screening can do much to ensure that this will happen.

Here is an example of a screening form I sometimes use. This form can be adapted any number of ways. Please note information in these forms is confidential and can not be shared with other participants without the consent of the client. It can be shared with other medical personal in the event of an emergency or illness. (AMC page 28)

THE NOBLE GIFT

WESTFIELD STATE COLLEGE Movement Science Sports and Leisure Services
Wilderness Leadership Program

HEALTH AND MEDICAL RECORD

_____
Last Name   First Name   Middle   Birth date

_____( )_____
Home Address (Number & Street)   City or Town State   Zip Code   Home Phone #

_____( )_____
Emergency Contact Name   Emergency Phone #

Do You Have Health Insurance?   No   Yes

_____( )_____
Health Insurance Company   Address   Phone #

_____
Name of Insured   Policy Number

NOTICE

The Wilderness Leadership Program at WSC integrates both classroom style teaching and physical activity into the instructional curriculum. Each participant is encouraged to choose their level of active participation in the programs offered by this program. The ability of each participant to manage his or her emotional and physical well-being, and for the group to support the individual decisions that are made by each participant is essential for the success of our programs.

To assist you in assessing your ability to succeed safely in our programs, and to enable us to assist you in case of an emergency, please complete this Health and Medical Record. Please note WSC does not administer medications (unless to children), except in emergencies, and we accept no responsibility for determining an individual's fitness to participate in the Experiential Education programs. **Any questions you may have about your ability to participate should be directed to your physician.** The information you are providing in this Health and Medical Record will be treated confidentially. It will not be released to anyone without your permission, except in an emergency situation where you are unable to otherwise communicate your wishes.

I hereby certify that the answers set forth here are true. The Wilderness Leadership Program is a tobacco-free and substance-free program—tobacco products, alcohol or drugs not prescribed by a physician are prohibited. I am aware that as a participant I am required to follow the policies and guidelines set by the staff / faculty and instructions from the leaders. I understand and agree to all policies and procedures. In the event I need to leave because of physical injury, illness, emotional or other reasons before the

TAYLOR SCOTT COOK, PH.D.

completion of the trip, or if I do not adhere to the policies or procedures, I may be removed from the program. I understand that I am responsible for making travel arrangements and paying travel costs for my early return home.

I hereby certify that I am aware that specific personal equipment is necessary for my participation in this program and that it is my obligation to provide this equipment. I acknowledge that my failure to provide the necessary equipment may prevent my full participation in this trip. I also understand that I am responsible for and must return any WSC equipment that I rent or use for this trip. I understand that there is a specified fee associated with participating in this trip and that I am responsible for paying that fee. I hereby grant permission for any photos that are taken during this activity to be used by WSC in promotional or other materials.

Should an accident or emergency occur, I hereby give permission to the physician selected by the WSC staff to hospitalize and/or secure proper medical treatment for me, except as noted below.

I agree to hold only myself liable for these noted exceptions.
Exceptions for treatment/hospitalization:

Any questions I have regarding this agreement have been discussed with the trip leader and/or the WSC Staff

_____

Signature and Date

1. Please rate your current level of physical activity

Activity	Times Per Week	Times Per Week	Times Per Week
Walking	1-2	3-5	5+
Jogging	1-2	3-5	5+
Cycling	1-2	3-5	5+
Aerobics	1-2	3-5	5+
General Sports	1-2	3-5	5+
Swimming Ability	Beginner	Intermediate	Advanced

Do you currently experience any **Allergies?**   No   Yes   *Do you carry personal **medications?**   No   Yes
Have you ever experienced an **Anaphylaxis Reaction?**   No   Yes

*Allergy	Reaction	Treatment

THE NOBLE GIFT

Do you currently experience **Diabetes**?   No   Yes   Do you carry personal **medications**?   No   Yes

*Type of Diabetes	Reaction	Treatment

Do you currently experience **Asthma**?   No   Yes*   Do you carry personal **medications**?   No   Yes

*Type of Asthma	Reaction	Treatment

Do you currently experience **Seizures**?   No   Yes*   Do you carry personal **medications**?   No   Yes

*Type of Seizures	Reaction	Treatment

Do you currently have **Cardiac Symptoms**?   No   Yes*   Do you carry personal **medication**?   No   Yes

*Cardiac Symptoms	Reaction	Treatment

Pre-existing condition information: C = **Current** (within last 12 months)   P = **Past**   N = N/A

Have you ever had	C	P	N	Have you ever had	C	P	N
Complete/partial hearing loss				History of heart disease (in family)			
Head injury				Palpitations (heart)			
Heat related illness				Heart murmur			
Orthopedic injury				Chest pains with or w/o exercise			
Ever dizzy or faint during exercise?				Bleeding disorder			
Shortness of breath with or w/o exercise				Stroke			
Ever told not to participate in sports?				High Blood Pressure			

Additional comments or information if checked a current or past condition.

_____

_____

_____

_____

TAYLOR SCOTT COOK, PH.D.

2. Please list any additional illnesses or medical / physical conditions for which you are currently being treated.

_____

Condition   Year Diagnosed   Treatment

_____

Condition   Year Diagnosed   Treatment

3. Please list any operations or hospitalizations you have had in the past year.

_____

Reason   Hospital   Doctor   Date

_____

Reason   Hospital   Doctor   Date

4. Please list additional medications you are now taking.

_____

Name of Medication   Dose   How Often/Reason

_____

Name of Medication   Dose   How Often/Reason

Physician Consultation

If you responded affirmatively to any of our requests for medical information, we urge you to contact your physician to discuss your ability to participate in our Experiential Education programs. If you or your physician requires additional information regarding these activities, please contact us.

I have consulted with my physician about my participation in the Experiential Education program?

                                                                   No   Yes

If you answered yes to the previous question, please provide the physician's recommendation:

- ☐ Advised to participate
- ☐ Advised not to participate
- ☐ Advised to use caution while participating in certain activities

THE NOBLE GIFT

6. Any Additional Comments

_____

_____

_____

_____

_____

The foregoing information is true and correct to the best of my knowledge.

Date: _____ Signature _____

This form has been adapted from The AMC in the "Mountain Leadership Manual"

CHAPTER 5

LEARNING STYLES

Photo by Ryan Crockett

A self motivated learner and awesome leader!

Learnership

What is learnership?
It is when a leader takes a learner through a variety of skill and interest evoking activities. The outcome is a learner who is skilled and who takes ownership in his or her learning potential. T. Scott Cook, Ph.D. 6/18/2005

As a leader of countless people in a variety of settings, I need to remind myself, that my job is not to lead people on a path I seek for them, but to show them what their options are and empower each to seek his /her own path. With confidence, courage and compassion burning deep inside my new found learner, I can sit back and watch, sometimes in amazement that my learner is a better student than I am a teacher. Have I done my job?

When we try to think out of the box we need to remember, we have years of boxes built around us and our students, we have many layers of walls, ceilings and floors to break down, personally as well as find ways to help my learner out.

Do all people want to become accomplished learners? No, just like all people don't want to become leaders, teachers, politicians, etc.

Is it idealistic to think learners who take ownership in their learning will grow to be more motivated, more self aware, self disciplined, goal oriented? Will they have a clearer picture of their goals, values and personal ethics? Will they be more sincere, better listeners, will they have a deeper understanding of meanings that elude those who are taught to scratch the surface? Will the value of this new understanding be felt on society?

Can we put a price tag on this education? Will its value inflate with the times?

Can we measure these things? Can we evaluate the effectiveness of those who find their own path and pursue their learning like a swimmer training for the Olympics?

Our goals as apprentices with the learners is to merely facilitate growth. I think teachers should shed the label "teacher" for the more dynamic, less restrictive title " facilitator!"

If cognitive ability is the skill of gathering knowledge, what is the ability of those who are shown how to seek knowledge and then put it to use in self motivated ways?

What of the subject of accountability? Do we ignore the time proven pass and fail structure? If so what do we replace it with? I favor self imposed, binding contracts made with oneself. If a learner has truly set out to learn, and they are self motivated, they are likely to be critical to the point they are harder on themselves than a test would be.

How does a person in power (the teacher, professor) let go, to empower the learner?

It's easy, LEADERSHIP! By studying the lessons of leadership, teachers are in a better mindset and skill set to reach out to their learners and empower their efforts at self directed education.

What skills are required of the learner in a traditional classroom? What learning styles are being met? If students put themselves on the path toward self directed learning, what level of comprehension is being met? What life lessons are being clarified?

Will the mental agility of a learner be greater than that of a student? Will they be more likely to seek a variety of ideas, viewpoints or depth of understanding before clarifying their position on a subject?

I have asked a lot of questions, that is my job as a facilitator. I hope only to empower you to seek your answers. Good luck.

(Cook, T. Scott "Learnership" 2005)

What is required of the leader/facilitator?
1. Ethics
2. Competency
    a. Hard skills
    b. Soft skills
3. Never loose your sense of wonder. Leave teaching doctrines behind to become a co-discoverer.
4. Become a Guiding Light. But not the only light. The learner needs their ahh moments, yet the leader needs enough clarity to know when the lesson good or bad needs to be taught and how it will be taught.
5. Be the commander, the captain of the moment. Seize the moment and then delegate the tasks.
6. Be a navigator. But not the pilot of each learning experience.
7. Be a kid. You just have big feet! If you have a hard time with this go back to # 3 and work on that for a while.
8. Be a conductor. Orchestrating all the different ways we learn, into one magic piece of work,

THE NOBLE GIFT

where the audience (the learner) gets swept away in each moment, looking forward to the next stanza.

9. Become a banker. Storing feedback, ideas and visions for use with different learners in different situations.
10. Become a Gardner. Know what seed you are planting and what it will look like in the grand scheme of things, you also need to know what nourishment will be required. When your effort come to bear fruit, seek only satisfaction from the beauty of your creation. Not, look what I did!
11. Be the Kindergarten teacher. We knew if our world was tumbling in, he/she would be there. We could count on them!
12. Be the family pet. No matter what kind of day you have had, be happy to greet each new discovery. How can it get any better?
13. Become the bumble bee. He shouldn't be able to fly, he's too big and his wings are too small. But he doesn't know it so he flies anyway!
14. Blend and bend into your environment. Like water, have the courage to stay the course, the patience to work thru the slow times and the sense of adventure to charge headlong into the next canyon, not knowing what's around the bend. As a leader you do not always needs to know the outcome.
15. Be the Sheriff. If you see something that is wrong, have the courage and sense of self to speak up.
16. Be a beaver. Hardworking, tireless, energetic, creative and just a bit manipulative. The beaver has a grand idea, and a vision behind all its hard work. So too should you!
17. The Oak tree stands silently watching the world, silently adding its special gifts. Remember in each acorn lays the potential of amazing growth and strength. So too is this true of a learner you have the ability and the wisdom to put each learner in fertile soil, and then watch as each branch grows and the interests of the student reach for the sky hungry to meets its potential.
18. Use all of your senses. But at times it might be wise to cut certain senses off to accentuate others. Let different senses guide you, don't guide your senses.
19. Be a resource. That is stable and willing to accept questions in a safe supportive manner.
20. Be a painter. Use the full pallet, and never let one color or mindset dominate your work. Be open to new visions, new expressions, and different views of the same scene.
21. If they learn one concept and follow it true, your job is done! Teach respect, because somone who respects all living things, others and themselves, will seek ways to enrich and understand all things large and small.

Cook, T. Scott "Learnership " 2005

What can we expect from our learners?

1. A sense of wonder.
2. Silence is OK! Truly gifted learners take the time to listen to their heart and head, not to mention the world around them, and to what others have to say.
3. Realize life is connected. We are a part of a circle, the circle of life.
4. Share yourself, your ideas, your needs, your wishes and your dreams. Realize too that nature is willing to share with you. Accept the gifts and offerings from all who are willing to share. Sometimes a Hummingbird may have more to teach than a four hour class.

5. Discover what motivates you! What makes you the happiest, saddest, most comfortable, the most uncomfortable.
6. Find your personal value system, question and clarify as needed.
7. Respect age, but don't worship wisdom that does not deserve respect.
8. Look at the world and subsequently each lesson with awe.
9. Find courage.
10. Find compassion for all living things.
11. Be willing to be put into situations that might require you dig a little deeper to find comfort, understanding and value.
12. Take chances and step out of the mold and set up your own mold of who you are and what you will become. Never let the world define you!
13. Take initiative, great things are not going to just happen. You have to begin making great things happen. If you see something that needs to be done, studied or talked about, don't wait, don't ask, do it! If you screw up, oh well, see # 13.
14. Take your time as your results may take years. Think like an Oak tree.
15. Take safe risks, socially, emotionally, educationally, personally.
16. Shut the door only on ignorance.
17. Understand hard work pays off.
18. Seek not to get recognized, seek to recognize.
19. Control the ebb and tide of your learning.
20. Keep alive your youth-like sense of wonder. If you have a hard time with this go to # 1 and start all over. Because children are our most accomplished learners.

Cook, T. Scott "Learnership" 2005

Some more traditional views about how people learn.
The ways people learn can effect our groups and how our message is perceived. An awareness of Cognitive Style is important. A well proven and often used tool to measure Cognitive Style is the Myers-Briggs Type Inventory (MBTI). This summary of cognitive style is adapted from the work of *Richard W. Scholl, Professor of Management, University of Rhode Island Revised: September 5, 2001*

A good homework assignment would be to go on-line and take a MBTI inventory test to see what your learning style is.

1. Behavior is a function of the interaction of situational forces and dispositional forces. The relative strength of the situation and the disposition (e.g., personality variables) determine the resultant behavior. The MBTI can be used to measure **cognitive style**, a dispositional variable that involves the ways in which the individual processes information.
2. There are a couple of points that must be kept in mind when attempting to interpret MBTI scores.
    a. The MBTI is an instrument that attempts to measure cognitive style. While it has strong validity and reliability measures, its accuracy is dependent on the honesty (sometimes this means honest with oneself) of the individual completing the instrument. Also the frame of reference (work, social, family) one takes when completing the instrument, affects one's score.

THE NOBLE GIFT

   b. Cognitive style, as a variable, measures the strength of your preference for the manner in which you process information. It is different from cognitive skill. You can develop skills that are not necessarily in line with your preferences. You can also cognitively over-ride your preferences and act in a way that may appear to be inconsistent with your style. Therefore, do not view your score as a set of handcuffs.
3. One's cognitive style generally operates in an unconscious manner, that is, while an individual may be aware of the outcome of the information processing process he or she is often unaware of the mental processes used to acquire, analyze, categorize, store, and retrieve information in making decisions and solving problems. Some typical behaviors which can be attributed to cognitive style are:
   a. You feel uncomfortable when asked a question in an open meeting. After you respond, you spend a lot of time thinking about what you should have said.
   b. In discussing problems in a meeting, one group member gets upset and storms out of the room, yelling all the way.
   c. After analyzing a group of job candidates against the advertised criteria for selection, you are uncomfortable with the top ranked candidate and actually offer the position to the third ranked candidate.
   d. You find yourself getting upset when Professor A does not follow the syllabus.
   e. Professor B seems to jump from one topic to another and from one example to another. You do not see the connection, but to some in the class, he makes perfect sense.
   f. After working on a project in a meeting, the leader of the team adjourns the meeting stating that she is happy that the group has developed a workable plan. You feel uncomfortable because, from your perspective, the plan contains only broad policy statements and the operational issues have not been worked out.
   g. Your study team has finished your term project. You feel satisfied with your group's product. The night before you are scheduled to hand in the project, you get a call from a group member suggesting that the group re-works the solution because he found some new material on the Web.

EXTRAVERSION (E):
- Processes information through social interaction.
- Develops and builds on their ideas through interaction with others.
- Verbalize ideas in order to reinforce them.
- Responds to questions quickly, as if thinking out loud.
- Prefers face-to-face meetings to memos and written communication.

   ### Group Decision Making Issues
   - Prefers to make decisions and work on assignments in the study group setting
   - Feeds to reaction to his/her comments by other group members
   - Brainstorms case ideas verbally

INTROVERSION (I):
- Processes information internally.
- Develops ideas and makes decisions in isolation.

- Does not always verbalize ideas and opinions
- Responds only after reflection
- Prefers written forms of communication to presentations and meetings.

   Group Decision Making Issues
   - Is likely to have *worked through* a case or assignment before coming to a meeting.
   - Introvert will generally prefer to look over a completed written document describing the plan before finally deciding.

SENSING (S):
- Collects data through five senses.
- Uses primarily inductive reasoning.
- Focuses on details.
- Learns experientially.
- Sees the differences between two concepts.

   Group Decision Making Issues
   - Tends to focus on operational issues
   - Looks for explicit evidence, looks to past experience to guide analysis
   - When data conflicts with theory; goes with data.

INTUITION (N):
- Develops knowledge through deduction.
- Prefers to view things globally.
- Sees the similarities between two concepts.
- Sees the connections and integration between parts of a system.
- Learns theoretically.
- Connects processes with goals.
- "Knows" something (cognition) because it is a logical deduction or extension of a theory/concept

   Group Decision Making Issues
   - Tends to focus on strategy issues.
   - Looks for model or theory to guide analysis.
   - When data conflicts with theory; goes with theory
   - Once overall strategy is developed, often closes shop without developing operational plan.

THINKING (T):
- Decides analytically by examining facts.
- Logical, objective
- Examines cause and effect beliefs to make decisions.
- Relies on cognitive component of attitude over the affective component.

FEELING (F):
- Decides on the basis of feeling.
- Uses logic to support feelings.
- Relies on the affective component of attitude over cognitive component.

JUDGING (J):
- Primary emphasis is on making decisions and coming to closure.
- Uses cognitive schema as a basis of perceiving in order to shorten information gathering process.
- Prefers order and structure.
- Creates environments that are ordered, regulated and controlled.
- Knows "right way" and "wrong way," that is, committed to one best way.
- Difficulty with multi-tasking. Likes to finish one task before starting another.
- Plans activities entirely before commencing.
- Prefers *vertical thinking*, that is, when confronted with an obstacles concentrates on removing that obstacle so that the original plan can be implemented successfully.

Group Decision Making Issues
- Pushes for closure and completion
- Will look for the *format* or *formula* to use in developing a problem or case solution

PERCEIVING (P):
- Primary emphasis is on perceiving, or gathering of information.
- Has difficulty coming to closure.
- Constantly looking for new information before making decision.
- Moves from one project to another.
- Prefers to remain flexible and avoid fixed plans, to keep options open.
- Prefers *lateral thinking*, that is, when confronted with an obstacle tends to go around it by developing solutions targeted at meeting the initial goal rather than implementing the proposed plan

Group Decision Making Issues
- Will attempt to keep group analysis and diagnosis alive, attempting to *re-open* analysis if new information surfaces.
- Push to find new ways to solve problems (Scholl)

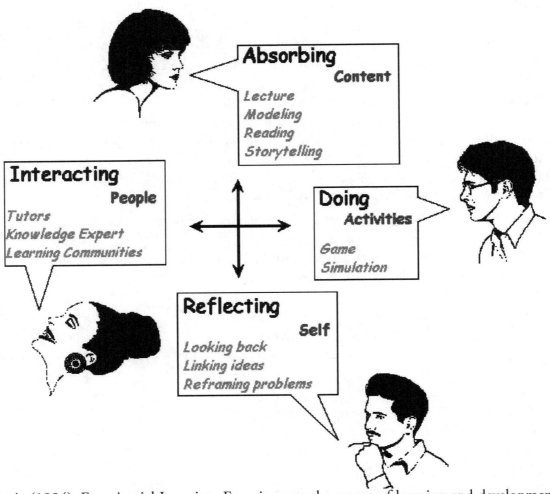

Kolb, D. A. (1984). Experiential Learning: Experience as the source of learning and development. New Jersey: Prentice Hall

Kate Larson in the article "LIFESTYLE Mindsets: Understanding Yourself Better"-
Presents another model of peoples learning styles is very simple to remember and to relate to.

1. **The Doer**—Always wants to be doing, is generally impatient to get started. Easily cuts out when there are too many directions, this is a problem when directions need to be heard and understood. The Doer needs to act on her goal immediately. The Doer needs to make the call, set the appointment, pack her workout bag and clear an hour out of her schedule. Responding with a sense of urgency to the changed Mindset is important. The Doer is looking for productivity.

    As a leader, these can be your best students—you show them, they do it! On the other hand they can be your most difficult; a happy medium in your teaching style would be to briefly present material and guide the class through the discovery phase. This student wants to see progress, dislikes wasting time and will work hard for task accomplishment.

    Obstacles—The Doer needs to be aware of being busy vs. productive. Thoughtfully following through on goals and recommendations is important. Understanding why you are doing the things you are doing will prevent you from shifting into a Struggler Mindset.

2. **The Thinker**–Collects and analyses information from many different sources, he / she watches and listens to what is being said and what is going on. A Thinker wants to make a decision. She thinks through problems, sometimes can be too analytical. The Thinker needs information. A Thinker may sound like a Struggler. "I think I need a personal trainer to get going, but it's probably too expensive." Right now, this individual is a Thinker thinking about whether a personal trainer would be worth the expense. Without more information, a decision can't be made. Suppose this Thinker calls and gets information on training. Their Mindset may then shift to any of the others. For instance they may slip into the Struggler's mindset, "Oh gosh, that's so much, I couldn't possibly spend that much on training." (Forget the amount they just spent on a New Years outfit, new golf clubs or shoes that weren't really needed.) Or the person may become an Achiever, "You know what, I'm tired of feeling tired! When can we get started?" Same information, different Mindset. As a leader to a thinker you need to give them things to think about, and then focus on helping them learn a physical skill.
Obstacles–If you are a Thinker, motivation is your challenge. If you're still stuck "thinking" about getting healthier, you haven't discovered a compelling goal that motivates you.

3. **The Watcher/ Seer**–Usually stands back, this behavior can be mistaken for being aloof. In actuality the watcher is taking in the visual picture. This learner just wants you to show them, and can grow impatient with too much discussion. When they have taken in the picture and are comfortable with the situation they will often welcome observations or solutions. Their mindset can now shift to any of the others, when given too much to watch or not enough, it can cause this learner to get stuck "watching."
Obstacles–The watcher can get stuck watching and never come out of this mindset. A leader needs to pull people along into one of the other mindsets, which with some coaxing usually works.

4. **The Feeler**–Needs to feel the skill. This is the kinesthetic learner. The leader needs a hands-on approach and will move their body through the range of motion. The learner will appreciate the direct approach.
Obstacles–Like the doer, they do not do well in a lecture format. You will often see them with their eyes closed rehearsing with their body, what they will be expected to do.

5. **The Struggler**–In order for the Struggler to shift mindsets, he often needs a new perspective, a "wake-up call." When your perspective changes about the value of something, often your struggling ends. When the options are either, start exercising, start learning to relax or have a heart attack, the Struggler often shifts his Mindset. Discovering you are borderline diabetic may help shift your Mindset from a Struggler to a Doer. Yet, that is not a guarantee.
Obstacles–Fear often keeps a Struggler stuck in a Mindset.

6. **The Achiever**–The Achiever is looking for progress and often needs a partner / support resource. As a leader, clients may use you as a resource to help them accomplish their goals, and to make their lifestyle changes last. They partner with you to design a plan that brings the fulfillment, energy, hope and fun back into their life.

    The Achiever says, "I want to lose weight the smart way. I'll agree to the recommended workout program. I'll agree to review my choices daily and monitor my progress." This is the person who may or may not lose all the weight they were determined to in a given time frame, but is more excited about the progress than the numbers on the scale.

The Achiever wants their relationships to be healthy, dynamic, and playful. They also know that this goal takes time and needs a plan to achieve.

Obstacles–Feedback from others and self can be a powerful force, both positive and negative. The achiever can slip into a struggler style and get stuck.

Adapted from the works of Tom Foster, Outdoor Center of New England, ACA Instructor Trainer Clinic and the work of Kate Larson; *in the article LIFESTYLE Mindsets: Understanding Yourself Better*

Now that we have looked at the ways that people learn, remember the challenge is to develop your "Noble Gift" so that you have many tools, theories and styles in your bag of tricks. There is no one solution to all the different styles and needs people have. Our best leaders are the ones who can switch styles with the "purposeful winds of change." A dangerous trap that unfortunately many leaders and teachers get stuck in is teaching in only the style they are most comfortable with. This approach excludes and even isolates those that do things differently.

Challenge yourself and create methodologies that consider the above theories. Nobody said it was going to be easy. If I am doing my job you are becoming a motivated, self directed learner! You are already looking for ways to create, adapt, discard and develop your Leadership Style. Your "Noble Gift."

CHAPTER 6

ETHICS

"Honesty is the first chapter in the book of wisdom"
—Thomas Jefferson

To be the leader of others, to share your "Noble Gift" your cause must be balanced by sound ethics. We have all seen leadership corrupted. Even where the cause is morally unacceptable, yet people follow. How powerful a gift this leadership is! An influential leader can persuade his /her followers to compromise their values, beliefs, moral character and the like. History has shown us the good, bad and the ugly of leadership. You must know yourself so well that you are unswayable on issues of ethics. Yet as we will see not all issues are cut and dry. There are many sides to ethical issues and sometimes we must count on what we will call ethical reasoning, to make the best decision for the situation.

Scenario 1
You are a counselor at a summer camp and a camper confides to you, that a family member has been sexually abusing him. This situation is easy from an ethical view point. You are a mandated reporter. Report the situation to the Department of Social Services and let the case take its course.

Scenario 2
At the same summer camp you are a counselor and have a very good friend who is on staff as well. The camp director has made it very clear, that no one is to leave their assigned sleeping area at night without reporting their whereabouts. Your friend has told you that she has been sneaking out to meet her boyfriend every other night.

You are caught in an ethical dilemma. What are the issues and how do you react? How about this situation from the Camp Directors View point? What if the boyfriend is a minor?

Scenario 3
You are a graduate student leading a backpacking trip. Where there is a very nice college sophomore. You have lots of things in common and you seem to enjoy each other's company a great deal. The idea of a romantic interlude occurs to you. You are both adults, the others on the trip will never know. You decide to go for it. The student is crushed that you would come on to her. The rest of the trip is very tense and you fear being reported to the wilderness trips coordinator who forbids this type of action.

What are the ethical issues at hand? How could you have dealt with them differently? What are the possible consequences of your actions?

As you can see, ethical issues are not cut in stone, but the resolve to do the correct thing needs to be as strong as the foundation of your castle. Otherwise you risk loosing the respect, the trust of those who look up to you. People need to know that above all else "YOU" will do the right thing.

Ethics

Ethics, in simple terms, is the study of morality. James Neil in an article entitled "Outdoor Education, Ethics, & Moral Development" posted on www.wilderdom.com refers to ethics and this morality as the "rightness" or "goodness" of matters. The following work is cited from James Neil's exhaustive research - From one point of view, whether something is right, good, or valued, is a subjective judgment is to be made based on particular situations (or *ethical subjectivism*, Hunt, 1990). From another point of view, there are some absolutes, for example the view that "killing another human being is bad" is always true (or ethical objectivism, Hunt, 1990). Many particular viewpoints derive from these two differing, underlying types of philosophy.

Further, for some people, the rightness or goodness of an action or decision is based on the consequences of the action or decision (*consequentialist theory*, Hunt, 1990). For others, the rightness or goodness is to be judged on the nature of the action or decision, independent of the consequences (nonconsequentialist theory, Hunt, 1990).

Outdoor education, once the can of worms is opened, reveals itself as having a minefield of potential and ethical issues and dilemmas as any other field. Perhaps the most commonly discussed ethical issues involve weighing up the relative human and ecological benefits (e.g., see Bureau of Land Management, 2002) of outdoor education activity. For example, how we can justify all the expensive gear, travel resources, impact on environment, and so on, for the human pleasure of a high-end adventure trip? The trash strewn up and down Mt. Everest, can it be morally justified? Can we morally take students into environmentally sensitive areas for their benefit only for them to cause significant damage to that environment?

Other common ethical topics include the ethics of leisure-class lifestyles, ethics of the use of risk and deception for educational, developmental, or therapeutic purposes, ethics of choice or compulsion with regard to participation in challenges, and the ethics of diversity and accessibility.

What are Some Examples of Ethical Issues in Outdoor Education?

In a book dedicated to the topic of experiential education and ethics, Hunt (1990) provided an introduction to the use of philosophy for resolving ethical dilemmas in experiential and outdoor education, with in-depth chapters on some particular ethical scenarios in outdoor education settings related to:

Informed Consent: It is ethical to disclose the content and risks of activities to students, so that they can make informed decisions regarding their participation. But when, if ever, is it appropriate to go ahead without informed consent, if its without the interests of students to do so?

Deception: Sometimes in outdoor education, deception is used for supposed benefit of students. There is often an element of intentional surprise, of purposely telling students misleading information, so that students encounter and work through challenges themselves. However, deception of others is a ploy fraught with danger - so when and how can it be ethically justifiable?

Secrecy: Sometimes instructors in outdoor education intentionally without information for supposed benefit of students. For example, giving students a map without roads marked and not telling students

THE NOBLE GIFT

where water can be found is to keep this information secret. When and how can the practice of secrecy be ethically justifiable in outdoor education?

Captive Populations: A captive population has no choice in their participation. For example, if an instructor leads a group intentionally into a difficult situation on an expedition and then gives a group two options - to go one way or another, now the group is being forced to choose from two options it may not have chosen had it been given that choice much earlier on. The people are captive to the situation and must choose one way or another. A person is 'captive' for example when up in a high ropes course. They are often faced with choices, such as down the zip line or climb down the ladder, when they may not have chosen either if they were in a non-captive situation. Sometimes participants are sent onto programs and required to complete programs (such as with delinquent youth). Thus they are captive in the program and not entirely of free will in their participation. Is this ethical?

Sexual Issues: For example, participants in an outdoor education program who didn't previously know one another begin acting on their sexual attraction to one another, including having sexual intercourse at night during the program. The two participants are open with others about their relationship. Some of the participants feel uncomfortable about the situation and approach the instructor and ask her what she thinks should be done about the situation.

Environmental Concerns: For example, a physically disabled participant on an outdoor education program involved in a ten day river rafting trip defecates in his pants and requests the assistance of an instructor to help him wash himself in the river, without the other participants in the group knowing, to avoid embarrassment. The instructor discusses the situation with another instructor who points out that this is a particularly environmentally sensitive river ecosystem and that there are strict park regulations that no fecal contamination whatsoever is allowed to enter the water stream. What would you do and why? (see also Yerkes & Haras, 1997)

Individual versus Group Benefit: This is a very common dilemma that occurs when there is a conflict between what might be optimally beneficial for the group as a whole versus what might be optimally beneficial for particular individuals. For example, a difficult summit might be an ideal challenge for the development of some individuals, but represent too great a challenge for the group as a whole. Sometimes these matters can be easily resolved (e.g., make the summit optional), but a lot of the time outdoor educators find themselves challenged to compromise group or individual benefits in making a decision.

Students' Rights: For example, if instructors withhold letters written to students by family and friends, because they believe it is beneficial to students to spend time only with the group and the environment, is that ethically justified? What are students' rights?

Social Implications: For example, a nuclear power plant company approaches a financially struggling outdoor education company and request a program to improve the teamwork of their managers as they are preparing to engage in a major new phase of production and they want their managers to work more effectively. The nuclear power plant company has been subject to criticism by environmental surveillance agencies for possibly contaminating the local environment. The company officials say that as part of their new phase of more efficient production that this will allow them to eliminate any negative impacts they may have had on the local environment. When the financially lucrative opportunity to provide teamwork programs for the nuclear power plant company is presented to the outdoor education company's staff, they are divided about whether or not to conduct the program. Some staff said no, because the organization should not be associated in any way with a nuclear power company that has such a poor environmental record. Others said yes, because we need to keep the organization alive and to help fund programs for local youth. Others who said yes, want to do the program and try to change the value-system of the managers. Still others said yes, we should do the program and treat the managers as they would any other participants, as they are human beings on their own merits, regardless of their race, gender, height, weight, religious affiliation or professional affiliation. What would you do and why? (see also Yerkes & Haras, 1997)

Paternalism: Paternalism refers to taking away an individual's right and capacity to make a decision, supposedly in the interests of that person's well-being. For example, if a participant wants to leave a program, but a powerful other, e.g., course director, talks and coerces the person into staying on the program. Or a person wants to use a different, well-proven, safety technique in which he/she has considerable expertise during a program, and an instructor refuses saying his/her technique is better. What are ethical approaches in these kinds of situations?

Other Examples
Perhaps some of the examples so far are overly dramatic examples and may seem far-fetched, but such situations do occur, as do a myriad of many less dramatic ethical issues. For example:
- Is it ethically sound to spit toothpaste into the woods? Should participants be required to swallow their toothpaste, even though it may make some people feel a little sick? For example, I participated in a backpacking trip on the Appalachian Trail with students who drank every single drop of waste water, including toothpaste and washing up water, in order to look after the environment.
- Is it ethically sound for an instructor to provide developmental experiences for participants who have value systems that the instructor opposes? For example, I struggled with my relationship with a student on a course I was instructing who revealed himself to me in confidence that he was a sexual offender. The child he was accused of raping was the same age as my daughter at the time.
- Is it ethically sound for the instructor of an outdoor education group to spend more time talking with some participants because he/she feels more comfortable with those participants? For example, in almost every teaching situation and outdoor education leadership situation I observe that the leader prefers to spend a greater amount of time with particular students with whom he/she gets along well and is comfortable with. Is this an ethical approach to teaching?

Adapted from the work of James Neill- "Outdoor Education, Ethics, & Moral Development" posted on www.wilderdom.com

Skip Armstrong & School kids in Costa Rica- Rio Toro
Photo Ryan Crockett

Sample
Code of Ethics & Mission Statement

The Professional
I will, to the best of my capability, assist, promote, and otherwise maintain the profession of Outdoor Leadership and make every effort to provide competent and consistent service to my customers.

The Environment
I will promise a professional standard of wilderness travel and low-impact environmental usage. I will attain a useful knowledge of local natural history, and the ability and willingness to impart this knowledge to my customers. I will maintain neat, sanitary and environmentally respectful camps at all times.

Respect for Rules
I will fully cooperate with all officials, law enforcement officers, private landowners and public land management agencies. I will abide by and advise my clients of all applicable conservation, regulations, and will not pardon their violation.

Equipment and Services
I will provide clean, well-maintained, functional equipment and gear that is adequate for all conditions likely to be encountered. I will employ competent and courteous personnel in sufficient number to care for the comfort of my clients. I will offer well-prepared and balanced food for clients and employees in keeping with the nature of the trip.

Accurate Information
I will accurately advise my clients of the demands and conditions involved in achieving their goals. This includes weather conditions, terrain, and the equipment, physical endurance and skills required for the activity to be undertaken.

Safety
I will at all times provide for the safety of clients and employees.

Truth in Advertising.

I will not misrepresent rates, service and/or accommodations, nor otherwise mislead prospective clients through false advertising.

Sample Mission Statement

Our Vision Statement defines The *Adventure Leadership Institute (ALI)* as an idealistic "waking dream" of how we would like our profession to evolve. It is a hope, or even a wish for the future.

The A.L.I. Mission: To enhance the outdoor leadership profession with the highest standards of honesty, safety, and professionalism by providing skilled leaders with quality competency based leadership training.

The A.L.I. Schools: To be an internationally recognized association of the world's best and most respected outdoor leaders.

The A.L.I. Schools Values: A.L.I. schools will uphold and live by the following values:

- **Integrity:** we firmly adhere to the stated values and established principles of the A.L.I.
- **Individuality:** we understand that each person or group has an inherent worthiness, distinguishing them from the A.L.I. Schools as a whole.
- **Respect:** we accept that people and processes are considered worthy of our high regard, and regard others as we would wish to be regarded. All living things, other people, plants, animals and myself are worth the greatest amount of respect, I can offer.
- **Teamwork:** we value the benefits of people working together, understanding that groups working toward a common goal may sometimes accomplish more than separate individuals.
- **Ethics:** we accept our moral duties, obligations, and principles of conduct, consistent with the A.L.I. Code of Ethics and everyday right and wrong.
- **Responsibility:** we accept accountability for providing answers to questions that affect the profession, and accountability for our conduct.
- **Fellowship:** we share interests, experiences, or feelings in a company of equals or friends.
- **Courage:** we persevere in mental and moral strength, and in our determination to do the right thing at the right time.
- **Commitment:** we agree and pledge to meet our associated and personal obligations to the best of our ability.
- **Excellence:** we strive to meet and surpass our previous achievements or accomplishments.
- **Personal Growth:** we continue to assimilate the knowledge and experience of others, to foster our own growth and the growth of others.

(Adapted from works by New York State Outfitters Guides Association and WEU inc.)

ETHICAL REASONING

Ethical leaders do the right things for the right reasons all the time, even when no one is watching. But figuring out what's the "right" thing is often, to put it mildly, a most difficult task. To fulfill your job, you must be able to reason ethically. Like it or not the US Army must do a lot of research, because their leaders are faced with huge ethical problems on an ongoing basis. The following is adapted from an officers training manual:

Occasionally, when there's little or no time, you'll have to make a snap decision based on your experience and intuition about what feels right. For leaders, such decisions are guided by personal values, the institutional culture, and the organizational climate. These shared values then serve as a basis for the whole team's buying into the leader's decision. But comfortable as this might be, you should not make all decisions on intuition.

When there's time to consider alternatives, ask for advice, and think things through, you can make a deliberate decision. First determine what's legally right by law and regulation. In gray areas requiring interpretation, apply Personal values to the situation. Inside those boundaries, determine the best possible answer from among competing solutions, make your decision, and act on it.

The distinction between snap and deliberate decisions is important. In many decisions, you must think critically because your intuition—what feels right—may lead to the wrong answer. In high stress situations especially, the intuitive response won't always work.

The right action in every situation you face may not be in any leadership textbook. Even the most exhaustive research and planning can't predict every situation. They're designed for the routine, not the exceptional. One of the most difficult tasks facing you as a leader is determining when a rule or regulation simply doesn't apply because the situation you're facing falls outside the set of conditions envisioned by those who wrote the regulation.

You are hiking with a group of teenagers. The going has been slow with blisters, heavy packs and the weather has slowed you to a point that you will not make your scheduled and permitted campsite. Even though your permit is very clear where you should camp every night, you decide to camp off the trail tonight. A ranger comes by and yells at you for camping off the trail. You attempt to explain your group's condition, but to no avail. It's too late to move, the ranger issues a citation you agree to pay it when you return to the trailhead. Your group thanks you. The course director is going to be upset, still you feel you made the right decision.

What ethics did you uphold? What ones did you compromise? What would you have done differently? What ethics was the ranger trying to uphold?

So at times you should apply values, your knowledge, and your experience to any decision you make and be prepared to accept the consequences of your actions. Study, reflection, and ethical reasoning can help you do this.

Ethical reasoning takes you through these steps:
- Define the problem.
- Know the relevant rules.
- Develop and evaluate courses of action.
- Choose the course of action that best represents relevant values.

Ethical reasoning isn't a separate process you pull out only when you think you're facing an ethical question. It should be part of the thought process you use to make any decision. Your participants count on you to do more than make sound decisions. They rely on you to make decisions that are ethically sound as well. You should always consider ethical factors and, when necessary, use relevant values to gauge what's right.

That said, not every decision is an ethical problem. In fact, most decisions are ethically neutral. But that doesn't mean you don't have to think about the ethical consequences of your actions. Only if you reflect on whether what you're asked to do or what you ask your people to do, will you develop that sense of right and wrong that marks ethical people and great leaders. That sense of right and wrong alerts you to the presence of ethical aspects when you face a decision.

Ethical reasoning is an art, not a science, and sometimes the best answer is going to be hard to determine. Often, the hardest decisions are not between right and wrong, but between shades of right. Regulations may allow more than one choice. There may even be more than one good answer, or there may not be enough time to conduct a long review. In those cases, you must rely on your judgment.

Define the Problem

Defining the problem is the first step in making any decision. When you think a decision may have ethical aspects or effects, it's especially important to define it precisely. Know who said what—and what specifically was said or demanded. Don't settle for secondhand information; get the details. Problems can be described in more than one way. This is the hardest step in solving any problem. It's especially difficult to make decisions in the face of potential ethical conflicts. Too often some people come to rapid conclusions about the nature of a problem and end up applying solutions to what turns out to be only symptoms.

Know the Relevant Rules

This step is part of fact gathering, the second step in problem solving. Do your homework. Sometimes what looks like an ethical problem may stem from a misunderstanding of a regulation or policy, frustration, or over enthusiasm. Other times, a difficult situation results from trying to do something right in the wrong way. Also, some rules leave room for interpretation; the problem then becomes a policy matter rather than an ethical one. If you do perceive an ethical problem, explain it to the person you think is causing it and try to come up with a better way to do the job.

Develop and Evaluate Courses of Action

Once you know the rules, lay out possible courses of action. As with the previous steps, you do this whenever you must make a decision. Next, consider these courses of action in view of relevant values. Consider the consequences of your courses of action by asking yourself a few practical questions: Which course of action best upholds my values? Do any of the courses of action compromise my values? Does any course of action violate a principle, rule, or law identified in Step 2? Which course of action is in the best interest of my participants and the environment? This part will feel like a juggling act, but with careful ethical reflection, you can reduce the chaos, determine the essentials, and choose the best course—even when that choice is the least worse of a set of undesirable options.

Choose the Course of Action That Best Your Values

The last step in solving any problem is making a decision and acting on it. Leaders are paid to make decisions. As a leader, you're expected—by your supervisors and your participants—to make decisions that solve problems without compromising values.

General and personal values and ethical decision making provide a **"moral touchstone"** and a workable process that enables you to make sound ethical decisions and take correct actions confidently. Find a place in your castle to put your touchstone. So that at all times, happy, sad, scared, alone, mad, confused or confident, you can turn to it for guidance. (US army officers training manual)

CHAPTER 7

SETTING GOALS

Time to look within; Time to look for new horizons; Will others follow? TS Cook

"If one advances confidently in the direction of his dreams, and endeavors to live the life which he has imagined, he will meet with a success unexpected in common hours."
Henry David Thoreau

Life's up and downs provide windows of opportunity to determine your values and goals.
Think of using all obstacles as stepping stones to build the life you want.
Marsha Sinetar

In the beginning, your quest to become a leader may have looked daunting, the objective clearly out of reach. Most people never accomplish their goals because they fail to set them. In this chapter we will look at how to bring to fruition your vision. We will also explore how to set reasonable goals for your program and its participants.

As you have spent considerable effort to develop your "Noble Gift" and to build your castle, so too should you spend time setting goals, because leadership without goals is destined to falter, lost without direction. Leadership without direction is not leadership, its we're lost together. Your participants will appreciate the clarity and the sense of purpose you give them. Together you can attain new heights and do things you believed possible. This is a fundamental strength of any quality leader.

Before you can attempt to meet your goals, you have to know what they are. That's a lot more complicated than it sounds. Your goals to this point may have been very short term, but now you are going to make decisions that *could* affect the rest of your life. That can be a very scary thought, but if you think things through and prioritize, you can set Specific, Measurable, Attainable, Realistic, and Timely goals - then meet them.

"I don't have any goals?" Not likely. Everyone has goals. You may not have them in clear focus right now, but you do have them. Picture yourself 5,10,15 years from now. Where are you living? What does that look like? Are you married? Where are you working? Whatever you are picturing yourself doing, then those are your goals. Think about them and keep refining them until they are specific.

Are there barriers to my goals? Write down what you perceive the hurdles to be. Now, determine if these stumbling blocks are real or imagined. Are they true barriers like not having the money to go to school or are they imagined like thinking you aren't smart enough. If they are imagined, change your thinking, you have control of your thoughts. Don't get trapped into negative self doubt belief patterns. Remember if you don't believe in your abilities nobody else will either. If they are real, explore different options like a cheaper school, a grants, scholarships or perhaps night school, so you can work during the day. Be creative with your thinking and your strategies.

"I don't know how to accomplish my goals?" Read the rest of this chapter, ask someone else. Speak with someone who has been doing what you want to do. Find out how she / he got there and do what they did! Use this individual as an adviser.

Set SMART Goals! By the end of the Season I want to Cartwheel!

SMART Goal Setting

I encourage you to pick up a pen and piece of paper and jot down the goals you want to reach. Look at each goal and **evaluate** it. Make any changes necessary to ensure it meets the criteria for a **SMART goal**. The following is adapted from an original work by 2004 Arina Nikitina http://www.goal-setting-guide.

S= Specific
M= Measurable
A= Attainable
R= Realistic
T= Timely

THE NOBLE GIFT

Specific

Goals should be straightforward and emphasize what you want to happen. Specifics help us to **focus our efforts** and **clearly define what we are going to do**.

Specific is the What, Why, and How of the SMART model.

WHAT are you going to do? Use action words such as direct, organize, coordinate, lead, develop, plan, build etc.

WHY is this important to do at this time? What do you want to ultimately accomplish?

HOW are you going to do it?

Ensure the goals you set are very **specific, clear and easy**. Instead of setting a goal to lose weight or be healthier, set a specific goal to lose two inches off your waistline or to cross Country Ski five miles at an aerobically challenging pace.

Measurable

If you can't measure it, you can't manage it. In the broadest sense, the whole goal statement is a measure for the project; if the goal is accomplished, there is success. However, there are usually several short-term or small measurements that can be built into the goal.

Choose a goal with measurable progress, **so you can see the change occur**. How will you see when you reach your goal? Be specific! "I want to read five chapters from my Emergency First Responders Book before my birthday" shows the specific target to be measured. "I want to be a good rock climber" is not as measurable.

Establish concrete criteria for measuring progress toward the attainment of each goal you set. When you measure your progress, you stay on track, reach your target dates, and experience the joy of achievement that spurs you on to continued effort required to reach your goals.

Attainable

When you identify goals that are most important to you, you begin to figure out ways you can make them come true. You develop the attitudes, abilities, skills, and financial capacity to reach them. Your begin seeing previously overlooked **opportunities** to bring yourself closer to the achievement of your goals.

Goals you set which are too far out of your reach, you probably won't commit to doing. Although you may start with the best of intentions, the knowledge that it's too much for you means your subconscious will keep reminding you of this fact and will stop you from even giving it your best effort.

A goal needs to stretch you slightly so you feel you can do it and it will need a real commitment from you. For instance, if you aim to lose 20 lbs in one week, we all know that isn't achievable. But setting a goal to loose 1lb and when you've achieved that, aiming to lose a further pound, will keep it achievable for you.

The feeling of success which this brings helps you to remain motivated.

Realistic

This is not a synonym for easy. Remember if it's easy, everybody would do it! Realistic in this case, means **do-able**. It means that the learning curve is not a vertical slope; that the skills needed to do the work are available; that the task fits with the overall strategy and goals of the organization. A realistic mission may push the skills and knowledge of the people working on it but it shouldn't break them.

Devise a plan or a way of getting there which makes the goal realistic. The goal needs to be realistic for you and where you are at the moment. A goal of never again eating sweets, cakes, crisps and chocolate may not be realistic for someone who really enjoys these foods.

For instance, it may be more realistic to set a goal of eating a piece of fruit each day instead of one sweet item. You can then choose to work towards reducing the amount of sweet products gradually as and when this feels realistic for you.

Be sure to set goals that you can attain with some effort! Too difficult and you set the stage for failure, but too low sends the message that you aren't very capable. **Set the bar high enough for a satisfying accomplishment!**

Timely

Set a timeframe for the goal: for next week, in three months, by fifth grade. Putting an end point on your goal gives you a **clear target** to work towards.

If you don't set a time, the commitment is too vague. It tends not to happen because you feel you can start at any time. Without a time limit, there's no urgency to start taking action now.

Time must be measurable, attainable and realistic.

Everyone will benefit from goals and objectives if they are SMART. SMART is the instrument to apply in setting your goals and objectives. (Nikitina)

Goal Setting

Goal setting is a very powerful tool that can yield strong results in all facets of your life and your group's life.

At its simplest level the process of setting goals and focus points allows the group (or you) to decide where it wants to go and what it wants to accomplish. By knowing precisely what your group wants to attain, they know what they will have to focus on and improve, and what is merely a disturbance. Goal setting gives you long-term vision and short-term motivation. It focuses the group's acquisition of knowledge and helps to organize its resources.

By setting SMART, clearly defined goals, the group can measure and take pride in the accomplishment of those goals. They can see forward progress in what might previously have seemed like meaningless toil.

By setting goals you and the group can:
- Achieve more
- Improve performance
- Increase motivation to achieve
- Increase pride and satisfaction in achievements
- Improve self-confidence
- Plan to eliminate attitudes that hold the group back and cause unhappiness

Research (Damon Burton, 1983) has shown that people who use goal-setting effectively:
- suffer less from stress and anxiety
- concentrate better
- show more self-confidence
- perform better
- are happier and more satisfied.

Goal Setting Helps Self-Confidence

By setting goals, and measuring their achievement, the group is able to see what they have done and what they are capable of. The process of achieving goals and seeing their achievement gives confidence and self-belief that the group will need that. Your group will be able to achieve higher and more difficult goals. This is a Core Competency of any Leader, and a good leader is able to teach this skill to their participants thus making the learning transferable into other parts of people's lives.

Providing that the group has the self-discipline to carry it through, goal setting is also relatively easy. The following section on goal setting will give you effective guidelines to help you to use this technique effectively.

To summarize, a good objective answers the following questions:
1. What will be different?
2. How will I know it when I see it?
3. What is the optimum performance level?
4. What is the minimum performance level?
5. What constraints, if any might affect performance

Setting goals for the group? Having the group set its own goals? Both are fine options, both depend on the style of leadership you are operating under. The following is copied from the book: *Mental Skills Training for Sports* Rushall, B. S. (1995).

Steps in Goal-setting

There are a number of steps that should be followed when setting goals. They are explained briefly below and are included as the steps for setting each goal-type included in this section. These steps were first described by Lars-Eric Unestahl of Sweden.

   1. Goal-awareness. Former goals which have and have not been achieved should be listed. This leads to better goal-setting skills and establishes an historical framework for developing realistic goals for the individual.

   Example; On our last trip to the White Mountains we were unable to climb Whiteface, Let's give it our best effort this trip.

   2. Goal-inventory. The group should establish a list of possible goals. This could be done in consultation with the leader and should include all types of goals including those with a low-probability of attainment. This step defines the range of possible goals.

   3. Goal-analysis. The goal-inventory should be evaluated with each goal being assessed for its appropriateness and possibility. A hierarchy of possible goals should be established for each classification.

   4. Goal-selection. The hierarchies of possible goals should be evaluated and the goals selected. The criteria for selection are that they be:
   - as difficult as possible but reachable while erring on the side of being too difficult rather than too easy;
   - agreed upon by the group member and leader;
   - established in priorities when more than one goal exists;
   - aimed at improving performance, not merely maintaining it or causing it to regress;
   - related to performance, not vague entities such as pride or confidence; and measurable.

5. **Goal-formulation.** When goals are selected, they should be formulated and analyzed according to the following characteristics:
- be expressed positively (no negative or avoidance wordings);
- be appropriate for the group and the individual members (not restricted to what the leader wants);
- have optimal probability (the group and the individuals should be able to justify why each goal can be achieved);
- have maximum believability (no doubts, all factors are controllable); and
- be measurable and observable.

Multiple goals. If possible, there should always be more than one goal established for a classification. The intent of teamwork should always be to achieve a number of outcomes. The reason for establishing multiple rather than single goals is that the incentive value of goals accumulates. The selection of multiple goals should always ensure that the attainment of the majority of them is highly probable. This will produce a positive orientation towards high expectations of success. The higher the expectation of success, the better the groups performance.

The setting of goals is not a simple task. It is not purely giving the instruction to "make up some goals" with the leader leaving it at that. It is a series of involved procedures that affects participation in a dramatic way. Because of that it is worthwhile to take the time to establish goals with the group according to the criteria that have been described above and the procedures indicated below. If that is not done, then goal-setting will be a feature of effective leadership that has been neglected. (Rushall page 3.1—3. 6)

Now that it is clear to everyone, what you hope to accomplish, you have added purpose to the mission (vision), your participants will be willing to work hard for the accomplishment of challenging tasks.

One summer Reggie and I had our group of Waukabiashi's camping out. During the night there was a fierce storm, but we had chosen our campsite well and were (relatively) assured we would be OK. As the night went on, I was pleased all group members were doing fine; however, when we awoke we found several trees had blown down in camp.

Not wanting to let the trees death go to waste, we formulated a vision of creating a totem pole. So out of the bottom 15 feet of the very large white pine that had fallen we set our goal. Convincing the Camp Director to buy some chisels, we had to make our own mauls out of other pieces of the tree. Each camper made his own maul and we then set out to create our masterpiece. The campers got so into chipping and carving, that they would work for hours, give up their free swim, stay after the buses just to follow their mission to completion.

By creating a vision, setting goals, and working hard the group was able to "plant" their totem pole. This totem pole told the story of the Waukabiashi's and it stood at the top of the hill that looked down on all of camp. This project would watch over camp for the next decade. After that year, every time one of our original Waukabiashi's would walk up that hill at the end of a long day, Reggie and I could feel the pride pour out of each of our young men.

As a leader you need to be prepared to dream, reach, set goals and work hard for their accomplishment. When you have mastered this process you will continue to grow as a professional, but also the people who you lead will grow in untold ways. This is the strength of your gift. Use it to help people become more confident, self aware, and more goal oriented.

CHAPTER 8

PREPARE TO LEAD

Up until now we have laid our foundation, added theory, purpose and values to our castle. With the walls, doors and windows added, we are ready to add the substance of your leadership. This will sustain you and allow you to share your "Noble Gift" with others.

In this chapter we will explore what we need to prepare ourselves to lead. We will look at; who we are leading, why we are leading them and what is needed as well as after the trip considerations.

A competent outdoor leader needs to be totally prepared for all eventualities on any given excursion. This may again seem daunting. However as we learned in our last chapter, if you set SMART goals in your planning process, you will most likely avoid poor planning. This in turn leads to a better run, more organized, dynamic, and a safer more enjoyable trip.

Any trip must have plans, we will learn about we can call Time Control, Energy Control, Emergency Control and Climate Control plans. As essential as these may seem, many outdoor leaders fail to consider one or even worse two or three of these areas. The result, misadventure, discomfort, pain, fear, disorganization or panic. As you will learn, a little work here, and some preparation can go a long way.

As leaders, you need to know who you are leading, so we will look at pre trip information questionnaires, medical screening, and the precursors to your risk management program.

Your day started simple enough, prepare the rafts, equipment, meet the group and then guide them down the remote class 3—4 gorge in the Western part of your state. Now you are on the side of the river administering CPR! What has changed? Could this have been prevented? Was this an appropriate trip for a person who is on heart medications? You now wish your agency had started the medical screening program you proposed for this and many of the other trips you lead! Your co-leader has left to get help as there is no cell service in this remote gorge. It is going to be at least an hour and a half before help arrives so the group will not get off the river until after dark. You now fear for the safety of group members as everyone is cold and scared. You have enough space blankets for the victim, but that's it. There is no staff left to get a fire going, and you can't stop CPR!

Could better pre-trip planning have helped here? What would you have done differently?

What steps needed to be thought about? What plans needed to be strengthened?

The Boy Scouts of America use the Motto "Be Prepared." A very simple yet encompassing set of skills, thoughts and work go into living up to this simple credo. In the book "Outdoor Leadership theory & practice" by Martin, Cashel, Wagstaff, Breunig. 2006 Human Kinetics they use the acronym "PREPARE" by using this acronym we can break down the steps of planning for any outdoor trip. By taking the Scout Motto and expanding it the authors simplify a very challenging set of tasks.

As a leader, remember the empowering skill of delegation. You need to allow other people, leaders and participants the opportunity to step up to the challenge and learn in the process. If you intend to run a country club trip, then you will do everything for the clients, but you must ask yourself the question "What are they learning?" As others accomplish their tasks, it is still up to you to check and recheck the details of the trip plans. The GO PREPARE system should help. The following is adapted from the book "Outdoor Leadership theory & practice" by Martin, Cashel, Wagstaff, Breunig.

GO PREPARE SYSTEM

An outdoor leader must take into consideration the following planning components by answering the related questions in order to develop a quality plan:

Information Explaining the GO PREPARE System

Each aspect of the GO PREPARE system will be studied at length so that the aspiring outdoor leader possesses the tools to design a comprehensive expedition plan. Finally, in this chapter we will discuss the importance of trip logistics and their place in the planning process. All trips require some level of logistical support. Logistics include transportation to and from the program site. Food drops, equipment exchanges, shakedowns and trip termination procedures. Smooth, well planned logistical support ensures that the trip plan is conducted in a competent manner.

Trip Purpose

The foundation of an effective trip plan revolves around well defined program goals and objectives. Outdoor leaders must understand organizational philosophy and program goals before attempting to develop a plan. Organizational philosophy and program goals vary significantly among agencies within the outdoor recreation industry. A competent outdoor leader is able to operationalize philosophy and goals through the expedition plan.

Trip Goals and Objectives (G.O.)

Developing expedition goals requires the same thought process used when creating goals for any program or educational lesson. Goals represent broad, intended outcomes to be experienced by clients as a result of participation. Trip goals reflect larger program goals which are guided organizational philosophy. Therefore, expedition goals should reflect the purpose of the organization by putting the philosophy into operational terms.

Goals provide direction for outdoor leaders and participants as they engage in a trip experience. Several objectives should be created to accompany each goal. Objectives represent specific, measurable outcomes related to each goal. Outdoor leaders are encouraged to use the SMART: specific, measurable, achievable, realistic, and time-bound method of objective development. Objectives serve as targeted outcomes to assess goal accomplishment. Well developed goals and objectives create measurable criteria necessary for program evaluation. Trip success and improvement can be determined through well written goals and objectives.

Outdoor leaders must take the time to craft quality goals and objectives when developing their trip plans. Well written goals and objectives serve the same purpose as a good map. Leaders are able to focus on a specific path or direction as they create and execute a trip. If leaders are forced to make tough programming decisions during the trip, goals and objectives will assist in the decision making process.

PREPARE System

Once the outdoor leader establishes trip goals and objectives, the leader must PREPARE for the expedition by engaging in a formal trip planning process. As learned earlier, a proper trip plan ensures safe, quality and environmentally sound experiences. It is recommended that an actual trip plan be compiled that addresses the following: participants, resources, equipment and clothing, a plan, access, rationing and an emergency plan.

Addressing these issues will alleviate many potential problems during the expedition. These components are not listed in order of priority or importance. Seasoned leaders work on issues simultaneously to bring the entire plan together as information falls into place. In some cases, trip planning may require the leader to begin several years in advance. For example, obtaining a permit for a trip location can take years if a waiting system or permit lottery is in place. However, the planning process may only take several days if components of the PREPARE system are in place. For example, an outdoor leader working for an established wilderness camp may experience the benefit of administrative support and a well established tripping program.

In this scenario, participant information, food, permits, routes and emergency procedures may already be in place. This wilderness leader simply needs to gather equipment and follow the standardized program format. The amount of trip planning required varies in any situation. The competent outdoor leader fully understands the GO PREPARE system of planning and creates a trip planning document. The following seven sections encompass the PREPARE system of trip planning. Each of the seven components should be included in a comprehensive trip plan.

1. Participants

"Who are the participants?" Any outdoor leader involved in the planning process must ask this critical question.

Many of the trip's parameters hinge on this important question. The competent outdoor leader views this question on several levels. An analysis of participant characteristics includes the following factors: age, group size, gender, health, prior experience and motivational level. Careful consideration of these factors enables outdoor leaders to design the appropriate trip.

Age

Developmental level by age is a logical consideration. Experiences designed for teenagers will vary from experiences designed for older adults. For example, the outdoor leader might keep the itinerary very busy and packed with numerous activities in order to keep the teenager engaged. Older adults might appreciate a less defined schedule with more opportunity to control their own time and pace. An in-depth discussion human development characteristics is beyond the scope of this chapter. Outdoor leaders without this knowledge would benefit from further research in this area.

Group Size

The number of participants represents a critical planning factor. Group size dictates equipment decisions, food amounts, permit restrictions, etc. Group size also influences environmental factors. Larger groups should not be led into environmentally sensitive areas to reduce issues such as vegetation trampling and perceptions of overcrowding. Large groups (twenty or more) can be split into patrols to increase hiking efficiency. This technique requires more leaders and first aid kits. These issues would be considered during the planning process.

Gender

Gender characteristics of a group also influence trip planning decisions. Is the group all males, females or coed?

Serving a co-ed group (especially youth) may require the leadership team to be co-ed. Co-ed groups influence risk management and equipment decisions. Leaders must consider tenting arrangements. Purchasing food for a group of teenage boys may vary from the quantity of food purchased for a group of adult women.

Health

Leaders must know the physical and mental condition of their participants. Medical and personal data forms collect this information. Leaders should have access to these forms during the trip planning process.

Information such as physical limitations, diet restrictions, medications and past medical history will influence all aspects of the trip plan. For example, if a participant has a documented physical restriction, the outdoor leader may have to adapt an activity or modify equipment to met individual needs.

Prior Experience

Knowing a participant's prior experience allows the leader to make informed decisions in all aspects of planning. For example, a known group of experienced whitewater kayakers allows a leader to design a paddling trip at an advanced level. Beware; leaders must have an accurate screening system to predetermine experience.

Participants who underestimate or overestimate their own ability provide poor information to design the perfect trip. Remember to plan trips that are safe enough for the weakest member of your group. As far as your skills go you should always be in your comfort zone, IE: Not Challenged.

Motivational Level

Knowing or understanding a participant's motivational level also helps when designing a trip. Many leaders will ask participants well before the trip to describe their personal goals and reasons for participation. Trips can then be designed around personal needs. Many organizations institute an admissions or screening process. If a participant's goals and motivations are not congruent with trip goals, other experiences and organizations can be recommended.

2. Resources

In most cases, resource availability determines trip design. Creating and balancing a trip budget should be reflected in the trip plan. Minimally, competent leaders create a simple budget to account for anticipated expenditures. In addition to budgeting, creativity is also a handy skill needed to compile resources. Equipment may be borrowed, traded or rented to supplement trip resources. For example, some organizations do not have the resources to purchase specialized outdoor equipment. Therefore, agencies require participants to bring specialized equipment such as personal kayaks or mountaineering equipment. Or, one agency will trade specialized equipment with another agency such as vertical caving gear for snow shoes as opposed to investing and maintaining an inventory of both items. Outdoor leaders must take into consideration all possible resources in order to execute fiscally sound expeditions.

3. Equipment and Clothing

A quality trip plan includes a personal clothing list. Because we as humans essentially try to carry with us our own environment, a leader should determine the appropriate clothing and equipment for any given trip and distribute a recommended personal clothing and equipment list to participants. This is the Climate Control Plan. This plan takes into consideration several different factors: equipment, clothing, climate, conditioning and environment. In our next Chapter we will look at specific equipment recommendations for several different types of activities.

The dress WISE layering system serves as the primary guideline for clothing selection:
- **W** = Wicking Layer—the layer worn next to the skin to wick moisture away and to insulate. Long underwear, liner socks and gloves and stocking cap.
- **I** = Insulation Layer—this layer traps warm air against the body to ensure adequate warmth. Wool or fleece pants, fleece jacket and gloves.
- **S** = Shell Layer—this consists of a water/wind proof outer shell such as rain and wind gear made of treated nylons or breathable/water proof fabrics.
- **E** = Extra Clothing—extra layers should be packed according to environmental conditions and types of activities.

Trip equipment falls into two categories: (1) Personal equipment and (2) Group equipment. A quality trip plan includes both equipment lists. The contents of these lists vary depending on organizational philosophy and resources. For example, some organizations believe standard gear should be issued to all participants to alleviate feelings of inequity. Feelings of inadequacy and privilege are reduced if everyone has the same rain gear, sleeping bag and backpack for example. Some organizations maintain no equipment inventories and require participants to supply all equipment.

Outdoor leaders know that weather plays a major role in expedition planning. Leaders must research the historical weather patterns for a given area. This information is easily accessible by internet to discover record temperature highs, lows, wind speeds and averages. With this information, leaders anticipate the absolute worst and best case weather scenarios and prepare properly. A leader who plans a trip based on a current, long term forecast is asking for trouble. Leaders do not forget to check current environmental conditions too. Snow pack, water levels, fire hazard, etc. also affect equipment and clothing choices. For example neglecting to bring snowshoes and gaiters when needed could adversely affect the trip. The worst should always be anticipated.

4. Plan

A quality trip plan includes both an itinerary and a time control plan. Itineraries vary in detail and length. The leader's objective is to provide a basic overview of trip flow through these tools. Some leaders create a detailed, daily schedule delineated by a timeline of all activities. Others create a broad overview of activities on a daily basis without time constraints. A quality trip plan includes some form of schedule to guide everyone involved in the process such as leaders, participants, administrators, parents, emergency contacts, permit providers, etc.

The Time Control Plan (TCP) composes a critical component of the trip plan. The TCP involves map reading and understanding the details of a route. Quality TCPs provide insight into the amount of energy and time required to complete a specified route in a safe fashion. TCPs also provide opportunity to develop topographic map interpretation skills. A competent leader develops a TCP that matches the goals and ability level of the group. A well calculated TCP helps leaders chose the perfect challenge for their group. TCPs can be developed for any adventure travel mode such as canoeing, backpacking, mountain biking, etc. This chapter discusses TCPs in the context of foot travel only. Adaptations can be made based on the leader's expertise to create TCPs for other travel modes. TCP plans typically include:

- Start time: the estimated time the group will start a hike
- Estimated walking pace: the estimated number of miles to be covered in an hour. (This calculation reflects many factors such as the group's level of fitness, weight of packs, weather, experience, etc. Average hiking speeds for a group of beginners with moderate levels of fitness and pack weights range from one to two miles per hour.)
- Linear miles to be covered: Route mileage is estimated using trip maps.
- Elevation gain and loss over the hike: The total amount of elevation gained and lost over the length of the hike is calculated. As a general rule, one hour should be added to the total hiking time for every 1000 feet gained and ½ hour will be added for every 1,000 feet lost (Ford & Blanchard, 1993). By using this calculation, leaders take into account the amount of energy required to hike over rough terrain. The amount of energy used is interpreted in energy miles. Another method used to determine actual energy miles states to add one mile for every 1,000 feet gained and ½ mile for every 1000 feet lost over the length of a hike. Note that high altitude conditions will affect this estimation and typically increase hiking time as groups gain altitude over 10,000 ft.
- Break time: estimate the average amount of break time expected per hour as well as additional breaks for food or other activities.
- Potential camp sites: identify daily destinations with backup options along the way.
- Identification of hazards and attractions
- Ending time: calculating the anticipated ending time for the hike allows leaders to estimate the total amount of time required to accomplish the hike.

5. Access

An important piece of any trip plan includes legal access to the intended trip area. Appropriate permission must be gained to travel on public or private lands. Leaders are responsible for ensuring that legal access is obtained.

This important task must occur far in advance to allow for adequate communication and administrative procedures. Fostering healthy relationships with land agencies and private land owners constitutes a critical leadership function. The following tips will help ensure excellent public relations with private and public land managers:

- Personally call or meet appropriate representatives to inquire about access.
- Complete all paperwork in ample time so not to inconvenience or pressure land administrators.
- Pay appropriate fees and maintain copies of all permits and letters of permission.
- Offer to send the agency or land owner a copy of your trip plan if not required.
- Thank individuals for their time as opposed to arguing if permission cannot be obtained.
- Strictly adhere to all regulations and wishes of the agency or land owner.
- Follow up with a thank you note once the trip is complete.

6. Rationing

The way to a group's heart is thru its stomach. This is the Energy Control Plan. Planning and packing the appropriate food rations can dramatically affect the success of any trip. Participants typically burn many more calories compared to engagement in everyday life activities. Ensuring enough calories and nutritional balance maintains energy levels as well as positive attitudes. Well nourished expedition members consistently make better safety related decisions as opposed to chronically tired, hungry participants. Meal time with great tasting food promotes relaxation and community building. Great satisfaction comes when participants develop their culinary skills and share with others. A competent outdoor leader is able to develop an appropriate rationing system.

The amount of care taken to ensure proper ration planning should increase as trip length increases. Basic nutrition rules exist that an outdoor leader must keep in mind. The average person consumes 2,500 to 3,000 calories when participating in average outdoor activities such as moderate backpacking or canoeing. Strenuous activities such as difficult backpacking or snow camping require consumption of 3,000 to 3,700 per day. Very strenuous activities such as mountaineering or extended time spent in cold weather requires 3,700 to 5,000 calories per day. Leaders ensure nutritional needs by adhering to the following guidelines. The average intake per person per day should be (50-80%) in carbohydrates, (10-15%) in proteins and fats (30%) in fats of which only 10% should be saturated fats (Pearson, 1997). Two different rationing systems lend themselves to sound trip planning. Each system is described in the following sections.

Menu Planning

Most people tend to be familiar with menu planning. Leaders systematically plan the contents of each meal over the course of a trip. Advantages of the menu system include outlining all meals to avoid confusion, an organized guide to prepare each meal, and a convenient way to plan short trips (two–five days). Leaders will discover that calculating calories and ensuring appropriate nutritional breakdown is more difficult when menu planning.

Bulk Rationing

Bulk rationing involves buying food in bulk based on the amount (weight) of food consumed per day. Food items purchased in bulk would include items such as pasta, beans, rice, flour, cereals, nuts, dried fruits, cheese, sugar, soup bases, spices, etc. found at a local grocery store or food co-op. Advantages of bulk rationing include avoiding extensive menus for long trips, allows for cooking creativity and caloric and nutritional calculations tend to be easier to compute. Using this system, participants consume anywhere from 1.5 to 2.5 pounds of food per person per day. Average activities require 1.5 to 2 pounds per person per day. Strenuous activities require from 2 to 2.25 pounds of food per person per day. Very strenuous activities range up to 2.5 pounds of food perperson per day (Pearson, 1997). Bulk food must be repacked into clear plastic bags to reduce packaging and additional waste generated in the field. Repackaging consolidates food into a more manageable system of transport. A convenient way to ration plan using the bulk method requires the use of a spreadsheet (Drury & Holmlund, 1997).

A short discussion comparing freeze dried food and bulk rationing is merited when faced with the choice.

Prepackaged freeze dried meals allow for quick preparation with minimal skills and time. These meals tend to be very expensive but very light if carried in a backpack. Beware that a prepackaged meal for four persons may satisfy only two hungry group members. The bulk rationing system is cheaper ($3.00 to $6.00 per person per day) Participants can get by with plenty of delicious food on $3.00/day and eat extremely well on $6.00/day.

Bulk rationing tends to be more financially feasible for institutional budgets and participant pockets. Prepackaged freeze dried food will double or even triple food costs and tends not to be as nutritional.

Fuel

When using camp stoves, fuel calculations vary depending on climate, altitude, size of group, food type and stove type. Leaders should start by consulting with manufacturer's recommendations. For example, a group of six using one white gas stove at high altitude in the snow requires much more fuel usage as opposed to a summer backpacking trip in the Great Smoky Mountains. A general rule used for a typical white gas backpacking stove for a group of three in the summer is as follows: Pack ½ quart per day for a group of three people backpacking in the summer time under moderate conditions (Harvey, 1999).

7. Emergency Plan

This is what I refer to as the Emergency Control Plan (ECP). Competent outdoor leaders include emergency protocol within a functional trip plan. Formalizing emergency procedures creates the framework for a quick, smooth response to any emergency situation. Of course, the best preparation for an emergency is prevention. Proper trip planning and quality leadership are two of the best defenses against emergencies. However, incidents do occur during outdoor expeditions. Leaders must have a formal E.C.P. to guide them through intense decision-making situations. Emergency protocol varies depending on the specifics of an organization's risk management plan. There are however fundamental components to an emergency plan. The following items are typically addressed in an emergency plan.

Emergency Contact List

Names, titles, primary phone numbers and alternative phone numbers for all potential must be compiled and carried during the trip at all times. Contacts to include: emergency rescue services for trip area, local sheriff, land management agency or land owner, organizational emergency contacts, support staff, contractors and nearest hospital or medical services. This list should be duplicated and waterproofed to be carried in the first aid kits and with the leaders.

Evacuation Procedures

If an evacuation is required, leaders must decide if outside assistance is needed or if self-evacuation is feasible.

Protocol related to either decision must be developed before the trip. For assisted evacuations, protocol might reflect the process for landing a helicopter, how information is relayed over a phone or radio, how teams of runners/messengers are managed and how jobs are assigned to group members to assist. For self evacuations, protocol might reflect when to use a litter and how to protect other members of the group. It should be clear to the leaders who will pay for an assisted evacuation. Knowing this up front will avoid confusion and allow the leader to obtain the appropriate resources if he or she is responsible. For example, some organizations require participants to obtain additional insurance to cover costs of evacuations.

Evacuation Routes
At all times during a trip, leaders must be aware of the nearest evacuation route. Topographic maps, guide books and research will provide this information. Evacuation routes are documented by marking each location on a map.

Communications
Contingency plans must be made to contact appropriate authorities in the event of an emergency. Satellite and cell phones may not always work. Backup plans must be developed so that leaders are not totally dependent upon technology. Along with evacuation routes, knowing where the nearest land lines are remain important information to know.

First Aid Procedures
Competent outdoor leaders seek training in wilderness medicine. Wilderness First Aid, Wilderness First Responder or Wilderness Emergency Medical Technician make up one of three certifications most outdoor leaders possess. Outdoor leaders should follow the protocol learned during these trainings and provide first aid at the level dictated by their training. The number of first aid kits and their contents should reflect the type of trip, environmental conditions and caregiver's expertise. For example, a leader not trained to inject epinephrine for anaphylaxis shock should not carry syringes in her/his first aid kit.

Record Keeping Procedures
Accident reports must be maintained by trip leaders. These forms typically are carried in the first aid kits. These documents are designed to be used in a variety of ways as discussed in the risk management chapter of this text. Leaders are responsible for completing and maintaining these forms in the case of an emergency. In some cases, copies of these forms are sent out with runners during a self-evacuation to properly inform response teams of the emergency.

Additional Considerations
Emergencies will be handled in a smooth, efficient manner if leaders are aware of all emergency related protocol. As stated before, protocol will vary among agencies. Therefore, competent outdoor leaders have knowledge of the following issues: severe weather protocol, loss of life protocol, sexual harassment and dealing with misconduct or psychological evacuations. Copies of the trip plan should be left with the appropriate individuals back home so others have comprehensive information to assist when needed.

Logistics
Finally, GO PREPARE but don't forget about logistics! Once a leader establishes a quality trip plan based on the GO PREPARE system, trip logistics are required to carry that plan out. Logistics involve administrative issues, transportation, food drops, equipment transport as well as post trip procedures. A successful expedition relies on well planned logistical support. Leaders may be able to manage their own logistics during a shorter or less complex trip. Longer trips that integrate numerous adventure activities over a long period of time require more complex logistical support. Some organizations specifically hire staff to serve in a logistical role.

Logistics staff duties may include purchasing and packing food, issuing and cleaning gear, transporting participants and equipment. Logistics staff sometimes conducts food drops during long expeditions. For example, a 30-day expedition may be divided into three different (10-day) food rations. Once the group nears the end of a ration period, logistics staff may horse pack food to a designated meeting point or meet the group at a convenient road head. Leaders that arrange their own logistics must plan accordingly. If there are multiple ration drops for example, food can be hidden in a cache to be picked up along the route later. If leaders serve as transportation drivers, do secure places exist to leave vehicles and equipment at the road head? With no outside logistical support, leaders may have to design a trip so that the group loops back to vehicles. Private shuttle services can also be contracted to meet transportation needs. The point to be made is that leaders must design appropriate logistical support to execute trip plans. Goals and objectives, resources, routes choices, itineraries, equipment needs and other trip planning components affect logistical choices. For example, leaders may simplify a trip plan to minimize logistical costs. Transportation, food and equipment considerations compose three critical logistical concerns.

The following considerations are stated in the form of questions. No exact answer will exist for each question.

The leader must put each question into the context of her or his situation to arrive at an appropriate solution.

Transportation

1. What resources are available to transport participants and equipment? Do leaders have access to agency buses or vans? What is the vehicle carrying capacity and does this number affect group size? Does the option exist for participants to transport themselves to the trip area? Are trailers or other modes of transportation available to carry equipment?

2. Who will drive? Are specific qualifications and training required to drive vehicles? Is it possible for qualified participants to serve as drivers on long road trips? If a shuttle service is contracted, are they reputable and safe?

3. What will be the status of vehicle access and security? Will vehicles be parked at trailheads and be accessible during and after the trip? Will these vehicles be secure if left unattended for long periods of time? If vehicles are not left at trailheads, how will transportation be arranged?

Equipment

1. How are equipment needs to be met before the trips start? Who will inventory, organize and issue equipment before the trip? Who will ensure proper equipment functioning before equipment is taken into the field? Do the leaders conduct a visual inspection of participant's personal gear before the trip start to ensure preparedness?

2. Who is responsible for equipment during the trip? Who will pay for damaged or lost equipment during the course of a trip? If the trip consists of numerous adventure activities, how will kayaks, caving gear, climbing gear and other specialized equipment be made available when needed? How will personal and group equipment be transported to the trip site?

3. How will equipment be dealt with after the trip? Who will inventory, clean, repair and store equipment once the trip is over? How will lost or damaged equipment be replaced and made ready for the next trip?

Food

1. How will food acquisition and preparation be handled? Who conducts initial menu or bulk ration planning?

Who purchases the food? Where is the best place to purchase needed items? Who will organize and repackage food? How will food be distributed to participants? If a long trip requires multiple rations, how will the food be divided, packaged and stored?

2. How will food issues be handled during the trip? Will the participants be divided into smaller cook groups or will cooking occur in one large group? How will the food be divided and carried during the trip? How will food drops be arranged during the trip if needed? What will be done with left over food at the end of a ration period or at the end of a trip?

Pre-Trip Considerations

Beyond the major issues of transportation, equipment and food, other logistical concerns face the outdoor leader. Administrative functions influence logistical considerations. Leaders must obtain and review participant information as discussed in the PREPARE system. This information can be obtained from medical forms or from participant applications. Participant information and special needs influences logistical decisions. For example, a participant with special needs may require the leader to adapt or modify equipment in advance. Dietary restrictions will influence food planning. Leaders typically conduct some type of participant orientation before going into the field. Pre-trip meetings, telephone interviews and information packets are common orientation techniques. Once participants arrive, leaders should consider an inspection of participant's personal gear. Double checking the participants' clothing selection, sleeping system, hiking boots, etc. allows leaders to spot inappropriate or unsafe equipment. Arrangements for additional clothing or new gear can be made before entering the field.

Many programs will integrate a "shakedown" experience into the programming format before the actual trip begins. Shakedowns involve taking participants into the field for a short period (one to seven nights) to test gear, experiment with clothing and develop initial skills before embarking on a full-blown expedition. Leaders identify faulty or inappropriate equipment that will be exchanged while equipment remains accessible.

Participants learn quickly if rain gear, footwear and other personal items are adequate. Participants also have the opportunity to experience the rations during a shakedown. Some organizations require the participants to package their own rations after the shakedown. Exposure to the food during the shakedown allows the participants to make more informed decisions about food packing. Better decisions regarding food choices, quantities and packaging techniques can be made. Before starting a shakedown or trip, it should be made very clear who will be responsible for lost or damaged equipment. Leaders will prevent future misunderstandings if this issue is addressed up front. For example, some organizations check equipment out to individuals and hold them responsible for each issued item. Some allow groups to share in the cost of lost or damaged equipment. Other organizations absorb the costs based on budgeting techniques to account for damaged/lost equipment. Finally, do not forget to leave a copy of the trip plan with logistical support. The plan serves as a handy reference to meet deadlines and to problem solve when issues arise.

Post-Trip Considerations

Finally, leaders need to account for logistical issues once the trip ends. How will the leaders handle final evaluations? For example, an organization requires that all participants complete a course and instructor evaluation. Leaders must arrange access to evaluation forms and schedule an appropriate amount of time for completion. Leaders must also consider the logistics of a closing ceremony and the supplies needed to conduct the ceremony. For example, certificates and patches may be awarded to the participants. How will leaders obtain these supplies and decide when and where the ceremony will be conducted. Leaders may want to consider a closing banquet. Whether it means visiting a restaurant or purchasing fresh food, these arrangements must be considered. Many times participants wish to have group member contact information upon trip completion. Leaders should consider facilitating this process so that participants can foster bonds developed during a trip.

Of course leftover food and equipment issues must be dealt with in order to support logistical planning for the next trip. Equipment must be inventoried, cleaned and stored properly. Adequate washing and drying space must be made available. Participants may or may not be part of the cleaning process. For example at the end of an outdoor leadership training experience, it would be an educational objective for students to have this important experience. At the end of a guided, commercial trip, equipment cleaning and repair would be the guide's responsibility. Finally, if additional fees need to be collected for equipment damage, trip photographs, tee shirts, mugs, etc. this must be factored into the overall logistical process.

GO (Goals and Objectives)
    Content Required:
        a. List of group's goals and objectives for the trip

P = Participants (Who are the participants?)
    Content Required:
        a. Brief description of participants in your group
        b. Names and contact information
        c. Health Information

R = Resources (What resources are available to support an expedition?)
    Content Required:
        a. Budget

E = Equipment and Clothing (What equipment and clothing will be needed?)
    Content Required:
        a. Personal Clothing List (Item and material make up—Use WISE Format)
        b. Group Gear List

P = Plan (What is the itinerary and time control plan?)
    Content Required:
        a. Time Control Plan (Daily hiking schedule, distance, time, etc.)
        b. Copy of map with campsites

A = Access (How does the group obtain proper access?)
    Content Required:
        a. Copy of permit or letter of permission
        b. Rules and regulations of the area

R = Rationing (How will menu be determined and food packed?)
    Content Required:

   a. Menu
   b. Food List
   c. Fuel Needs
E = Emergency Plan (What is the emergency plan?)
  Content Required:
   a. Personal emergency contacts
   b. Evacuation routes
   c. Contact information for land agency, local emergency response, sheriff and RU

LOGSTICS
  Content Required:
   a. Transportation plan
   b. Route to the site that includes a map

Adapted from the work of;
Martin, B., Cashel, C., Wagstaff, M., Brenig, M. (2006). *Outdoor Leadership: Theory & Practice.* Human Kinetics: Champaign. IL.

Works Cited in original work;
Drury, J. & Holmlund, E. (1997). *The camper's guide: To outdoor pursuits.* Sagamore Publishing: Champaign, IL.

Ford, P., & Blanchard, J. (1993). *Leadership and administration of outdoor pursuits* (2nd ed.). Venture Publishing.

Harvey, M. (1999). *The National Outdoor Leadership School's wilderness guide.* Simon & Schuster: NY, NY.

Pearson, C. (1997). *NOLS cookery.* Stackpole Books: Mechanicsburg, PA.
Priest, S. & Gass, M. A. (1997). Effective leadership in adventure programming. Human Kinetics: Champaign, IL.

The Leave No Trace Center for Outdoor Ethics recommends the following principles for all groups and individuals entering the out of doors.
 Keep campsites small. Focus activity in areas where vegetation is absent. ***In pristine areas;*** Disperse use to prevent the creation of campsites and trails. Avoid places where impacts are just beginning.

1. DISPOSE OF WASTE PROPERLY
  Pack it in, pack it out. Inspect your campsite and rest areas for trash or spilled foods.
  Pack out all trash, leftover food, and litter.
  Deposit solid human waste in cat holes dug 6 to 8 inches deep at least 200 feet from water, camp, and trails. Cover and disguise the cat hole when finished.
  Pack out toilet paper and hygiene products.
  To wash yourself or your dishes, carry water 200 feet away from streams or lakes and use small amounts of biodegradable soap. Scatter strained dishwater.

2. LEAVE WHAT YOU FIND
Preserve the past: observe, but do not touch, cultural or historic structures and artifacts.
Leave rocks, plants and other natural objects as you find them.
Avoid introducing or transporting nonnative species.
Do not build structures, furniture, or dig trenches.

3. PLAN AHEAD AND PREPARE
Know the regulations and special concerns for the area you'll visit.
Prepare for extreme weather, hazards, and emergencies.
Schedule your trip to avoid times of high use.
Visit in small groups. Split larger parties into smaller groups.
Repackage food to minimize waste.
Use a map and compass to eliminate the use of marking paint, rock cairns or flagging.

4. TRAVEL AND CAMP ON DURABLE SURFACES
Durable surfaces include established trails and campsites, rock, gravel, dry grasses or snow.
Protect riparian areas by camping at least 200 feet from lakes and streams. Good campsites are found, not made. Altering a site is not necessary.

In popular areas;
Concentrate use on existing trails and campsites.
Walk single file in the middle of the trail, even when wet or muddy.

5. MINIMIZE CAMPFIRE IMPACTS
Campfires can cause lasting impacts to the backcountry.
Use a lightweight stove for cooking and enjoy a candle lantern for light.
Where fires are permitted, use established fire rings, fire pans, or mound fires. Keep fires small.
Only use sticks from the ground that can be broken by hand.
Burn all wood and coals to ash, put out campfires completely, then scatter cool ashes.

6. RESPECT WILDLIFE
Observe wildlife from a distance. Do not follow or approach them.
Never feed animals. Feeding wildlife damage their health, alters natural behaviors, and exposes them to predators and other dangers.
Protect wildlife and your food by storing rations and trash securely.
Control pets at all times, or leave them at home.
Avoid wildlife during sensitive times: mating, nesting, raising young, or winter.

7. BE CONSIDERATE OF OTHER VISITORS
Respect other visitors and protect the quality of their experience.
Be courteous. Yield to other users on the trail. Step to the downhill side of the trail when encountering pack stock.
Take breaks and camp away from trails and other visitors.
Let nature's sounds prevail. Avoid loud voices and noises. (Leave No Trace Center for Outdoor Ethics).

THE NOBLE GIFT

The Wilderness Education Association has been involved in training outdoor leaders. They have broken down effective Leadership of others into the following 18 point curriculum.

Good judgment is the umbrella that covers the 18 points. It is the pervasive leadership quality that grows from the exercise of decision making in a leadership role. The development of good judgment is the philosophical and educational objective underlying all 18 points.

1. Decision Making and Problem Solving
2. Leadership
3. Expedition Behavior and Group Dynamics
4. Environmental Ethics
5. Basic Camping Skills
6. Nutrition and Rations Planning
7. Equipment and Clothing Selection / Use
8. Weather
9. Health and Sanitation
10. Travel Techniques
11. Navigation
12. Safety and Risk Management
13. Wilderness Emergency Procedures and Treatment
14. Natural and Cultural History
15. Specialized Travel / Adventure Activity
16. Communication Skills
17. Trip Planning
18. Teaching, Processing and Transference

Source and for more information; Wilderness Education Association 900 East 7th Street - Bloomington IN, 47405 E-mail: wea@indiana.edu

Let's look closely at participant screening. This breaks down into three areas you should be concerned with, physical attributes and therefore a readiness to learn and participate in the activities you propose to lead. Another category would be a medical concern. Clearly someone could have the physical readiness to participate, but have a medical condition that would make it unwise for that person to come on your trip. Conversely, you need to be willing to adapt as appropriately as possible. The last category we should concern ourselves with would be psychological readiness to benefit from your program. Here too, you want to make sure your activities are readiness appropriate for your clients.

Confidentiality is an area you need to be concerned with. In some medical screening questionnaires the client and their parents will be sharing with you information of a confidential and personal nature. Be aware of your professional responsibilities in this area and share only this information on a need to know basis. Others should know about a medical/ physical/ psychological condition of a participant, only if that person will be in a direct position to effect a safety system or treatment of that person in the event of an emergency.

Example; You have been told that Dan has epilepsy. He clearly can not do your SCUBA camp, but he does want to learn to swim. Who on your staff do you share this information with?

The following are some questions Outward Bound uses for one of its programs; you should consider adapting these questions for your Medical Screening Questionnaire;

OUTWARD BOUND

Women of Courage; This questionnaire is written to help you understand the challenges of the Women of Courage Program and to support you in preparing emotionally, physically and mentally.

This information is **confidential** and will allow your instructors to know about any situations that may arise during the course.

Once we have received your completed application we will contact you to arrange a telephone interview. This interview provides a chance for you to ask questions and for us to review your application with you.

Pre-Course Questionnaire
Your Name:_____
Address:_____
Phone:_____ Emergency Contact:_____

Please use additional paper as necessary.

1. How did you find out about the Women of Courage program?

2. Why do you want to participate in Outward Bound's Women of Courage?

3. What do you hope to gain from your experience at Outward Bound?

4. What excites you about the program?

5. What are your initial fears about participating in this program?

6. You may have never been on a canoeing trip before. Perhaps you have experienced trauma in a rural or wilderness setting. Please describe any particular concerns you have about the course setting (e.g. unpleasant memories, fear of water, fear of the dark, worries about being away from home and/or conveniences).

7. Women of Courage is designed to be a challenging experience. While you will be having fun, there will also be many activities that can be hard on your body and emotions such as getting up early, sharing a tent with other women, peeing in the woods, canoeing, climbing and portaging.

What will be your biggest emotional challenge?

What will be your biggest physical challenge?

How will you take care of yourself during times of stress?

8. Have you been in individual counseling or therapy?   Yes   No
In the past?   Yes   No
Currently?   Yes   No
For how long? _____

Tell us about your therapy. How many sessions did you go to? What were some of the issues you dealt with?

9. Have you been in support or therapy groups?   Yes   No
In the past?   Yes   No
Currently?   Yes   No
For how long? _____

Tell us about the group sessions. How many sessions did you go to? What were the topics you talked about?

10. Tell us about your support system you have when you go home after the course.

11. Is there anything else you would like to tell us about? Is there anything going on in your life right now that might add to the challenge of an Outward Bound course?

Thank you for your time and honesty.

Pre- Medical Questionnaire
Name:
Course Code:
Course Dates:

We look at all medical forms carefully to ensure participants are fully prepared for a successful Outward Bound course. Before we ask you to go to a doctor for a physical exam, which often costs money, we use this form to get an initial medical history. Please complete the form accurately and completely. Every question must be answered. Please note that none of the following conditions will automatically eliminate you from the program.

Women with a wide variety of medical conditions and physical abilities have attended Women of Courage.

If you circle yes to any question below please describe in detail.

1. Do you have any current medical problems? [Describe]
    Yes   No
2. Does your health prevent you from participating in any physical activities? [Describe]
    Yes   No

3. Are you taking prescription or non-prescription medications? [List medications, dosages & reasons for taking]   Yes   No
4. Do you smoke? [If so, how much?]   Yes   No
5. Do you have asthma or shortness of breath?   Yes   No
6. Do you have diabetes?   Yes   No
7. Do you have high blood pressure?   Yes   No
8. Have you ever had seizures?   Yes   No
9. Do you require a special diet? [Please specify]   Yes   No
10. Are you pregnant? [What trimester?]   Yes   No
11. Do you have problems with you neck, back, knees or joints that limit your activities? [Describe]   Yes   No
12. In the last two years: A) Have you been in therapy or treatment for any of the following issues:
a. Suicide or self-harm   Yes   No
b. Depression   Yes   No
c. Chemical Dependency   Yes   No
d. Anger or Physical Aggression   Yes   No
e. Eating disorders   Yes   No
B) Have you received in patient psychiatric hospitalization or psychotropic medication?   Yes   No
13. Please describe the physical activity do you do on a regular basis.

14. Please describe any other conditions that may have a bearing on your health or your ability to participate in the Women of Courage course.

15. Your height (inches or centimeters)
16. Your weight (pounds or kilograms)
17. Your clothing size:
Shirts:

Pants:

18. Please list any fears you feel limit you.

19. State your comfort level in new situations. Do you have any fears, in the water, dark spaces, in closed areas, or in the woods. You may have to go to the bathroom in many different places. Will this present any problems for you?

Your birth date?

Skill Screening

Like medical and physical screening a good skill questionnaire can help avoid potential problems. It helps you get to know the strengths of your group. You can see experience level, who has what skills, and perhaps linked with the other surveys might suggest who is ready for your trip.

Another purpose in screening is to limit group size. Certain locations have regulations on the maximum number of people traveling and/or camping together. Note that if neither you nor your co-leader has done the trip before it will be more difficult to screen since the physical requirements will be less clear. In this case you may need to set a higher experience level and requirements.

If your trip is advertised here are some important points to keep in mind:
- Be prepared for a phone call anytime. Avoid screening via email unless you know the person and their abilities. A direct conversation is preferred since it is more interactive and allows you to get a better sense of a person's true abilities and experience.
- Have a list of questions to ask (see below). The conversation should not be an exercise in wearing each other out. You may need to explain why you are asking these questions (as the leader you are responsible for the group and want everyone to be safe and to have a good time). Develop your own style. A relaxed conversation that encourages the potential participant to volunteer information about themselves is better than just hitting them with a battery of questions.
- If they qualify for the trip, provide initial information (follow-up later with email or printed information sheet).
- Remember that screening does not end until the trip actually begins—be sure to check equipment/clothing at the trailhead or starting location.

The following questions can be used to screen participants for outdoor trips.
The difficulty level of the trip will determine which questions to ask.

QUESTIONS:
1. What is your name? (spell if necessary)
2. What is your address?
3. What is your telephone number?
4. Can you tie a retrace figure 8 knot?
5. Do you know anyone else on the trip?
6. What is your experience level? Explain the trip rating system if necessary and one exists.
7. What is the longest trip you have been on?
8. Have you gone with a group before?
9. What other trips have you been on and who led them? What trips have you done in the past six months? What kind of exercise do you do regularly? How often?
10. What kind of equipment do you have?
11. What is the worst problem you have ever had on a trip?
12. Do you have any special medical problems or are you taking any Medications? Allergies?
13. Do you have any medical training?
14. Where have you Kayaked/climbed/hiked?
15. Can you cook?
16. What was your best group experience? Did the leadership play any part in this?
17. What was your worst group experience? Did the leadership play any part in this?
18. Do you have any questions?

YOUR RESPONSES:
After obtaining answers, you may then decide whether the trip will be beyond the level of skill or the

individual. If they wish to participate in too-easy a trip, that is their decision but if they wish to go on a trip that is beyond their ability that is your decision. For an advanced trip it is best not to accept someone that you do not know until you have a chance to check their references, others they have gone with on trips and their leaders. As a leader, it will be your responsibility to recommend that they do not participate. If they persist, you may have to refuse to take them. Explain that the trip includes certain risks (mention them) and that an inexperienced participant could create a possible burden on the leader and other participants. Encourage them to try another easier trip so they can build up their skills. If their equipment is incomplete or inadequate, you may require them to obtain the proper gear, for their own comfort and safety and that of the group.

If they qualify for the trip, mention the requirements, such as deadline for deposit, cancellation policy, length of trip, where and when to meet and what type of snack or food to bring. Explain how long after the set meeting time you will wait for all to appear.

Remember that a well-planned trip and well-prepared participants make for an enjoyable and safe experience for all. Good screening can do much to ensure that this will happen. This is truly the start of an efficient risk management program. (AMC page 28)

I have said for years that once the trip starts, that is the easiest part of the entire experience, only if you have done your work while planning. Good luck, Remember GO PREPARED.

CHAPTER 9

GEAR LISTS

The most important essential, however, is not on the list— **"Common Sense."** Having the right gear is one thing, knowing how and when to use it is quite another. Most often, it's not a person's equipment that saves their bacon. It's their experience, know-how, and good judgment.

Conversely, it is generally inexperience and lack of good judgment that gets people into trouble. Not only must we have the proper equipment—including the ten essentials plus four—and know how to use them. We must also cultivate knowledge and wisdom related to the backcountry activities that we engage in through self-study, courses, and leveraging off the experiences of others.

The Ten Essentials: An Annotated List

By far, the best known outdoor equipment list is the so called list of Ten Essentials. The list was first suggested in the 1930s in an article which appeared in the newsletter of the <u>Mountaineers</u>, a Seattle-based outdoor club. Since then it has been reprinted in various forms and is used often by outdoor educators as a teaching tool.

The original ten items, along with helpful notes, are listed below. Even though the Ten Essentials list is revered by many in the outdoor field, it shouldn't be taken as gospel. It is a good starting point, but you should add to the list depending on circumstances- where you are going and what you will be doing. Suggestions for additional items are included at the end of the list.

1. Matches. Use **"Strike-anywhere"** matches. Whatever you do, don't use "Strike-on-box" matches. It is impossible to light "Strike-on-box" matches on anything other than the special striker strip on the box. If you don't have the match box or if the box gets wet, you are in big trouble. Try it out for yourself, and you'll be amazed. They simply won't light on anything else. Be very careful when shopping for matches. It's easy to get the two different types of matches mixed up at the store. The boxes look the same. Always double-check and make sure you buy the right matches. Once you're sure that you have the right matches, place the matches in a **waterproof case**—small plastic waterproof match containers sold at sporting goods stores work fine—and include a **striker**. A piece of emery board makes a good striker. In very wet conditions, you'll want to have a dry striker along with your matches. When you need a fire, you don't want to mess around trying to light matches on wet rocks. Matches, which weigh nothing and easily fit in your pocket, are one of your most important survival tools. Not only does fire allow you to survive a cold, miserable night, but it is an important morale booster as well.

2. Fire Starter. Always include fire starter with matches. Always. There are times when even the best woodsman or woodswoman will not be able to make a fire without it. Fire starter assures that you can get fire going quickly, no matter how bad the conditions. Place some fire starter in your pack, but also put a *small chunk of fire starter* along with your *matches* and a *striker* in a *waterproof case*. Carry the case in your pocket. Never put your waterproof match case in your pack. If you do and if for some reason, you get separated from your pack, you're in trouble.

3. Map. Many people who have been rescued could have easily gotten themselves out of trouble by simply having a good map along. I can name three times, when I would not have made it out of the woods without a map. Believe me, those were three nights I did not want to spend in the woods alone.

4. Compass. Even if you carry a GPS device, you still need a compass. Although, GPS units provide a reasonably accurate fix of your location, they do not provide accurate bearings. If you know how to follow a compass bearing, you can guide yourself out of thickly forested areas, featureless winter landscapes, foggy sagebrush areas, etc.

5. Flashlight, Extra Batteries and Bulb. A flashlight—or better yet, a headlight-is another one of those tools, like a map, that is simple and cheap insurance. Should night overtake you, it gives you the ability to find your way back to the trailhead.

6. Extra Food. Having extra food is critical in emergency situations. It helps ward off hypothermia in cold, wet weather, and it keeps you thinking clearly in a crisis.

7. Extra Clothing. Even if it's a sunny day and you're on a short day hike, you should carry at least a rain jacket. It keeps you dry and also serves as wind protection. A good hat - wool or fleece, is also high on the list of extra clothing, since a large amount of body heat is lost through the head and neck area. When deciding what to take, stay away from cotton which is worthless when wet.

8. Sunglasses. Good sunglasses are particularly important when you are in snow country. Snow or sun blindness can completely disable an individual.

9. First Aid Kit. Be prepared for emergencies. Carry basic first aid supplies such as sterile gauze and pads, band-aids, moleskin, etc. See <u>lightweight first aid kit</u> for ideas.

10. Pocket Knife. With a pocket knife—a multi purpose Swiss Army knife is ideal—you can make field repairs, shave branches to make kindling, punch holes to repair a tarp, cut nylon cord, etc. Source; The Mountaineers Article www.mountaineers.org

Other Essentials

Here's some other important items that you'll want to consider in addition to those listed above.

Shelter. The Ten Essentials' list has one glaring omission. It lacks the materials to build an emergency shelter. When all is considered, the best way of surviving wet or snowy nights is to have some type of roof over your head and a dry floor under you. One of the best shelter options is a combination of a **lightweight nylon poncho, nylon cord and a lightweight space blanket.** The poncho can be tied to trees or placed over a rudimentary snow shelter to keep out wind and weather—and in a pinch it doubles as a rain jacket. Use a *nylon* poncho or tarp. Avoid plastic ponchos and tarps. They rip easily and become brittle in cold weather. For a dry floor underneath you, a lightweight space blanket is a good choice. They are inexpensive, light, and when folded aren't much larger than the size of a bar of soap. Since such lightweight space blankets, however, can tear easily, they are best used as a floor and not depended upon as a tarp over your head.

Desert Travel Considerations. Don't forget one or more *containers of water* (an important item for any outdoor travel) and *a piece of plastic* for making a solar still.

Winter Travel Considerations. For winter travel, make sure you have *adequate extra clothing*. You'll also want to carry enough *repair supplies* to be able to fix a broken snowshoe or ski. A *headlight* is doubly important in the winter since days are short and night comes quickly. It's hard to get to water in the winter—lakes are frozen and streams are under a deep layer of snow—and you'll need a *metal cup* to use for melting snow. A *portable shovel* is an important winter survival tool. With one you can dig snow caves or snow trenches in which you can survive a bitter, cold night. Moreover, in avalanche terrain, a shovel is a must. It is nearly impossible to dig someone out of an avalanche without a shovel. Lastly, in avalanche country, always carry an *avalanche transceiver* along with your shovel.

Walk-up Mountaineering. If you enjoy climbing mountains without using technical equipment, it is still good practice to carry at least 50 feet of lightweight rope for emergencies.

Lakes and Rivers. For water related activities, a life jacket is a must. Hypothermia is always a concern and you'll want plenty of high energy food, rain gear and synthetic clothing. Carry a throw rope rather than a coiled rope. They are far easier to use and are less apt to get tangled. And, of course, no self respecting river rat ever leaves home without a roll of duct tape.

Compiled by RonWatters reprinted with permission. http://www.isu.edu/outdoor/ten.htm

Ultralight Backpacking Equipment List

"ALL" DAY HIKES:

Start with the 10 Essential, Then add:

DAY PACK

Large enough to fit all your gear inside, and preferably with compression straps, sternum strap, padded belt and back.

HIKING BOOTS

Appropriate for the terrain you'll be in. Remember to treat them before you go, with Nikwax or some other waterproofing agent.

BASE LAYERS: NO COTTON!
- ___Lightweight thermal underwear top
- ___Lightweight thermal underwear bottom

INSULATION:
- ___Light Fleece Jacket—200 or 300 weight
- ___Light Fleece Vest—200 or 300 weight (optional, use your good judgment)

SHELL:
- ___Windproof, waterproof, highly-breathable parka or jacket—pit zips, 2-way zipper, and pack pockets for ventilation; and preferably with adjustable hood and hem, large enough to allow layering underneath.
- ___Windproof, waterproof, highly-breathable pants—full-length side zips for easy entry and ventilation.

OTHER BACKPACKING ESSENTIALS:
- ___Hiking Socks and Liners (+ extra pair)
- ___Quick-drying hiking shorts (wear over the thermal underwear in cool weather)
- ___Thin fleece gloves (e.g., lightweight Patagonia Synchilla)
- ___Fleece Cap or Balaclava (must cover ears)
- ___Baseball cap (wool, synthetic—cotton ok in warmer weather)
- ___Toilet Paper

FOOD: Take enough for the day and extra for 24 hours
- ___Gorp (nuts, seeds, dried fruit, m&ms)
- ___Hard Cheese (lasts longer)
- ___Jerky (beef/turkey) or salami
- ___Cookies
- ___Crackers
- ___Tiger's Milk Bars
- ___Licorice Sticks
- ___Kudos
- ___Bear Valley Meal Packs
- ___Power Bars (Berry)
- ___Chewing Gum
- ___Gatorade
- ___Bagels, English muffins
- ___String cheese (individually wrapped)
- ___Chocolate and candy
- ___Dried fruit (raisins, apples, pears, peaches, bananas)
- ___Dried meat and fish
- ___Giant pretzels
- ___Raw fruit/vegetables
- ___Nuts
- ___Pop Tarts
- ___Fig/Peach/Apple Newtons

OPTIONAL:
- ___Hiking Staff or trekking poles

THE NOBLE GIFT

___Bandanna (cotton ok)
___Sit pad
___Gore-Tex Socks (in damp environs, keeps feet warm and dry)
___Gaitors (long for snow or short for scree)
___Pack Rain Cover
___Pack Towel (1)
___Camera & extra film
___Parachute Cord (many uses)
___Duct Tape (many uses)
___Monocular or Binoculars
___Reading Glasses
___Field Watch
___Altimeter / Barometer (especially if going offtrail)
___Moleskin (if not part of First Aid Kit)

"ALL" OVERNIGHT HIKES:

___Start with the Fourteen Essentials.
___Add DAY HIKES gear. Then add the following:

BACKPACK

___In lieu of the day-hike daypack, you'll probably need a pack with more capacity to carry the additional over-night gear. A pack with approximately 3000 to 4000 cubic inches is satisfactory for long weekends and packs with 4400 + cubic inches are generally used for week-long treks. You'll need to experiment to find what works for you.

SLEEPING SYSTEM:

___Sleeping Pad if on snow, consider closed-cell / open-cell combination—e.g., full-length, closed-cell Cascade Design RidgeRest 3/4 length, ultralight, open-cell Thermarest
___Sleeping Bag: 3-Season light 20 degree bag should be enough most of the time
___Sleeping Bag: Winter If you have only one bag e.g. the 20 degree bag above, you can add warmth to it by using it together with a bivy sack and/or by wearing some or all of your clothes to bed. If you can afford it, and go out in the Winter frequently, you might want to invest in a winter bag e.g. a zero degree bag; dryloft will keep your insulation dry; a draft collar is a must.
___Tent (3 or 4-season) or Gore-Tex Bivy Bag if it snows at night, you might need to knock the snow off your three-season tent. If you go out frequently in the Winter, you might want to invest in a bomb-proof four-season tent.

COOKING:

___Lightweight Trail Stove (white gas—e.g., Whisperlite; or butane/propane—e.g., Primus Titanium)
___Stove Fuel—white gas or butane/propane canister (if melting snow for water, take more fuel).
___1 medium pot w/lid & pot handle
___Lexan spoon

FOOD: Here are some suggestions for you to choose from, these work well and are inexpensive

Breakfast:
___Hot chocolate

___Coffee, Tea
___Instant Hot Cider
___Instant Oatmeal (variety)
___Instant Cream of Wheat
___Malt O' Meal (w/brown sugar)
___Granola
___Nature Valley Granola bars (variety)
___Dried fruit (apples, raisins)

Lunch:
___Gorp (nuts, seeds, dried fruit, m&ms)
___Bagels
___String Cheese
___Hard Cheese (lasts longer) ___ Jerky or salami
___Cookies
___Crackers

Dinner:
___Instant soup (Lipton's Chicken Noodle & Cream of Chicken)
___Freeze-dried dinners (cook in their own foil container = less cleanup)
___Mountain House: Lasagna, Spaghetti, Pasta Primavera, Chili Mac
___Mountain House (All Natural): Noodles & Chicken, Chicken Polynesian, Beef Stroganoff
___Mountain House Freeze-dried desserts (Fruit Crisps—peaches, strawberries)

Dinner Spices (keep dry in small transparent canisters)
___onion powder
___garlic / chili powder or other spices you enjoy at home
___pre-mixed, ground dried herbs
___pepper (red or black)

Other Non-Cook Nourishment—Good for Snacks
___Tiger's Milk Bars
___Licorice Sticks
___Kudos
___Bear Valley meal packs
___Power bars (Berry)
___Chewing Gum
___Gatorade
___Bagels, English muffins
___String cheese (individually wrapped)
___Chocolate & candy
___Dried fruit (raisins, apples, pears, peaches, bananas)
___Dried meat and fish
___Giant pretzels
___Raw fruit / vegetables
___Nuts

THE NOBLE GIFT

    ___Pop Tarts
    ___Fig/Peach/Apple Newtons
    ___Crackers
OPTIONAL
    ___Optional if going light and fast overnight with Bivy: Lightweight Tarp for rain/snow cover
    ___Candle Lantern
    ___Miniature playing cards; cribbage set, etc.
    ___Therm-a-Rest'R Lite Chair Kit (weighs 10 oz and fits all 20-in-wide Therm-a-rest mattresses)

ADDITIONAL GEAR FOR SPRING & FALL
BASE LAYERS: (NO COTTON !)
    ___Mid weight thermal underwear top
    ___Mid weight thermal underwear bottom
OTHER ESSENTIALS:
    ___Mid weight fleece gloves or mittens
    ___Waterproof over gloves or mittens
OPTIONAL:
    ___Snow Shovel
    ___Avalanche beacon
    ___Snowshoes and Poles w/touring baskets
    ___Ice Axe (for mountain trips in snow & ice)

ADDITIONAL GEAR FOR SUMMER
OPTIONAL:
    ___light shorts for swimming
    ___synthetic T-shirt (e.g., coolmax)
    ___light water shoes (e.g., Speedo Surfwalker, Nike Water Shoes)
    ___sun hat w/neck shroud

ADDITIONAL GEAR FOR WINTER
BOOTS:
___In addition to substantial leather boots, appropriate for winter conditions, you can also consider plastic boots and sorel insulated boots, as possible options.
BASE LAYERS: (NO COTTON !)
___Midweight or Expedition-weight thermal underwear top
___Midweight or Expedition-weight thermal underwear bottom
OTHER ESSENTIALS:
___Mid weight or Expedition-weight Insulated fleece gloves or mittens
___Waterproof over gloves or mittens
OPTIONAL:
___Down Sweater
___Insulated Boots (e.g., Sorel Bighorn—rated to -40 degrees).
___Hand and ToeWarmers (e.g., *Grabber Mycoal* air-activated warmer)

___ Snow Shovel
___ Avalanche beacon
___ Snowshoes & Poles w/touring baskets
___ Ice Axe (for mountain trips in snow & ice)
___ Insulated Water-Bottle Blanket

© RonWatters reprinted with permission. http://www.isu.edu/outdoor/ten.htm Hiking Gear Inventory & Ultralight Backpacking Equipment List.

Suggested Equipment List for Backpack Trips
The following equipment list is a guide to help you prepare for backpack trips. More items are listed than you will actually need but it will give you an idea of some of the equipment possibilities.

Dressing in layers is the best choice for outdoor activities. As you get warm, you can take off layers, and as you cool down during breaks, you can put them back on. The term synthetics on the clothing lists, below, refers to materials such as pile, capilene, synchilla, lycra or polypropylene.

Note also that some of the items can be shared. The tent and stove can be split up among the party. Repair and first aid kits can also be shared. Feel free to make copies of this list and pass it out to the members in your party.

Clothing–Inner Layer
- ☐ Synthetic underwear
- ☐ Inner socks (wool or synthetic)
- ☐ Swim suit

Clothing–Insulating Layer
- ☐ Pile shirts or jackets
- ☐ Down or synthetic fill jackets
- ☐ Down or synthetic fill vest
- ☐ Wool shirt
- ☐ Wool sweater
- ☐ Pants (preferably synthetic)
- ☐ Hiking shorts & t-shirt
- ☐ Wool or pile socks (2 pairs)
- ☐ Wool stocking hat
- ☐ If you expect cold weather: mittens or gloves (wool or pile)

Clothing–Protective Layer
- ☐ Wind breaker or parka with hood
- ☐ Rain jacket or poncho
- ☐ Hat for sun protection

Other Clothing Items
- ☐ Suspenders, belt or webbing
- ☐ Bandana
- ☐ Gaiters (if you'll be traveling through snow)

THE NOBLE GIFT

Pants Pockets
- ☐ Matches (with striker in waterproof container)
- ☐ Knife
- ☐ Fire starter

Feet
- ☐ Hiking boots
- ☐ Sandals or Tennis Shoes (nice in camp or for river crossings.)
- ☐ Insoles
- ☐ Extra socks

Haulage
- ☐ Pack
- ☐ Stuff bags with toggles for clothing, food and gear
- ☐ Day pack (if you plan to do day hikes from a base camp)

Bedroom
- ☐ Sleeping bag
- ☐ Sleeping pad
- ☐ Bivouac bag
- ☐ Tent (poles, snow stakes, fly, guy lines) OR Tarp and Ground cloth
- ☐ Candle or candle lantern

Kitchen
- ☐ Stove
- ☐ Matches in stove
- ☐ Fuel bottle (with gas)
- ☐ Funnel
- ☐ Pots
- ☐ Pot gripper
- ☐ Cup
- ☐ Spoon
- ☐ Corkscrew
- ☐ Food
- ☐ Water container(s) & water
- ☐ Water purification system (filter & accessories, purification tablets)
- ☐ Bear-proof food container (in bear country)

Repair Kit
- ☐ Sewing needle
- ☐ Nylon thread or dental floss
- ☐ Duct tape
- ☐ Vice grips (5" size)
- ☐ Clevis pins (for external frame packs)
- ☐ Bailing wire
- ☐ Extra stove parts (gaskets for stove, fuel cap, etc.)

Emergency Kit
- ☐ Matches (and striker in waterproof container)

- ☐ Fire starter (solid fuel pellets, candle, pitch wood, etc.)
- ☐ Compass
- ☐ Map
- ☐ Knife
- ☐ Whistle
- ☐ Nylon cord

First Aid Kit

- ☐ Two gauze rolls (2" wide)
- ☐ Moleskin for blisters
- ☐ Chapstick
- ☐ Sunblock
- ☐ Two triangular bandages
- ☐ Six sterile pads (4"x4")
- ☐ Anti-acid tablets
- ☐ Ace bandage
- ☐ Band-aids-assorted sizes
- ☐ Butterfly closures
- ☐ Safety pins
- ☐ Aspirin
- ☐ Two-inch first aid tape
- ☐ First aid book
- ☐ Personal medications

Also see Lightweight First Aid Kit.

Personals

- ☐ Lotion
- ☐ Toothbrush/paste
- ☐ Glasses or contacts
- ☐ Comb
- ☐ Mirror

Miscellaneous

- ☐ Sunglasses
- ☐ Sun block
- ☐ Headlamp or flashlight (spare batteries and bulb)
- ☐ Extra candles
- ☐ Rope (particularly important in bear country to hoist food into a tree)
- ☐ Watch
- ☐ Notebook/pencil
- ☐ Book
- ☐ Wire saw
- ☐ Thermometer
- ☐ Toilet paper
- ☐ Insect repellent

Revised 6/24/98. Compiled by R. Watters http://www.isu.edu/outdoor/packlist.htm

THE NOBLE GIFT

Check-off List for Day Hiking Trips

Here's a handy check-off list you can use when planning day hikes. You'll need to adapt the list to your needs, but make sure that you carry enough that you'll able to survive the night out if something goes wrong. (See the <u>Ten Essentials'</u> list for more details on important survival items).

- ☐ Matches -Use "<u>Strike Anywhere</u>" matches. Place matches & fire starter in a waterproof case
- ☐ Firestarter - Always take firestarter along with matches, always.
- ☐ Striker for Matches- If things are wet, a striker is a godsend. Emery board works well.
- ☐ Waterproof Case - Place matches, firestarter, striker in waterproof case & carry in your pocket.
- ☐ Map
- ☐ Compass
- ☐ Headlight or Flashlight, Extra Batteries & Bulb
- ☐ Food - Lunch, energy bars, & candy which is very important in hypothermic conditions
- ☐ Water or Sports Drink
- ☐ Extra Clothing -Take, at least, gloves, wind breaker—better yet, rain jacket—and stocking hat.
- ☐ Gaitors - If hiking in snow
- ☐ Sun Glasses
- ☐ Sun Screen
- ☐ Pocket Knife
- ☐ First Aid Kit (See <u>Lightweight First Aid Kit</u>)
- ☐ Lightweight Nylon Tarp—For Emergencies (See information on emergency <u>shelters</u>)
- ☐ Space Blanket—For Emergency Ground Cloth (See information on emergency <u>shelters</u>)
- ☐ Nylon Cord - Use to tie up the tarp for emergency shelter
- ☐ Day Pack or Hip Pack

Revised 6/24/98. Compiled by R. Watters http://www.isu.edu/outdoor/packlist.htm

Mountain Bike Day Trips

Be prepared when you go on your next mountain bike ride. Here's a suggested list of items that you'll want to consider carrying with you.

- ☐ Mountain Bike
- ☐ Helmet
- ☐ Gloves
- ☐ Clothing–Be sure to take at least a wind shell or rain jacket in the event the weather changes.
- ☐ Food–Snacks, energy bars
- ☐ Water or Sports' Drink - At least 6 ounces for every 2 hours
- ☐ Sun Screen
- ☐ Sun Glasses
- ☐ First Aid Kit (See <u>Lightweight First Aid Kit</u>)
- ☐ Headlight–for longer rides
- ☐ Matches & Firestarter in Waterproof Container (Hey, it's light & could be a life-safer)
- ☐ Space Blanket–The kind that packs down to the size of a bar of soap
- ☐ Extra Tube
- ☐ Patch Kit–glue or adhesive patches, patches, sandpaper

- ☐ **Tools:**
    - ☐ 6, 8, 10 Hex Wrench Set,
    - ☐ Duct Tape
    - ☐ Chain Tool
    - ☐ Adjustable Wrench
    - ☐ OR Combination Tool like a "Cool Tool"
    - ☐ Quarters for Telephone (Just in case!)

Before Getting Underway:
- ☐ Check Wheels - Spin wheels and make sure they are true.
- ☐ Check Quick Releases - Quick releases should be tight.
- ☐ Check Headset - Make sure headset is free of sand and not sloppy.
- ☐ Check Brakes - Brakes should pull correctly and pads should be aligned on rim.
- ☐ Check Peddles - Shake peddles & make sure they are secure.

Revised 6/24/98. Compiled by R. Watters http://www.isu.edu/outdoor/packlist.htm Contributors: Michelle Byrd, Mat Eperlding

Suggested Equipment List for Multi-day Kayaking & Rafting Trips

The following lists are suggestions. The actual equipment that you carry will depend on your likes and dislikes. The lists include most of the items that might be carried on a luxurious-style raft trip where weight isn't much of a problem. If you are going on a lightweight raft trip or on a self-supported kayak trip, then pare down and choose those items which will meet your needs yet still enable you to be safe and self sufficient. Feel free to make printed copies of the list and check off items as you are getting ready for the trip.

Adapted from: *The Whitewater River Book: A Guide to Techniques, Camping and Safety*

Rafting

Boats and Accessories
- ☐ Inflatable raft and various parts (thwarts, bow and stern lines, boat bag, etc.)
- ☐ Frame, if used, and straps or cord for lashing frame to boat
- ☐ Oar boat: oars, oar stops, oar- locks or thole pins and clips, extra oars in addition to oar locks
- ☐ Paddle boat: paddles for everyone, plus a couple of extras
- ☐ Pump
- ☐ Waterproof bags and/or rigid containers to carry gear and food
- ☐ Bailing buckets
- ☐ Straps, cord, carabiners, or clips for lashing gear above floor of boat
- ☐ Tarp to cover equipment on boat

Repair Kit
- ☐ Duct tape
- ☐ Patching material, glue, solvent (all items should be compatible with materials used in your raft)
- ☐ Scissors to cut material
- ☐ Brush to apply glue

- ☐ Sandpaper
- ☐ Rag
- ☐ Carpet thread or dental floss, and carpet needle to mend bad tears (sewing awls also work)
- ☐ Boat with a frame also would include:
- ☐ Tools (vise grips, pliers, screwdriver, wrench, hand drill, hammer, bits, small saw)
- ☐ Bailing wire
- ☐ Pipe clamps
- ☐ Extra screws, bolts, nuts, nails, washers to fit parts on frame
- ☐ Epoxy
- ☐ Replacement parts for any breakable item

First Aid Kit
- ☐ Triangular bandages
- ☐ Gauze rolls (two inches wide)
- ☐ Moleskin for blisters on hands or feet
- ☐ Assorted Band-Aids
- ☐ Sterile pads (four by four inches)
- ☐ Butterfly closures
- ☐ Safety pins
- ☐ First aid tape (two-inch size)
- ☐ Ace bandage
- ☐ Aspirin
- ☐ Antacid tablets
- ☐ Snake bite kit
- ☐ Tweezers
- ☐ First aid book
- ☐ Personal medications
- ☐ Drugs (if you carry drugs, work with a doctor to learn correct dosages and possible side effects)

Also see Lightweight First Aid Kit.

Clothing
- ☐ Wetsuit or dry suit
- ☐ Wet suit booties or wet shoes or booties-shoe combination
- ☐ Hat and/or helmet
- ☐ Windbreaker or paddling jacket
- ☐ Wind pants or rain pants
- ☐ Rain gear (jacket and pants)
- ☐ Shorts and/or swimsuit
- ☐ T-shirt
- ☐ Wool or pile shirts or jackets or sweaters
- ☐ Wool pants
- ☐ Wool or synthetic long underwear
- ☐ Underwear

- ☐ Synthetic fill or down jacket
- ☐ Wool stocking cap or balaclava
- ☐ Dry pair of shoes and clothing for in camp
- ☐ Leather gloves or Pogies

Personal Equipment
- ☐ Waterproof bag to carry personal clothing and equipment
- ☐ Life jacket
- ☐ Sleeping bag
- ☐ Sleeping pad
- ☐ Tarp or tent with poles, stakes, etc.
- ☐ Flashlight, with spare batteries and bulb
- ☐ Candle for light in tent
- ☐ Personal items (toothbrush, toothpaste, hand lotion, glasses or contacts, towel or washcloth, biodegradable soap, razor, etc.)
- ☐ Eating utensils (cup, spoon, plate, etc.)
- ☐ Notebook and pen
- ☐ Knife, matches, fire starter (best if carried on your person)
- ☐ Water bottle
- ☐ Insect repellent
- ☐ ChapStick
- ☐ Sunblock
- ☐ Sunglasses with safety strap
- ☐ Fishing gear and fishing license
- ☐ Camera, with film, lenses, etc.

Safety and Rescue Equipment
- ☐ Life jacket (one extra life jacket per raft maybe required in some states or countries or by some agencies managing the river)
- ☐ Throw-rope rescue bags or ropes in each boat
- ☐ Signal mirror
- ☐ Winch with no stretch rope
- ☐ Knife attached to life jacket
- ☐ 4-5 Carabiners
- ☐ 4-5 Slings (six to twelve-foot lengths of one-inch tubular webbing)
- ☐ 4 Prussiks (6-foot lengths of 5-7 mm rope)
- ☐ Police whistle

Other Group Equipment
- ☐ Map with waterproof map case
- ☐ Compass
- ☐ Guidebook and other resource books about the river and area
- ☐ Water containers

THE NOBLE GIFT

- ☐ Purification tablets or other means of water purification
- ☐ Permit on rivers regulated by governmental agencies
- ☐ Matches and fire starter
- ☐ Ropes for lining boats
- ☐ Shovel
- ☐ Lantern
- ☐ Fire pan with grill
- ☐ Plastic garbage bags
- ☐ Burlap bags or nylon stuff bags to use over plastic garbage bags to prevent spills (also handy for carrying cooking pots, Dutch ovens, fire pan)
- ☐ Toilet paper
- ☐ Portable toilet system (toilet seat, chemicals to stop methane production, any other parts)

Cooking and Food Equipment

Lightweight trips:
- ☐ Pots ☐ Small stove and fuel ☐ One cup and one spoon per person ☐ Food and spices

Luxurious-style trips:
- ☐ Dutch oven
- ☐ Frying pan
- ☐ Coffee pot
- ☐ Griddle
- ☐ Buckets
- ☐ Coolers and other food containers
- ☐ Spatula
- ☐ Large spoon
- ☐ Pliers
- ☐ Knives
- ☐ Can opener
- ☐ Burlap bags to hold Dutch ovens and pots
- ☐ Charcoal & lighter (when wood is scarce)
- ☐ Propane or gas stoves if fires are not used, with fuel
- ☐ Paper towels
- ☐ Dish soap and scrubber
- ☐ Clorox for sterilizing dishes and utensils
- ☐ Eating utensils for each person
- ☐ Food and spices

Kayaking

Choose clothing and equipment from the previous list that best meet your needs, plus the following:
- ☐ Kayak or decked canoe
- ☐ Paddle
- ☐ Flotation bags
- ☐ Small, waterproof day storage bag to carry items that must be readily available

- ☐ Sponge
- ☐ Spray skirt
- ☐ Helmet
- ☐ Duct tape for repairs
- ☐ Spare break-down paddle
- ☐ Wet suit or dry suit
- ☐ Wet suit booties
- ☐ Cold weather gear: mittens, pogies, hood
- ☐ Paddling jacket
- ☐ Throw-rope rescue bag
- ☐ Water bottle
- ☐ Other rescue equipment:
  - ☐ 2-3 Slings (six to twelve-foot lengths of one-inch tubular webbing)
  - ☐ 2 Prussiks (six-foot lengths of 5-7mm rope)
  - ☐ 2-3 Carabiners
  - ☐ Knife attached to life jacket

Revised 5/10/04 Compiled by R. Watters http://www.isu.edu/outdoor/packlist.htm

Suggested Equipment List for Overnight Ski or Snowshoe Trips

The following equipment list is a guide to help you prepare for overnight winter trips. More items are listed than you will actually need to give you an idea of some of the equipment possibilities.

Dressing in layers is the best choice for outdoor activities. As you get warm you can take off layers, and as you cool down during breaks, you can put them back on. The term synthetics on the clothing lists below, refers to materials such as pile, capilene, synchilla, lycra or polypropylene.

Note also that some of the items can be shared. The tent and stove can be split up among the party. Repair and first aid kits can also be shared. Feel free to make copies of this list and pass it out to the members in your party.

Adapted from <u>Ski Camping: A Guide to the Delights of Backcountry Skiing</u>. Compiled by RonWatters reprinted with permission. http://www.isu.edu/outdoor/ten.htm

Clothing–Inner Layer
- ☐ Long john top and bottoms (wool or synthetic)
- ☐ Inner socks (wool or synthetic)
- ☐ Liner gloves (wool or synthetic)
- ☐ Vapor barrier (plastic socks or bags, etc.)

Clothing–Insulating Layer
- ☐ Pile shirts or jackets
- ☐ Down or synthetic fill jackets
- ☐ Down or synthetic fill vest
- ☐ Wool shirt
- ☐ Wool sweater
- ☐ Turtleneck

- ☐ Wool pants or knickers
- ☐ Pile pants
- ☐ Wool or pile socks (regular or knicker) (2 pairs)
- ☐ Wool stocking hat or balaclava
- ☐ Hood of jacket
- ☐ Mittens (wool or pile) (2 pairs)

Clothing–Protective Layer
- ☐ Windshirt or parka with hood
- ☐ Rain jacket
- ☐ Wind pants
- ☐ Overmittens

Other Clothing Items
- ☐ Suspenders, belt or webbing
- ☐ Bandana
- ☐ Face mask
- ☐ Gaiters

Pants Pockets
- ☐ Matches (in waterproof container). Be sure to use "strike-anywhere" matches.
- ☐ Knife
- ☐ Fire starter

Feet
- ☐ Ski boots
- ☐ Insoles
- ☐ Extra socks
- ☐ Boot wax
- ☐ Down or synthetic fill booties
- ☐ Overboots

Skis/Snowshoes and Accessories
- ☐ Skis and bindings or Snowshoes and bindings
- ☐ Poles (screw together type for avalanche terrain)
- ☐ Skins

Haulage
- ☐ Pack
- ☐ Stuff bags with toggles

Bedroom
- ☐ Sleeping bag

- ☐ Sleeping pad
- ☐ Bivouac bag
- ☐ Vapor barrier inner bag
- ☐ Tent (poles, snow stakes, fly, guy lines)
- ☐ Candle or candle lantern

Kitchen
- ☐ Stove
- ☐ 12"x12" ensolite pad for insulation under stove
- ☐ Matches in stove
- ☐ Fuel bottle (with gas)
- ☐ Funnel
- ☐ Pots
- ☐ Pot gripper
- ☐ Cup
- ☐ Spoon
- ☐ Corkscrew
- ☐ Food
- ☐ Water bottle and water

Repair Kit
- ☐ Sewing needle
- ☐ Nylon thread or dental floss
- ☐ Duct tape
- ☐ Sheet metal (5"x2") -for pole repair
- ☐ Epoxy
- ☐ Screwdriver which fits your binding screws
- ☐ Vice grips (5" size)
- ☐ Extra screws to fit bindings
- ☐ Ski tip
- ☐ Clevis pins (for external frame packs)
- ☐ Bailing wire
- ☐ Cables for cable binding users (skiers)
- ☐ Extra bail for pin binding users (skiers)
- ☐ Extra basket
- ☐ Extra stove parts (gasket for stove or fuel cap, etc.)

Emergency Kit
- ☐ Matches (and striker in waterproof container)
- ☐ Fire starter (solid fuel pellets, candle, pitch wood, etc.)
- ☐ Compass
- ☐ Map
- ☐ Knife

- ☐ Whistle
- ☐ Nylon cord

First Aid Kit
- ☐ Two gauze rolls (2" wide)
- ☐ Moleskin for blisters
- ☐ Chapstick
- ☐ Sunblock
- ☐ Two triangular bandages
- ☐ Six sterile pads (4"x4")
- ☐ Anti-acid tablets
- ☐ Ace bandage
- ☐ Bandaids-assorted sizes
- ☐ Butterfly closures
- ☐ Safety pins
- ☐ Aspirin
- ☐ Two-inch first aid tape
- ☐ First aid book
- ☐ Personal medications

Also see Lightweight First Aid Kit.

Wax Kit (for those with waxable skis)
- ☐ Waxes (two-wax system or assorted waxes)
- ☐ Cork
- ☐ Scraper
- ☐ Wax remover (often overnight skiers will use white gas which is normally carried for stoves)
- ☐ Hand cleaner
- ☐ Rag

Avalanche Safety
- ☐ Pocket hand lens
- ☐ Shovel
- ☐ Avalanche transceiver

Personals
- ☐ Lotion
- ☐ Toothbrush/paste
- ☐ Glasses or contacts
- ☐ Comb
- ☐ Mirror

Miscellaneous
- ☐ Snow saw

- Sunglasses
- Sun block
- Goggles
- Headlamp or flashlight (spare batteries and bulb)
- Extra candles
- Watch
- Notebook/pencil
- Book
- Wire saw
- Thermometer
- Toilet paper

http://www.isu.edu/outdoor/skilist.htm

The Do-it-yourself Coffee Can Survival Kit

This is a compact kit that can be carried in the car, on the boat, or in a pack for hunting, hiking, exploring, etc. Most of the contents will fit in a one-pound coffee can which doubles as a pot for melting snow and device with which to dig an emergency snow shelter. (However, if you can carry it, include a small shovel. It is far, far better than trying to use a coffee can.) You should be aware that if this kit is carried while on hiking or hunting trips, you still need to carry the other Ten Essentials not included below.

Keep three points in mind when putting together a survival kit. First, make it small enough that you'll actually carry it and not leave it home. Second, use the list as a guide and customize it to your needs. For instance, if you are allergic to insect bites, bring the appropriate medicine, or carry appropriate wrap if you have knee problems.

Third, bring enough to enable you to spend at least one night out. It is usually the first six hours that determine whether you'll be able to survive an emergency. If you can make it through the first night, then your chances are good that you can make it a few more nights if necessary.

Thanks to Allan Priddy for putting this list together, adapted by RonWatters reprinted with permission. http://www.isu.edu/outdoor/ten.htm

General Items
- Braided nylon rope (25 feet)
- Mirror
- Matches (2 boxes)
- Fire Starter
- Poncho (bright orange to attract attention)
- Toilet paper
- Candle (wrapped in aluminum foil)
- Paper and pencil
- Fishing line, hooks, split shot leads
- Knife
- Whistle
- Money (2 nickels, 2 dimes, 2 quarters, $20 bill: helpful for making phone call or paying for gas if broken down along highway)

- ☐ Garbage Bags (2 large size bags)
- ☐ Bright orange surveyor's tape

Repair Kit
- ☐ Sewing kit
- ☐ Dental floss (It's strong and useful as thread for sewing, or a fishing line or for lashing branches for improvised shelters.)
- ☐ Safety pins
- ☐ Wire (bailing wire)

First Aid Kit (**Also see** Lightweight First Aid Kit)
- ☐ Moleskin
- ☐ Sterile pads (2 x 2 and 4 x 4)
- ☐ Sterile Gauze
- ☐ Neosporin
- ☐ Band-aids
- ☐ Aspirin
- ☐ First Aid Tape

Nourishment
- ☐ Honey Packages (available in small foil packages available at convenience stores)
- ☐ Instant Soup or tea (a couple packages)

Optional
- ☐ Folding saw
- ☐ Compass (learn how to use)
- ☐ Hard Candy

Carrying container
- ☐ Coffee Can (1 lb size) or nylon stuff bag

All contents except the plastic bags and the optional items will fit in a 1 lb coffee can. (Or you can flat "Spam" cans or oval-shaped containers available at outdoor stores.) The plastic bags can be affixed to the outside of the can with a rubber band. To keep things from rattling in the can, wad up some wax paper and stuff it around the items. The wax paper stays dry and also doubles as a fire starter. To save weight the contents can be placed in a stuff bag and a metal cup can be used instead of the coffee can.

2/13/98. Compiled by Allan Priddy http://www.isu.edu/outdoor/survkit.htm

CHAPTER 10

RISK MANAGEMENT

Good plans shape good decisions. That's why good planning helps to
make elusive dreams come true.
—Lester R. Bittel

Every Nobleman has their dragons to slay. Some dragons are easier than others. Risk management is a two headed dragon we can not defeat; however, we can train it to behave. We as leaders can understand the outcomes and prepare for the eventualities. One head of the dragon is "risk" whether perceived or real we need to learn how to act, plan and prepare with risk in mind. If we fail to deal effectively with this head of our dragon, the other head will spin around and bite you in the "you know where." This head is liability. A true nobleman loves a challenge, but if you lose this match you may loose your entire kingdom! When an individual competes with another, the best usually wins. This is not the case when it comes to the legal system and liability. Risk Management is not a contest and I have no intention of referring to it as one, however there are concepts that when exposed show similarities. On one side you have you, your agency, your skills, certifications and perhaps accreditation. You also have your training, preparation, experience and your actions. On the other hand you have someone or a group of people who can say you did something wrong, and that caused injury! Some serious work is needed to stack the odds in your favor so you shall prevail in this challenge. You have too much to lose to not prepare for this likelihood.

As a prudent professional you need to prepare yourself for all aspects of your job, just as we have been doing in the previous chapters. Unfortunately, risk management is something we need to spend considerable effort on. I say unfortunately only because of the legal side of this game, not because of the prevention and preparation aspect of risk management. Managing risks is something we are basically fairly good at in our daily lives. We decide to stop at the stop sign, not eat the bacon fat and peanut butter sandwich, and we follow traffic rules when walking, running or riding our bikes. We realize our actions have consequences.

As leaders our actions have implications, responsibilities and consequences. Our challenge is to keep our management efficient so that we can seamlessly interact with the environment and our participants, while managing the risks and following certain standards of care.

The weather is fine, there is a light snow falling, perfect for the snowshoeing trip you have scheduled. You have gone over the medical forms and the participants should arrive prepared as you sent them a gear list two weeks ago. But just to be sure, you will go over their personal gear and then hand out the snowshoes.

Your trip will take you into a forest you have never been in before. You can't believe the day is so perfect. Off you go. You put some miles behind you and then stop for lunch. You break out your stove and serve up some hot chocolate. It is snowing harder now! You remember you meant to check the weather forecast, opps! By the time the group loads back up after lunch, one participant has trouble getting his shoes back on and your ungloved hand nearly freezes in no time. It has gotten very cold and the snow is really coming down.

You are ready to leave now, and you realize you are really turned around! No problem we will just follow our tracks out. Except during lunch, the drifting snow has covered your tracks. You dig into your pack for a compass, not sure what good it will do you, because you didn't take a bearing before you started the hike. To your dismay there is no compass, radio or even a cell phone. You forgot to check your own equipment before going out. "What a rookie mistake" you mutter. But you are really thinking "OH SHIT!"

After some searching, you find some tracks sheltered by a pine tree, and they give you a general sense of which way to go. The wind is coming from your right as you travel straight out of the woods. You've done it. You've gotten the group to a trail and you don't know which way to turn. The wind tells you to turn left, you do and two miles later there is the van. It appears to be stuck, but you have lots of strong adults with you and you are on your way.

You get back, and you feel like you did your best under tough circumstances. True, but the circumstances were made more difficult by you and your lack of preparation. Let's change the scene now.

You got out of the woods to the trail and took a right. You hiked 2 miles before you realized you were wrong. You are now tired and cold with darkness approaching. One member twists his knee. You are going to have to spend the night. During the night one group member succumbs to hypothermia, and it is now your day in court. The judge looks down at you and asks you if you checked the weather. What gear did you bring with you? Did you let your agency know exactly where you were going? Did you have a map? A compass? Did the participants know what they were getting into? Did they sign a liability release?

Your day in court did not go so well! The nice thing about this story is we can change the ending. But we can't change what happens, to make things better again. Looking ahead at all aspects of each program helps us avoid liability, misadventure, fear, discomfort, injury and even death.

A well planned Risk Management program (RMP) helps us look at all aspects of what we do, how we do it, what we need with us, who we do it with, why we do it and if we should do it. The RMP should clearly explain, What happens if? Who does what?

The following information is adapted and reprinted with permission from the work of Rick Barnard.

Preface

Many people do not think of the insurance and risk issues involved in leading a group in the outdoors. Work place safety is a very important issue for groups and boards of directors to consider.

A comprehensive risk management and insurance manual needs to be prepared to provide agencies with a basic understanding of Proactive Risk Management and insurance coverage. This work begins with a review of the law and policy wordings, and ends with some sample guidelines of how groups policies have dealt with situations.

Insurance is purchased to protect against losses from acts that are *unusual, unintentional, and catastrophic.* Insurance companies have a difficult time assessing the risk associated with Outdoor Leadership & Recreational activities. Additionally, we conduct our activities in a litigious society, which can result in difficulty in obtaining insurance at a reasonable cost for certain activities (e.g. wilderness trips, canoeing, mountain biking, etc.).

It is important that all groups work together to ensure compliance with legal standards and current insurance requirements. In addition, all agencies need to create sound operating policies, which will help to safeguard each agencies assets and future.

We need to work together to ensure that all agencies and groups can obtain the insurance coverage necessary to enable them to fulfill their mission to "explore, enjoy and protect the wild places of the earth."

Risk Management

- Organizers have both a legal and practical reason for ensuring the event is safe.
- Reducing risk is good business.
- Ensuring an event is safe and fun for participants is often a matter of common sense.
- Failure to follow reasonable standards of conduct can lead to liability.
- Depending on the type of risk, a proper risk management plan can reduce, transfer, retain, or eliminate the potential loss or injury.

Your interest in ensuring the trip is safe comes from a practical standpoint. As a leader (assuming that one of your goals is to ensure that participants have a good time) this is often accomplished by creating an event that avoids dangers, which are not associated with the activity. If people have fun, they will likely want to return. Reducing risks and promoting safety is good business. Your desire to run a good expedition comes from both a positive business sense and a need to avoid liability.

Insurance is a necessary evil for most organizations, and is often an important part of a—and must never be thought of as an entire—risk management program. When it is combined with the other parts of a risk management program, insurance transfers responsibility for financial loss away from the organization to an outside source. Insurance is necessary in situations where the risk cannot be eliminated, reduced or absorbed. Insurance allows organizers to acquire adequate funds to compensate for potential losses.

Insurance, aside from covering losses, provides funds to cover the legal costs that result from injury litigation. Even if the organization is eventually found not to be responsible for the injury or loss, the legal costs can be extremely high. As of 1991, the average cost to defend a lawsuit against the directors and officers of an organization in Canada was approximately $250,000. In 1994, the average cost to defend a similar claim in the United States was more than $900,000. Most agencies can not absorb these costs.

The philosophy of risk management

A good risk management strategy performs four major functions:
- It <u>*reduces*</u> risk by limiting the chance of mishap. Enforcing rules is an example of risk education.

- It *transfers* risk by making others responsible for injuries or loss. For example, waivers and insurance transfer responsibility for injuries.
- It *retains* risk by being prepared for mishaps. Having an emergency action plan for example—ensures that if a mishap occurs the actual loss or damage will be minimized.
- It *eliminates* risk by stopping activities that will cause injury. By stopping an event when weather conditions become too dangerous, or changing and adapting the trip so it does not become unsafe, you ensure that injuries will not occur.

A good risk management plan reduces the chance of an injury occurring and, if an injury does occur, minimizes the potential for a lawsuit. If there is a lawsuit, the plan lowers the chances of the suit's success. Finally, if the legal action is successful, it reduces the financial consequences for the organizers. Ultimately, it makes the trip safer and more enjoyable for all involved.

Liability

As an organizer, it is helpful to understand your legal obligations. When a person is injured as a result of someone else's mistake, financial reimbursement may be obtainable through a lawsuit. The courts expect that a common sense approach will be brought to the situation at hand and reasonable care will be exercised in handling it. Failure to follow or enforce appropriate rules and regulations, not correcting dangerous situations, or improper preparation for foreseeable emergencies, are all scenarios that have the potential to result in liability.

Components

A comprehensive event risk management plan should include the following components:
- Identifying and training staff and volunteers;
- Ensuring proper documentation, including incident reporting, participant waivers, etc.;
- Securing insurance coverage and necessary permits;
- Undertaking thorough facility inspections;
- Providing on-site first aid and/ or medical coverage;
- Developing an emergency action plan; and
- Communicating—to and with everyone.

Waivers

- Is the waiver written as a contract?
- Is the waiver posted as a sign?
- Is the waiver printed on the admission ticket?
- Will children be participating?

Risk management considerations

- Agencies should keep an updated roster of all members.
- Agencies should have the volunteers and staff sign an acknowledgment of risk forms and waivers of liability for the more hazardous activities/services. (See "Waiver Form,")
- Members, volunteers, and staff should complete an activity registration form. This is used as documentation to establish who is involved, what activity/service they are involved in, and how they can be contacted.

- Agencies should have an incident reporting system that includes the completion of accident report forms should a loss or injury occur. All staff and volunteers need to know the reporting requirements. (See "Accident/Illness Report Form,")
- Directors and officers must check that trip leaders are qualified to lead and are properly trained to ensure a safe and enjoyable outing for all participants.
- Directors and officers must ensure that the operators of day camps or other children's activities are qualified (certified) counselors, teachers, or day care providers and that they are trained in CPR. All people who look after children must undergo a police check with the proper legal authorities. The parents/guardians of any minor participating in a group event/activity should submit a medical treatment authorization and consent form (see Medical Treatment form.)
- Certificates of Insurance must be obtained from service providers (e.g.contractors, companies, and/or individuals) hired to do work for the group. The organization should be added as an Additional Insured on the service provider's insurance policy. Only qualified contractors, companies, and/or individuals should be used.

Insurance and contract law

A liability insurance policy is not a medical or accident policy to insure members against losses from injuries. It is a contract insuring the agency, and its volunteers, directors, and officers—while they are acting on the agencies behalf—against liability to third parties for negligence and providing a defense against such claims must be able to establish three things:
- **The existence of a duty of care;**
- **A breach of that duty; and**
- **Damage caused by the breach.**

Individual trips, events, or activities are not covered by the policy if they are privately organized and not officially sanctioned by the agency.

Liability is equated with responsibility: it is the responsibility that falls upon persons by virtue of their actions or arising from their ownership or use of something. Liability is imposed by law.

Law imposes liability in three different ways:
1. **A finding of negligence.** This is when someone commits a tort (a wrong) against another person(s) causing injury or damage.
   - A tort is defined as an injury, other than a breach of contract, which the law will redress with monetary compensation.
2. **A finding of nuisance.** This is an English common law term dealing with land use, and private or public nuisance.
   - A private nuisance is the substantial and unreasonable interference with an occupier's use and enjoyment of the land being occupied.
   - A private nuisance may become a public nuisance if it affects a large number of persons.
3. **A breach of contract.**
   - One may attract liability by breaking a contract. With regard to negligence, a plaintiff is entitled to succeed if he or she is found to be in breach of contract.

Review of Specific Insurance Coverage

Our system of civil justice imposes responsibility (liability) to both individuals and corporations. Courts will judge each set of circumstances brought before them and attempt to compensate those who have suffered injury or damage due to the negligent action of others.

Over the years, as individuals and corporations became more aware of the responsibility they owe to others, they determine that they could not accurately predict, nor budget for, the amount of compensation that might be awarded. This compensation has become the subject of liability insurance. Its main purpose is to provide protection to the Insured with respect to certain types of injury or damage caused by their negligence.

Liability insurance takes many forms: the type and limit of coverage required by an organization depends upon its operations, the extent to which these operations may be subject to litigation, and the anticipated level of compensation that could result from such an action.

Since most organizations deal with the public by providing services or products, they have a greater chance of causing catastrophic harm to others than the average person who has very little contact with the public in his/her private life.

There are two types of insurance policy contracts dealing with tort liability coverage. The Commercial General Liability (CGL) insurance policy defends negligent acts that result in bodily injury or property damage to third parties. Directors and Officers Liability (D&O) insurance coverage defends the wrongful actions of the board of directors of an organization that result in financial harm and tort legal action from third parties. Together both insurance policies provide protection for most liability exposures but not all that an organization can face. Breach of contract, criminal acts, war, and environmental pollution for example, are not insurable in most situations. Liquor liability for the sale of alcohol products at events, and meetings is usually an excluded coverage. Refer to the contract wording and discuss it with your broker for more detail on what is covered in a liability insurance policy.

Commercial General Liability insurance policy

The duty to defend

In addition to providing protection to an Insured for damages suffered by a third party, liability insurance policies also contain provisions requiring the Insurer to defend certain types of lawsuits brought against the Insured. With respect to liability insurance, the limit stated in the policy is merely the maximum amount that will be paid to a third party on behalf of the Insured. In addition, the cost of providing a defense and this cost are not contractually limited. The costs resulting from lengthy investigation, initial court proceedings, appellate litigation, and the interest on judgments frequently exceed the amount of the loss and have the potential to exceed the limit of liability.

The duty to defend is always tied to the obligation to indemnify. In other words, the only claims that the Insurer must defend are those that, if proven, would fall within the scope of the liability coverage provided.

The Insurer is not obligated to defend claims that fall wholly outside the scope of coverage. Further, the duty of the Insurer to defend a claim or suit falling within the scope of coverage, ends when the amount paid in settlement of claims or suits reaches the limit of liability stipulated in the policy.

Unincorporated organizations

According to the law, unincorporated organizations do not exist; therefore, they can neither sue or be sued. If an accident occurred as a result of an activity organized by an unincorporated organization, the plaintiff would probably sue the officers or directors and attempt to establish personal liability. If negligence is proven, the individuals who face liability will not be able to hide behind the corporate identity of the organization.

Liability of an organization is established in two ways:
1. Vicariously through the specific negligence of its servants (e.g. officers, volunteers) or
2. Through direct liability for negligence on the part of the organization as a whole. In this case, it is important that your insurance policy define the officers, directors, and volunteers as Named Insured(s) on the policy.

Protected persons

Persons protected by liability policies will depend upon:
1. The type of liability coverage provided;
2. Contractual liability assumed; and
3. The nature of the operation. The Named Insured is always fully protected and subject to the policy terms, conditions, and exclusions. Other individuals or organizations may also be protected under the policy. The Additional Insured may be specifically named or unnamed, depending on their relationship with the Named Insured.

The Named Insured is the person or organization named in the liability policy declarations. In other words, it is the risk whose liability has been underwritten and accepted and to whom the insurance policy is issued.

The Named Insured must be a legal entity. In basic legal terms, an individual has legal status simply by being. To qualify as a legal entity, an organization must be recognized to some extent in legal terms as having a sufficiently separate existence that enables it to own property, conduct lawful business, enter into contracts, sue or be sued, and make or carry out decisions through its agents.

An insurable relationship is one in which a person or organization may incur tort liability simply because of:
- Its position, relationship or association with the Named Insured; or
- What the Named Insured is, does or has.

Usually a relationship is considered insurable if it is based on or involves:
- A position or job held or occupied with the Named Insured, such as a director, executive officer, employee or volunteer worker;
- A special relationship or association with the Named Insured or an additional insured, such as being the spouse, partner, stockholder, or member;
- A premises or other property owned, rented, leased, or borrowed by the Named Insured; and/or
- A financial interest in the business or property owned or operated by the Named Insured or work done by or for the Named Insured.

Additional Insured

The person or organization named in liability policy declarations is not necessarily the only person or organization protected under the contract. In addition to the Named Insured, certain other persons or organizations will be protected under various liability policies by virtue of their insurable relationship with the Named Insured. Although these persons or organizations may be afforded coverage under the liability policy, there are significant differences between them in the areas of rights, duties, and coverage.

Some or all of the following Additional Insured may automatically be covered under a liability policy:
- If an individual is named, that person and his or her spouse;
- Employees of the Named Insured (for acts within the scope of employment);
- Any person (other than an employee) or organization while acting as the Named Insured real estate manager;
- indicate which of the liability insuring agreements is being provided; or
- describe the insurable relationship or the liability exposures for which the additional insured is being provided coverage.

The principle reason to add someone as an additional insured to another's liability insuring agreement to give that person or organization a direct right to defense coverage provided by that agreement for claims or suits made or brought for covered liability.

Contractual liability assumed

In today's business environment, contracts play an integral role in the delineation and management of the contracting parties' responsibilities and obligations. The widespread use of contracts is evident with nearly all service, purchase, lease, or rental relationships governed by contract, whether written, oral, or implied. It is important to understand that even though the Named Insured may assume the liability of another party by contract or agreement, not all such contracts or agreements are covered within the scope of general liability insurance. Contractual liability is not covered by a separate insuring agreement. Rather liability for injury or damage assumed by the Insured under any contract or agreement will be specifically excluded.

Coverage is then granted for specific contracts or agreements by exception to this broad exclusion. Coverage that would have existed in the absence of a contract or agreement is also covered by exception. Contractual liability is the liability resulting from agreements to transfer liability. Such agreements are also referred to as "Hold Harmless" agreements. For written contracts, these agreements will usually be located under a section or clause that references indemnification. Although the contract language used to effect the transfer of liability varies, it can usually be recognized by the inclusion of such terms as "assume," "hold-harmless" and/or "indemnify." Most courts will not uphold a transfer of liability resulting from the sole negligence of the indemnitee or events that are beyond the control of the indemnitor. The argument against such a transfer is that the responsible party should be held accountable for liability resulting from their acts of sole negligence or control.

Medical payments

This insuring agreement covers reasonable medical expenses incurred by a third party without the need to prove negligence or establish any other legal obligation on the part of the Insured. In other words, it applies on a no-fault basis. Coverage applies to reasonable medical expenses incurred and reported to the Insurer within one year after sustaining bodily injury. The bodily injury must be caused by an event that occurs while the agreement is in effect and must result from business activities. The injured party must submit to any reasonable medical examinations by a doctor chosen by the Insurer.

Multi-media liability

The multi-media liability extension provides coverage for the association's publications including newsletters, magazines, videotapes, books, film, audio cassettes, for liability imposed by law as a result of one or more claims. It may arise out of any form of defamation related to disparagement or harm to the character, reputation, or feelings, of any person or organization. This includes libel, slander, and product disparagement. Coverage extends to members as an Additional Insured of the association with respect to their sanctioned "works," that are under the editorial control of the association

Alcohol liability

The Commercial General Liability wording in standard use in Canada does not exclude coverage for liquor liability; however, many groups need to review this exposure in the light of coverage restrictions. Many non-profit groups hold wine and cheese events as fundraisers or will have a dance or event at which liquor is sold. When a monetary charge is made, the organization is in the business of selling liquor for which there is no insurance coverage.

The following rules need to be applied: if you are holding a small social gathering with limited drinks served then the Commercial General Liability coverage will meet your needs. If you are organizing a special event where a charge is levied, then you need to purchase party alcohol liability coverage or hire professional bartenders who have the license and the insurance to serve liquor. A recent court case in Barrie, Ontario held the company liable for liquor served at an office party. The law states that if a person drinks your liquor you can be held responsible for their subsequent actions until the effects of the liquor are gone.

The laws that apply to alcohol liability exposures are common law, and provincial regulations which may vary by province. Ontario has very strict rules regarding office parties.

Automobile liability

Automobile insurance coverage is mandated by each State and mandatory insurance coverage is required for all vehicle operators as specified by the law in all states. Third party liability coverage is covered by these regulations; therefore, all operators and managers must understand their exposures under the law. There are several situations under which someone can have liability imposed by law: negligence, vicarious liability, under contract, and deliberate acts.

Negligence This is the failure to do what a reasonably prudent person would have done under similar circumstances, or conversely, doing something that a reasonably prudent person would not have done. This is the common law requirement setting out an individual's duty to others.

Vicarious liability This is liability resulting from the negligence (e.g. a master/ servant relationship) someone the Insured has permitted to operate the automobile. It has been established by law that if someone is working or volunteering for an organization, he/she is carrying out instructions for that organization's benefit. The organization must, therefore, be responsible for the actions of its employees or volunteers.

In the same vain, if the organization owns or rents a vehicle and lends it out to other people, it must take responsibility for their negligent actions.

The implications are that organizations must keep their policy limits high and educate and train staff and volunteers to be vigilant in their management and use of automobiles to transport people.

Confirm with your broker the automobile insurance coverage that your organization has in place and discuss what the group's needs for automobile insurance coverage.

Groups involved with the maintenance of trails and roads need to pay particular attention to their non-owned vehicle liability exposures and ensure that they have a loss control program in place to reduce and eliminate any exposures, and insurance in place to assume any inherent risk.

Groups involved in the transportation of children are required to be especially careful. Liability exposure involving children is absolute. Check the operator license, insurance, and government regulations regarding the busing of children.

There have been too many incidents, where agencies have placed children in dangerous situations with amateur operators, rather than hire a qualified, professional operator. The bad press, distress, and consequences caused by an accident far outweigh simply canceling an outing or event.

Insurers want to know how employees use their car for corporate purposes?

Is it truly an incidental exposure or occasionally running errands? Or is there a significant exposure, such as a service delivery operation. How many people and cars are involved? Does the Insured have contractors providing a delivery service and can it be argued that they are volunteers or employees? What is the hired car exposure? Are there situations where the insured employees are renting vehicles on a daily rental basis and are they buying adequate insurance coverage to protect themselves and the organization?

Under the law relating to vicarious liability, the organization may be held responsible for employees' and volunteers' actions in these circumstances.

It is, therefore, important that the organization takes control of situations by having policies in place to deal with them. This issue should be reviewed and discussed with your risk manager and broker.

Sexual abuse liability

Allegations of past abuse by employees or volunteers of organizations are one of the fastest growing areas of civil litigation. Recent legal cases have put a severe strain on the insurance companies defending these nonprofit organizations and resulting in coverage exclusions and restrictions. It is, therefore, more important than ever that the organization develop and follow a sexual abuse policy/guideline. It is always the offender that is 100% responsible for child sexual abuse. A recent study found that 85% of the offenders are known to the victim and that 92% of children accurately reported their sexual abuse. Management to minimize the risk of sexual abuse involves three tasks:

    Identifying the risk. How can a child be harmed here?

    Measuring the risk. How serious is the risk of harm?

    Controlling the risk. What is my group doing to prevent such harm?

Preventative medicine is the best way to reduce abuse claims. The following actions should be taken:

1. Rigorous recruitment screening, hiring, file documentation, and training practices.
2. Clear cut rules regarding contact between staff and clients.
3. Rules about not touching kids anywhere that would be covered by a bathing suit.
4. Employee/volunteers not allowed to bring clients to their homes.
5. Leadership training of employees and volunteers.
6. Protecting the child, believing it can happen, making them the first priority, and involving the police and Department of Social Services right away should something occur.
7. Boards of Directors must have a written code of conduct in place that assign responsibility, provides for incident investigation, and addresses media and community relations.

What to do in the Event of an Accident

The chance that you may have a claim is normally the only reason you purchased a policy, so it makes sense to think in advance what should be done and not done if the occasion arises.

You will be asked to prove that a loss took place or to document your actions in the event of a liability loss. To prove the amount may involve producing evidence of the present value of the articles damaged, destroyed, or stolen, as detailed in the accounting records.

In incidents where a person is hurt and has suffered a bodily injury it is important that they are looked after immediately with the proper medical care and transported to hospital to a doctors care if required. Information the participant has provided on their personal health form should be shared with these medical professionals. It is very important that care be taken at this stage to worry about the injured person and to not say or do anything that may upset them further. Many personal injury lawsuits are the result of mishandling an injured person at this stage or someone saying something that angers the injured person. The Leader should remain in control during the situation and document what transpired after the event for future reference in the event of a lawsuit.

In most loss situations the Insurer will appoint an adjuster. In the case of a severe loss they will want to visit the premises to inspect and access the damage, take pictures

and document the event. In addition they want to ensure that steps have been taken to protect the property to prevent further damage. Note it is important that you start clean up to prevent further loss at the time of an incident, but do not begin to effect repairs until the adjuster has given you permission to proceed. If you are advised of any form of

legal action against the organization or any of its affiliated entities, this information must be communicated to the Executive Director and to the insurance company immediately.

You should report threats of litigation as well as actual notice of suit.

Forms and Procedures

The forms and procedures in the following chapter are samples that have been used by agencies. These forms can be adapted and used for your own purposes.

Trip/Outings Waiver

Acknowledgment of group member responsibility, express assumption of risk, and release of liability

Trip Name:

Trip Date(s):

I understand that during my participation in the above Trip, I may be exposed to a variety of hazards and risks, foreseen or unforeseen, involved in the activities of the Trip. The risks include, but are not limited to, the dangers of serious personal injury to my person or property, or my death ("injuries and damages") from exposure to the hazards of travel in the areas the Trip will visit. I know that injuries and damages can occur by natural causes or activities of other persons, animals, trip members, trip leaders and assistants or third parties, and such injuries and damages can occur as a result of negligence or because of other reasons. I understand that risks of such injury and damages are involved in adventure travel Trips and I appreciate that I may have to exercise extra care for my own person as well as for others around me in the face of such hazards. I further understand that on Group Trips there may not be rescue or medical facilities or expertise that may be necessary to deal with the injuries and damages to which I may be exposed.

In consideration for my acceptance as a member on this Trip, and the services and amenities to be provided by the Group in connection with the Trip:

- I hereby waive, release, and discharge all claims for any such injuries and damages against the Group and its officers, directors, employees, agents, and leaders, even though such injuries and damages may result from the negligence of the Group and/ or its officers, directors, employees, agents, and leaders;
- I understand that this assumption of risk and release is binding upon my heirs, executors, administrators and assigns, and includes any minors accompanying me on the Trip;
- I confirm that I have read the outing rules and conditions applicable to the Trip and will pay applicable costs and fees for the Trip;
- I confirm that I have read this document in its entirety and I appreciate, understand, and freely and voluntarily assume all risks of such injuries and damages and notwithstanding such risks, I agree to participate in the Trip.

Name *(please print)*:
Signed: Date:
If you are accompanied by a minor, the minor's parent or legal guardian must sign this
Release on behalf of the minor.
Name of Minor *(please print)*:   Age:
Signature of Parent or Guardian: Date:

Accident/Illness Report Form
1. Person making report: Date: Address: Phone:
2. Identify outing as Club:
3. Date of Accident: Time: Weather Conditions:
4. Location of Accident:
5. Brief factual description of accident (state no opinions respecting cause):
6. Identity of ill or injured person:
Name: Age: Sex: Height: Weight:
Address: Phone:
7. Description of injury or illness:
   First Aid Given:
   By whom:
8. Copy of this report sent to appropriate manager.
   Name and Address:

Complete the following when rescue help and evacuation is needed, otherwise skip to 13 and complete.
9. Does injury or illness require immediate evacuation? Manpower and equipment available with injured party?
10. Exact place rescue party to meet?
11. Notify family? Yes No
Name: Relation: Address: Phone:
12. Agency contacted for rescue:
Call back phone numbers:
Person making rescue request?

Date request is made: Time:
Submit to Association with privileged information attached.
13. Witness(es) to accident and rescue *(use back of sheet for additional information if necessary)*:
Name: Address: Phone:

14. Full description of accident and rescue including discussion of preceding events and conditions *(use back of sheet for additional information if necessary)*.

15. Leader's evaluation. Give your opinion of the cause of the accident. Be specific.
Show sources of information and whether accident could have been prevented *(use back of sheet for additional information if necessary)*.

16. I, personally, have supplied the confidential information requested above for the association's legal committee:

Name *(please print)*:
Signature:
Date:

Confidential–DO NOT COPY

DO NOT COPY

Medical Treatment Authorization and Consent Form

Please complete and return this form to your trip leader.

The following form is designed for those situations where minors on a group activity are unaccompanied by either parents or legal guardians. This "Medical Treatment Authorization and Consent Form" gives authority to a designated adult (i.e. the trip leader), to arrange for medical care for a minor in the event of an emergency. This is extremely important in that medical care cannot be provided to a minor without approval by the parents or legal guardians, unless there is written consent authorizing an agent to give approval.

Minor's Full Name:
Minor's Address:
City: State: Postal Code:
Minor's Age:

The undersigned do hereby authorize _____ (Trip Leader's Name) or such substitute as he/she may designate as agent for the Undersigned to consent to any X-Ray, anesthetic, medical, dental, or surgical diagnosis or treatment and hospital care for the above named minor which is deemed advisable by and to be rendered under the general or special supervision of any physician and/or surgeon, licensed under the Provision of Medicine Practice Act or of any dentist licensed under the Dental Practice Act, whether such diagnosis or treatment is rendered at the office of said physician or dentist, at a hospital, or elsewhere.

Name of Parent/Guardian *(please print)*:
Address of Parent/Guardian:
Home Telephone: Business Telephone:

Parent/Guardian Signature: Date:
Witness:
Insurer: Account No.:
Family Physician:
Address *(in full)*:

Working for Wilderness Emergency Procedures

The emergency procedures below are to be followed by staff or volunteer leaders should an emergency arise. Common sense, discretion, and initiative are also to be used by staff or leader's to deal with serious situations as quickly and efficiently as possible and to ensure the staff or leader's actions are appropriate to the situation. Communication with the office is critical to ensure that the staff or leader (herein after the "leader") receives all support available during the emergency.

Emergency Procedures

The following constitutes a **major emergency** and must be reported to the office immediately:
1) Death;
2) Fracture of skull, spine, or pelvis;
3) Major fire at accommodation;
4) Any injury or illness that is life threatening;
5) Loss of limb;
6) Multiple injuries in vehicle accident;
7) Multiple poisonings or gassings;
8) A participant or leader lost for more than 12 hours;
9) A group that is 24 hours late at a scheduled pick-up/drop-off;
10) Evacuation for any reason;
11) Sexual, physical, or emotional assault;
12) Suicidal threat; or
13) Other as deemed an emergency by the leader.

The following constitutes a **minor emergency** and must be reported to the office as soon as possible:
1) Any incident that requires admission to the hospital that is not life threatening; or
2) Any incident that is not on the list of major incidents.

In the case of any emergency, the leader is expected to:

1) Control the situation while ensuring their own safety and making sure the situation is safe for all other group members and anyone else in the area. Injuries to oneself and other individuals are to be avoided as far as possible.

2) Locate a telephone. When you arrive at a site, ensure you are familiar with the location of the nearest telephones.

3) Deal with the situation as required, including application of first aid to the leader's level of training, and by contacting the ambulance, hospital, etc. Hand over responsibility for the emergency to emergency services when they arrive. Continue to maintain the safety and comfort of the rest of the group.

4) Call the designated Emergency Contact Person at the office. If they do not answer their telephone,

If the Emergency Contact Person is not there, or it is after hours, leave a message with the following information and then call them at their home telephone number:
- i) nature of the problem
- ii) your location
- iii) a detailed account of the emergency
- iv) how the situation has been handled to this point
- v) which participant(s) and/or leader(s) have been involved
- vi) number of people to be evacuated
- vii) phone number where you can be reached for the next 30 minutes, or a time when you will phone back

5) If the Emergency Contact Person cannot be reached at the office or at home, continue attempting to contact the Secondary and then Tertiary Contact Persons. When contact is made with a secondary or tertiary person, have them leave a message with the others to advise who is coordinating the emergency.

6) Write a factual report of the event. Ask every member of the group to do the same. This should be a report of the facts of the event only, not a subjective description. As far as possible, the reports should be completed independently. The enclosed accident report form will assist group members in recalling important details of the event. The reports should be forwarded to the Coordinator as soon as possible.

The leader should ensure their report contains:
- i) a chronological description of the incident
- ii) name of casualty
- iii) what happened
- iv) what injuries were received/incidents occurred
- v) where and when the event happened
- vi) what action was taken/has been taken
- vii) where the casualty is
- viii) a contact number for the group leader
- ix) the emergency contact number of the casualty, etc.
- x) communications with all other parties (including time and telephone numbers)

7) Complete any relevant paperwork (e.g. SOAP, insurance, etc.).

8) Make a decision as to whether or not the expedition will continue with Emergency Contact Person considering the safety and well-being of the rest of the group.

The Emergency Contact Person who is coordinating the emergency is expected to:
1) Follow the telephone contact instructions left by leader(s) (e.g. phone back immediately or wait for their next call);
2) Gather all information and facts from trip leader, and record on Incident Information Form;
3) Alert the Manager, and Director
4) Alert the Director who will inform the insurance company via the agent;
5) Alert the Executive Director in the case of a **major** emergency;
a) The Executive Director will then appoint a spokesperson, who is responsible for:
- i) gathering patient information and facts and preparing a statement
- ii) informing the Chair of the Board of the emergency

iii) calling the casualty's next of kin
iv) talking to news media
v) coordinating incoming information and passing it to Directors, next of kin, and media.

6) If you are the secondary or tertiary emergency contact, leave a message with the other contact people telling them you are managing the emergency. If you are the secondary or tertiary emergency contact and reach the primary emergency contact, follow the instructions of the primary contact person;
7) Keep a communications log of the events and the communications that occur
throughout the emergency, including the time of communications, telephone numbers, and parties spoken to;
8) Other responsibilities may include:
    a) Picking up and transporting group members;
    b) Helping prepare emergency plan;
    c) Helping re-route expedition;
    d) Visiting the group and the incident site;
    e) Considering the safety and well-being of the rest of the group;
    f) Deciding whether the trip will continue;
    g) Considering the need for legal advice; or
    h) Other duties as required or appropriate for the situation.

NOTE: *No one, including the spokesperson, will release any information that identifies responsibility for an accident without first obtaining legal counsel. Never speak with the media about emergency situations. Do not provide the media with information regarding the nature of the illness or injury, especially prior to diagnosis by a licensed physician. Do not release the names of casualties to the media, especially do not do this until the next of kin being notified.*

Following the incident, the leader and staff will:
1) Refer all media inquiries to the Executive Director;
2) Remember that the rest of the group requires attention as well as the casualty(ies);
3) Record all incidents in their written report;
4) Not apologize, as apologies can be taken as admissions of liability; and
5) Follow-up with the casualty, casualty's family after the event to confirm the interest in and concern about, the person and their health.

The following article "Outdoor Safety Management" is written by Rick Curtis it is presented in its whole form. Source www.outdoorsafety.org

1. The Outdoors as a Risk Activity
How do you define an accident? Definition - chance or what happens by chance; an event that happens when quite unlooked for; an unforeseen and un-designed injury to a person; an unexpected happening; a casualty; a mishap.
    Read "Thanksgiving Death in the High Peaks"—Why did this occur? Separate answers into Environmental Hazards and Human Factor Hazards. Use this to define the Dynamics of Accidents formula.
    What are some outdoor program risk activities? What is the highest risk? (answer–driving to the trailhead)

2. Theory of Accidents—How Accidents Occur
1) Dynamics of Accidents Formula

Dynamics of Accidents Model

Environmental Hazards
- Terrain
- Weather
- Equipment

\+

Human Factor Hazards
- physical condition
- experience
- skills
- fear
- communication

\=

Accident Potential

 +

These two factors can overlap to a greater or lesser extent. The greater the overlap the higher the Accident Potential. The effect of combining Environmental Hazards and Human Factor Hazards multiplies the Accident Potential rather than simply being additive. The greater the number of hazards, the more quickly the Accident Potential can rise. For example:

Accident Potential Increase
2 Environmental Hazards + 2 Human Factor Hazards = 4 times higher Accident Potential
3 Environmental Hazards + 3 Human Factor Hazards = 9 times higher Accident Potential

2) Examples of Hazards

Environmental Hazards
When assessing the potential environmental hazards you need to look at three factors.
1. ACTIVITY
- Static–activities in which the environment is relatively unchanging (e.g. hiking)
- Dynamic–activities in which the environment change very quickly in unpredictable ways (e.g. whitewater paddling, biking)

2. LOCATION
In remote locations you need to exercise additional precautions. One common method of accomplishing this is to increase the rating of the rapid by one class if you are in a remote setting. For example, a Class III becomes a Class IV. This helps take into account the increase in Accident Potential (see below).

3. SEASON/CLIMATE
Weather and the possibility of weather changes also have a significant impact on Accident Potential.

A) Environment
- Rocky trail
- Exposed ledges
- Cold temperatures

- Rain
- Darkness
- Overexposure to sun
- Poison ivy
- Beestings

B) Equipment
- Broken stove
- Boots not broken in
- Improper clothing
- Inoperative equipment

C) Driving/Transportation
- Bad road conditions
- Darkness
- Unfamiliar road
- Difficult road (CLASS I - VI)
- Other erratic drivers
- Pedestrians/cyclists

Human Factor Hazards

A) Participants
- No awareness of hazards
- No skills to avoid hazards
- Resistance to instructions
- Irresponsible/careless attitude towards self, others, equipment>
- Need to "prove" self, macho attitude
- Poor physical strength, stamina
- Fear, anxiety

B) Leaders
- Lack of knowledge of environmental hazards
- Inadequate skills to extricate group and self from hazards
- Poor safety judgment
- Poor teacher of necessary skills
- Instructions unclear
- Poor supervisor, does not correct problems
- Ineffectual under stress
- Lack of teaching plan

C) Drivers
- Poor driving skills
- Rushing to meet schedule
- Overly tired on long drives
- Not driving defensively

D) Group
- Group not yet formed, lacks cooperative structure

- Interpersonal frictions unresolved
- Poor communication patterns excessive competition
- Scapegoating or lack of concern for slow or different individuals
- Excessive pressure or stress to "perform" - macho
- No practice in working harmoniously under stress
- Lack of leadership within group
- Splintering into sub-groups

3) Sample Accident Scenarios

Here is an opportunity to test out your ability to analyze a situation for Environmental Hazards and Human Factor Hazards. Check of the Accident Scenarios page and see how you do. Also you can think of an accident or near miss situation that you have been in whether on an outdoor trip or in some other setting. Analyze the situation and list the Environmental Hazards and the Human Factor Hazards that led to the Accident Potential and determine what steps could have been taken to reduce the Accident Potential.

4) Teaching the Formula = Reducing the Accident Potential

It is essential to teach the Dynamics of Accidents Formula at the very beginning of any trip so that all participants are aware of how their behavior is directly related to reducing the possibility of accidents. Participants then can take some responsibility for their own safety. The formula gives you five basic things:
- A technique for evaluating risk potential in the field
- A tool for analyzing how accident potential can be reduced
- A decision making tool
- A rationale for why OA has paticular things we teach, particular rules and policies
- A rationale for why you make particular decisions

5) Environmental Briefing

A comprehensive Safety Program allows one to intervene to prevent Human Factor Hazards from overlapping with Environmental Hazards and thereby reducing the Accident Potential. In order to do this it is necessary to rethink from Day 1 of the trip *what is an environment?* In planning a trip the leaders must examine the environment and the activities of the trip in order to ascertain what the possible environment hazards of that trip are. This information must be communicated to the group in the form of an Environmental Briefing at the beginning of the trip with subsequent briefings when there is a change in environment or activity (e.g if a hiking group changes to canoeing the environment and activity have changed and there are different environmental hazards). The first Environmental Briefing should follow the leaders' presentation of the Dynamics of Accidents formula. On longer trips it may be useful to have the participants do some of the Environmental Briefings once they are familiar with the formula. This can be done with the help of the leaders. The Environmental Briefings set a a tone for safety and help inculcate the idea that the participant is responsible for his/her own behavior.

6) What If?

It is important to analyze the possible accident potentials from a what if perspective. Ask yourself what is the worst case scenario. Then ask yourself what you can do to reduce the accident potential.

7) Prepare a sample Environmental Briefing

You will be leading a hiking trip on the Appalachian Trail in the Delaware Water Gap in the first week of May. Write a sample Environmental Briefing for this trip.

3. Record Keeping

Record keeping is an important part of any safety program. Keeping records and reports allows your agency to find trends in situations that may lead to changes in training for leaders, equipment, activities, and routes.

1) Accident Reports–These are to be filled out whenever there is an accident on a trip. It documents how the accident occurred, where, when and what treatment was given to the injured person(s). These forms are to be filled out under the following circumstances:
- If there is an injury or illness which requires treatment for more than one day of the trip.
- If an injury or illness causes the person to miss some part of the trip (e.g. group has to wait 1/2 day for person to recover).
- If the person needs to be transported to a medical facility for examination and/or treatment (even if they are discharged).

2) Field Information Reports–These forms are filled out whenever there is a "near miss" accident - a situation in which no one was injured but which could have resulted in injury. It is also used to communicate any other useful information that someone traveling in that area would need.

3) Emergency Report Form–This form is filled out whenever there is an injury which requires outside medical assistance. The form is designed to be quickly filled out and to make sure that all necessary information is transmitted to authorities.

4. Pre-trip Planning

The essence of any safety program lies with pre-planning. It is essential to cover a wide variety of areas before the trip, during, and after in order to maintain maximum safety.

1) Pre-trip Planning

A) Route Planning
- Trail conditions
- Water availability and quality
- Rangers
- Emergency phone numbers
- Weather forecasts
- Daily evacuation plan
- File overall trip plan with program director

B) Application forms from all group members—informs leaders of previous experience, any medical problems, disabilities, allergies, food issues etc.

C) Teaching Plan - a teaching plan should be developed for each major activity that will occur on the trip. This plan should present a well thought-out and step-by-step plan for safely teaching skills. This should also be shown to the program director prior to the trip.

D) Equipment:
- What to bring - Leaders should examine what the equipment needs of the trip are based on activities, location, and weather (see Personal and Group Equipment Lists).

- Check it out - Leaders then need to make sure that all participants have the necessary equipment. If people are bringing their own equipment, it must be examined to make sure that it is in good shape. Also all equipment should be checked to make sure it is in good working condition.
- How to use it—Participants must be instructed on the safe and appropriate use of all equipment.

2) **During the Trip**
- Teach the Dynamics of Accidents Formula
- Give Environmental Briefing
- Teaching Skills
- Accident Response—n case of an accident react calmly and thoughtfully so as not to further injure or exacerbate the situation. Specific details of accident response are covered in CPR and first aid training
- Multiplication of Errors—through poor judgment/ overreaction - present an example.

3) **Post-trip Activities**
   A) Record and write up any accidents, near-misses or information to be transmitted. Report this information directly to the program director.

5. *Implementing Program Change*

Improving the safety of a program involves a combination of all the items discussed above. The basic model for change is as follows:

PRE-PLANNING——-> TRIP EVENTS——-> ACCIDENT RESPONSE——-> REPORTING ——-> ACCIDENT ANALYSIS——-> PROGRAM CHANGES——-> PRE-PLANNING

6. *Safety = Judgment*
1. Know your limits and group's limits. Be conservative.
2. Be flexible - (e.g. change route if needed) camp early if group tired (R. Curtis)

Special concerns about working with children

Working with children can present many and different challenges. We would all recognize that we have a particular degree of responsibility when we are working with children or they are under our care. For this reason there are a number of simple steps we need to take to ensure their safety and welfare and to ensure that the time they spend with us is positive.

Good Practice Guide for Instructors/Volunteers/All Staff

The following actions are intended to eliminate the incidence of abuse of children and help to shield staff and volunteers from false allegations being made by promoting good practice.
- Do not spend too much time alone with children away from others, **always have a witness.**
- Do not take children alone in a car on rides or on hikes, however short.
- Do not take minors or participants to your home or private quarters.
- If any of these are necessary, make sure they only occur with the full awareness and approval of someone in charge in the agency or the child's parents and have someone else with you.
- Design instructional programs that are within the ability of the child.

You should never:
- participate in rough, physical or sexually provocative games, including horseplay.
- allow or engage in inappropriate touching of any form, don't touch anywhere other than arms, hands, shoulders and top of head. Do not allow others to touch you, in any other places.
- allow children or staff to use inappropriate language unchallenged.
- make sexually suggestive comments or jokes to a child/ participant or in their presence, even in fun.
- let allegations a child makes go unchallenged or unrecorded; always act and document.
- do things of a personal nature that children can do for themselves.

It may be sometimes necessary for staff or volunteers to do things of a personal nature for children, particularly if they are very young or disabled. These responsibilities should only be carried out with the full consent of parents. Leave doors open, let people know where you are, have a witness. In an emergency situation, which requires this type of help, parents and a direct supervisor should be fully informed. In such situations, it is important to ensure all staff is responsive to the child and attend to personal care tasks with discretion.

In addition, medical consent should be obtained in the event where medication or treatment is required to be administered in the absence of the parent / guardian; this includes hospitalization. Your medical waiver should contain a release that allows you to seek treatment or to provide care. You should never give a child any type of medication, or over the counter or prescription, without parental permission, always document this permission.

In the article entitled Risk management for organizations: Keeping the ship afloat by: Preston Kline & Rick Curtis they offer the following review and assessment related to how the program went. These are just a few of the questions that you need to ask to establish how well your agency has planned and executed its mission.
- Did the program meet its goals and objectives?
- Was the program properly planned to facilitate meeting goals and objectives?
- Did the facility or location meet the programs needs?
- Were the staff and participants adequately prepared to deal with what they encountered? Do they need additional training?
- Were there accidents or close calls on the program? If so were they handled and how? Are there changes that need to be implemented? If so what?

All Leaders Get Old

All leaders get old. With regular upkeep and maintenance (constant review, reassessment) and through staying up to date on the latest standards and techniques of leadership (outdoor programming), professional leaders can stay safely in the field for years. There are leaders in practice, who were outdated by the time they started their career and never caught up with the field. There are also professional leaders who have stayed current and do the proper self and peer review and restructured what they do and how it is presented so they are always acting within current "standards of care." To not do this is especially problematic since staff often change frequently and don't develop lots of organizational history and experience. The administration, often the keepers of organizational history, may be too far removed from the field. They may be operating on outdated standards and approaches. "It has always worked for us that way," is a statement that has caused far too many tragedies and indefensible lawsuits. You need to think carefully about how you will keep your program afloat and sailing well for the long haul. In some cases you may decide either to completely retire a program or build a new one from scratch. You also might decide that the program, the staff and/or the participants are no longer appropriate for the type of conditions you have been putting them in, so you place them in a less demanding setting. This may provide you with a more than adequate level of risk management.

Our goal here has been to give you an overview of how Risk Management permeates all aspects of your program. It is not simply the job of a "risk manager" in your agency or some committee that meets twice a year. Everyone on the organization has to understand the big picture and their individual areas of responsibility within that big picture in order to make sure that risk is properly managed and that the overall goal of your job, a safe and beneficial experience for you clients, has been met. (Curtis and Cline)

CHAPTER 11

EMERGENCY READINESS

WEATHER, LIGHTNING, FIRST AID PROCEDURES, EMERGENCY SCENE MANAGEMENT, FIRST AID KITS

First Aid and Accident Scene Management
This chapter cannot cover all the required knowledge, judgment and experience to be competent in first aid and accident management. Anyone that is far from help, especially you with the additional responsibility of leading others, should seek instruction in wilderness first aid. The benefits of learning an orderly response to an emergency are too numerous to list. An organized approach and in the field practice scenarios are taught in all nationally recognized wilderness first aid trainings.

Wilderness First Aid (WFA) is a basic level certification, and is generally taught as a two-day, hands-on course. Wilderness First Responder (WFR), an eight to ten day course is generally the accepted training for Professional wilderness leaders. Wilderness Emergency Medical Technician (WEMT) is the most thorough training available and is highly regarded in the field. This type of wilderness training can also be very useful for those venturing to nations with less developed emergency medical care systems.

Contact information for organizations providing wilderness medical training can be found in the resources section at the back of this book. You can also check the web site from SOLO, Wilderness Medical Associates WMA or the American Red Cross, for listings of courses all over the country.

In this book we can only cover the very basic principles of emergency response. Suggestions for the first aid kit everyone in the backcountry should carry will also be made. The rest is up to you. Part of a good risk management program is having highly skilled, experienced leaders ready to deal with any eventuality that nature or your group can throw at you.

It's been a long trip, seven days backpacking with a group from the city. All has gone well so far, you are half way through the trip with the hard part ahead of you. The group of eight high school freshman are doing a great job, morale is high and camp is lively tonight.

You have a co-leader with you but it's her first trip with your agency. Abby is doing a great job and is very thorough in everything she does with the group. The trips logistics are working flawlessly, but you are tired. This is your third back to back trip with no real time off in between.

You ask Abby after dinner if you can take five and go down to the stream and relax. She says sure she's got it. The kids are busy cleaning up dinner and getting ready to settle down for a quick night fire and debrief the day. You will be back by then.

The stream is beautiful at dusk, you lay down to relax, soon you awake and it's dark. You know the way, but in your haste your first step you slip on the moss covered rocks. Your body falls onto a long ago downed hemlock tree below you and onto the rocks. When you come to, you feel blood on your face, your wrist is broken and it hurts to breathe. You can't get up, you have no whistle, no first aid kit, but you told Abby where you were going. She'll come looking.

Its not even two minutes more when two campers come looking for you, sent by Abby. You wave to them and the look in their face says it all. One goes to get Abby, as the other stays and gets his personal first aid kit out. He starts asking you questions, you realize that he is doing exactly what you taught him to do on day one of this adventure. With first aid kit in hand he controls the bleeding from your forehead. Out comes a space blanket and he wraps you up in it. "Smart kid" but why is he treating me for shock? The pain in your chest is now out of this world and breathing is getting harder. This student of yours now does something amazing. He cuts your shirt right up the middle, looks at your chest and gets a ziplock bag out of his first aid kit. He now tapes the bag to your chest, leaving one little corner untapped. Why is he doing that? I didn't teach him that? When you regain conscientiousness you are being loaded on a helicopter and the group is standing off in the distance with Abby.

Pride and pain is the emotion you feel as the helicopter speeds down the valley. The pride comes from knowing you did your job so well that members of the team had risen to a challenge and saved your life.

The bumps, breaks, bruises and your sucking chest wound all heal with time. Abby visits right away and you thank her. She says that the group did fine after the accident as they took the easy way out, they all took turns being the assistant leader for a day. What about Colin? I asked, "how did he know to do that with the bag?" Abby says, "Remember the book in the kids first aid kits, Colin stayed up each night reading another chapter, he had just read the night before the section on serious injury. He was so motivated that he put some duct tape and a ziplock bag in his first aid kit." I told "Abby that kid saved my life."

Colin stops by to see me three days later and you thank him. He surprises you by thanking you, and he explains, "When you taught us first aid, I knew what I was put on this earth to do. When I found you by the stream, I knew it was my calling to take care of people. I have signed up for a First Aid class at the Red Cross."

He went on to say that before the trip he was hanging out with the wrong kids and when you taught first aid it was "so interesting" that he wanted to know as much as you obviously did.

Your job was complete for this trip, but you have some healing and reflecting to do. "What if I didn't empower those kids with knowledge? What else happened that week, if we made such a profound effect on one kid?" With the power of my leadership, I was able to create a learner, who then went on to save my life. That's a full circle!"

First Aid in the Wilderness is different; it calls for knowledge, preparation, resources, and experience. One mistake many leaders make is to not share this skill and the knowledge that goes with it. Perhaps they fear by talking about emergency preparedness, a situation will occur. As you could see from the above story, it is my belief, that by empowering people with knowledge they respect their position and the environment all the more. One challenge you will face is how much do you share with your clients. You will need to answer that yourself. Each program has different goals and different time constraints; we could easily spend an entire week doing a first responders class and not accomplish our other goals. You will need to be creative, but make the time to teach some first aid skills.

Wilderness First Aid Kits

Every person engaged in an outdoor group should carry a personal first aid kit and one person in every group, usually the leader, should carry a master first aid kit.

THE NOBLE GIFT

There is no perfect first aid kit—they are always a compromise in space, weight, usefulness, and cost. Any first aid kit should not contain things you don't know how to use. It should contain items that serve multiple uses or can't be improvised. Good kits contain instruction cards or a first aid booklet—even if you are an EMT, no one's recollection is ideal all the time. It should contain a pen or pencil and a first aid report form (SOAP notes) or blank paper. You will use this to write down as much information as possible while you are administering care to a patient.

You can not have everything with you, so be prepared to improvise what you don't have in your kit. The kit will change with each season, or with the location, country and length of trip, in Costa Rica you might add a snake bite kit, but while in Maine you won't need one. The Master first aid kit should be crush proof and water proof and be able to withstand abuse—start with a heavy duty dry bag or dry box and pack items inside it in freezer-type zip-lock plastic bags. If you carry medications, make sure they have the clients name on them and they are labeled with directions from the doctor. The best way to accomplish this is to require medications to be in their original prescription bottle. Make sure these medications go where the participant goes, ie: the group splits for a night. Most products will remain useful over long periods of time, but you should check expiration dates periodically.

A good first aid kit can take a long time to create. Add things you wish you had the last time you needed the kit and throw out things you have never used. Commercial kits are expensive, and sometimes have things you won't need or can't use. They are a good compromise if you don't know where to start. Keep an inventory of your kit, review the contents and <u>refill it immediately</u> after each trip. If you use an issued first aid kit, check it before leaving because if the last person did not refill it you will run out of band aids on your trip.

First Aid Kits

The Article; "Emergency First Aid in the Wilderness, begins with your own personal first aid kit." Written by Ron Blackwood posted on the web site Outdoor Club.org. He makes the following recommendations for a First Aid kit.

The kit should be small and waterproof. A plastic or aluminum box with a tight fitting lid makes a good container. A heavy-duty ziplock or waterproof ditty bag may be used as well. It should contain the essential medical instruments and bandage materials listed. All items should be carried on backpack trips. Asterisked items (*) may be left in camp or automobile. The contents of a medical travel kit should be carefully chosen, using the type of trip, duration and distance from medical care as criteria. All medications should be stored in separate air-tight plastic containers and clearly labeled as to the name of the drug, dosage, and expiration date.

Medical Instruments & Bandage Materials In The Basic First Aid Kit
- Adhesive strips–1" x 3", 10; Adhesive strips–2" x 4", 5: Minor cuts & abrasions.
- Butterfly bandages/ Steri strips, with tincture of benzoin applicator, 10:
- Closure for minor cuts. Apply benzoin to make the bandage stick.
- Adhesive tape–1" roll, 1
- Battle dressing–4" x 4", 1: Large wounds or abrasions pressure dressing.
- Elastic Ace bandage–4", 1: Securing dressing, splints or wrapping sprains.
- Moleskin or Molefoam, 1 pkg.: Cover or prevent blisters.
- Gauze pads (Telfa pads & Vaseline gauze)- 4" x 4", 6: Cover large wounds.

- 30" x 4" piece of 1/4" wire hardware cloth with edges taped, 1: Splint for suspected fractures.
- #11 sterile scalpel blade with handle, 1: Removing splinters & other small foreign bodies from the skin.
- Hemostat or tweezers, 1: Removing splinters, cactus spines and other foreign bodies.
- Small scissors, 1
- Oral thermometer, 1
- Sling or triangular bandage, 1: Immobilize arm/shoulder if needed.
- Wilderness first aid manual and CPR card, 1
- Length of surgical tubing, 1: Constricting band.
- Snakebite extractor kit, 1: Remove snake or bug venom.
- Disposable gloves, 2 pr.: Avoiding contact with blood.

Medications In The Basic First Aid Kit

Aspirin–5gm or 325mg tabs, 50. Two every three hours as needed. This is a highly effective agent for relief of minor pain and for lowering fevers. It is an excellent exoskeletal anti-inflammatory agent. It will decrease fever; decrease the inflammation of tendinitis and sunburn. All brands are equally effective regardless of price. Purchase the 5gr USP size. Precautions: Use with caution if a history of ulcers, asthma, on anti-coagulants, or serious bleeding, Do not give to children without Doctor's orders.

*Antacid tabs, 20. As needed. Use to neutralize stomach acid in the treatment of indigestion, heartburn and ulcers. Precautions: May cause self-limiting diarrhea. It can be used as a mild laxative.

Antihistamine–Decontaminate, 20. Follow package directions. This group of drugs blocks the release of histamine, a chemical released during allergic reactions. Benadryl (diphenhydramine) is highly effective in the treatment of mild allergic reactions to insect stings and hay fever. It may also be used to control motion sickness, nausea, vomiting and insomnia. Precautions: Most antihistamines cause drowsiness.

Antibiotic Ointment, 1 oz. Apply externally as needed. Used to treat superficial bacterial skin infections. Bactracin Ointment is very effective and may be purchased over-the-counter. Precautions: Some individuals may be allergic to one component of the ointment.

*Tylenol tabs, 24. As directed. *Tylenol with Codeine 1/2 gm (or 32mg) tabs or Vicodin, 12. One every 4-6 hours for severe pain. May be used as an aspirin substitute but has no anti-inflammatory properties.

Liquid soap, 2-4 oz. Clean wounds.

Sunscreen SPF #15 or greater, 3-4 oz. As directed. SPF 15 or higher provides effective protection against sunburn. Banana Boat or Bullfrog are among the best products available.

Steroid Ointment or cream, 1-2 oz. Follow package directions. Used externally to decrease the inflammatory effects of insect bites and poison oak. Kenalog Ointment (0.1%) is very good but is available only by prescription Precautions: Do not use on skin infections.

Insect Sting Kit (if allergic or hypersensitive to hymenoptera insect stings.), 1. As directed, should be carried if you are severely allergic to bee or wasp stings. It contains epinephrine and is available only through a doctor's prescription. The Epipen Auto-Injection Kit is a good example and is used only for emergency treatment of anaphylactic reactions. It is injected intramuscularly to relieve breathing difficulties. Precautions: It may cause, headache, tremor, restlessness or anxiety.

Insect repellent, 2-4 oz. As directed. 50% or better DEET is a very effective insect repellent. Natural repellents such as citronella have proven to be very effective as well.

*****Throat lozenges, 10.** As directed.

*****Pepto-Bismol tabs, 24.** As directed. *Immodium tabs, 12. As directed. These are an effective treatment for diarrhea and soothe an upset stomach. Precautions: Use with caution if you have a history of ulcers, asthma, or are on anti-coagulant medications.

Lip Balm with sunscreen, 1 tube. As needed.

*****Cavit–7gm, 1 tube.** As needed. This is a pre mixed filling paste and is available from a dentist or a dental supply store. It relieves the pain of a chipped tooth or a lost filling. Precautions: This is a temporary fix only until you can get to a dentist.

Water purification tabs, 1 bottle: As needed.

Ibuprofen 200mg tabs, 24. As directed. May be used as an aspirin substitute. It is an effective anti-inflammatory and pain reliever. It may be used to reduce fever. Precautions: Should not be used by people who are allergic to aspirin.

*****Oral Rehydration Salt Packet, 2.** As directed for dehydration.

Diamox–250mg tabs, 15. As directed for prevention or treatment of acute mountain sickness.

The foregoing lists were prepared by Robert Vinton, M.D. who is a general practitioner, avid backpacker and bicycle tourist.

This information will give you an excellent first aid kit. No kit is any good without some medical training. I strongly suggest that you enroll in a first aid and CPR course if you haven't already done so. Additionally, read and understand the instructions on the medications before you have a medical emergency. There is no substitute for the old Boy Scout adage -"BE PREPARED!" (Blackwood)

Wilderness Experiences Unlimited recommends the following list for all participants in their Adventure Leadership Training Program.

Participant First Aid Kit Contents
Packed in Separate Zip Locks (each grouping) Medical Forms for all participants & Leaders with emergency contact information.

- Latex Gloves 3 Pair
- Personal Medications- In original Prescription Bottle—enough for the entire trip +2 days.
- Mole skin 1 ½ packages
- Mole Foam ½ package
- Water tablets (Porta Aqua 2 bottles)
- Waterproof Sunblock
- Bug Repellant
- Antibiotic Ointment
- Hyrocortozone Cream
- Band Aids- 8-12 assorted
- Adhesive Tape 1 roll
- Gauze Dressing- 5 min assorted sizes
- Rolled Gauze -Cling- 2-3 rolls
- Ace Bandage
- Cravats—2
- Tweezers
- Safety Pins
- Alcohol Prep Pads–10
- Needle
- Tylenol / Ibuprofen 1 bottle (50 tablets)
- Aspirin 1 Bottle (50 tablets)
- Pepto Bismol or Tums
- Antihistamine 20 tablets
- Compass
- Quarters for phone calls
- Lighter and Water Proof Matches & Emergency Candle
- Jello or high energy sugar supplement
- Duct Tape—Roll a few yards around a Pencil

There is no definitive first aid kit. Good Training is your best prevention.

Prevention, Self-Sufficiency and Accident Scene Management

A leader and the host agency should establish safety guidelines for each activity to be conducted on your trip. It is your job to follow these guidelines, and adapt to changes as required by the group, equipment or the environment. The following is adapted from; Jonathan Silver, AMC Mountain Leadership Manual

Prevention is like weather forecasting. You look at the obvious equipment, activity, behavior and then take into consideration the environmental factors, static and dynamic. Certain conditions also predispose you or your group to accident and illness, just like our seasons. Interpret the results and you have a plan to prevent. In the wilderness as soon as you have several risk categories stacking up against you, you are increasing your accident likelihood.

You are responsible for your participants. We have discussed this at length, however when an accident occurs, remember that you are responsible for the victim and the rest of the group. Make sure that you and at least one other individual (preferably a co-leader) are actively administering to both the needs of the victim and the needs of the group. The group members and you should make sure that everybody stays well fed, hydrated, and warm while the victim is being cared for. It is a good idea to appoint a group safety person, to attend to these details. This could easily be a well educated and skilled participant. Remember the rule to delegate; you can not do it all.

Make sure that you or another is actively documenting the incident—use a SOAP note and keep track of as much information as possible. Documentation serves as a record of trends; it also lets other personal know the status of what has been done. Should there be a lawsuit, it also will show up in court as such it must be accurate and timely documentation.

And remember—there are several ways that accidents can be prevented right from the start. As a leader, it is your responsibility to take all of these into consideration.

PREVENTION
Plan your outing carefully—If you have not figured this out by now go back to chapter one and start this book all over!
- If you have not traveled in the area before, educate yourself, ask other people or scout the trip.
- Gather useful information up to the last minute, such as a weather report.
- Make sure your trip description that you sent to participants, fits with the outing you actually undertake. "Oh by the way we will be hiking 20 miles a day" does not go over well, when the paperwork said the trip was easy to moderate backpacking.
- Inform participants of expected difficulties, behaviors and expectations that will be required from each of them during the trip and in the event of an emergency, near miss or incident.
- Set realistic objectives and be willing to adapt.

Be personally prepared
- Have the appropriate skills/fitness level for the outing. Your fitness is a primary concern you should never be challenged by the trip, if an emergency occurs you will need an amazing reserve of energy and fitness.
- Activities you lead should be well within your level of comfort, skills and fitness.

On the trip
- Use conservative judgment and common sense
- Be aware of major threats and preventive measures
    Hypothermia or Hyperthermia
    Drowning
    Lightning
    Falls
    Stream crossings or road crossings
    Pre-existing medical conditions
- Keep people within your group in contact

No solo travelers
- Know where you are
- Be willing to cancel the trip or alter the objective, any objective is secondary to safety and having fun

- Watch people for signs of problems before they become serious, don't be afraid to ask questions, and seek solutions to minor problems along the way. This is when you can still prevent an accident.

SELF-RELIANCE
Plan for emergencies:
- Know points of emergency contact
- Carry emergency phone numbers in your first aid kit.
- Know medical concerns in your group
- Carry appropriate equipment
    - Clothing
    - Shelter
    - Food/Water
    - First Aid Supplies
- Consider an appropriate level of First aid training
    - Teach the basics of first aid, and what to watch for personally. Utilize the resources in your group effectively
- Know who has skills and training that may be useful, especially medical training
- Be aware of the equipment and supplies carried in your group, make sure they do not get left behind, or stored improperly. All your safety gear needs to be readily useable when needed.

THE ACCIDENT SCENE
Scene safety- If the scene is not safe, do not enter, and put yourself in danger. Wait, or do something that will stabilize the scene so you can effect a rescue and remove the victim from the dangerous situation. If there was just a rock fall that hurt someone in your group consider the area unsafe and unstable.
- First priority is the safety of yourself and other potential rescuers
    - Avoid adding victims
    - Make sure others in the group are organized and in a safe place
    - Treat your patient (if it is a medical situation)
- Delegate someone to provide medical care (the best person may not be you) Some situations may require you to have a broader view of the picture organizing several tasks at the same time.
- Consider moving the patient if they are in a dangerous location, do this quickly andefficiently without causing further harm to the patient.

Delegate tasks to people
- Step back and analyze what is needed
- Do not leave people idling around
- Communicating with the patient/victim Consider the psychological needs of the patient, they are scared be reassuring.
- Recording care given to patient
- Assembling available equipment that may be needed This may include 1st aid supplies, shelter, food, water.

THE NOBLE GIFT

- Evaluating routes of evacuation or obtaining assistance Delegate 2 competent individuals if possible
  Evaluate the Scene
- Continue to make sure the delegated tasks are being carried out

EVACUATION
Consideration
- Does patient need to be evacuated?
  - Options for Evacuation
    - Walk out
    - Carried out by group
    - Carried out by rescue group
    - Evacuated by vehicle
  - Sending a messenger
    - With a note describing situation and location and your intentions
    - Map marked with location of patient and remainder of group
    - List of resources requested
  - Communications technology
    - Cell Phones can change much of this
    - Do not count on technology to assist you—consider them an aid only
      - Batteries run down
      - Service is limited, but you may have service at the ridge not too far away!
      - Phones break
      - Coverage is not complete
      - Little use if you don't know where you are. There are stories about people who have gotten hurt or lost in the backcountry and call for help on their cell phone, When asked where they are they don't know, they even go so far as get upset with the dispatcher, because they can't come and get them right away.

LEADERSHIP
The leader must control the scene—the scene must not control the leader.
- Empathize
  - Understand the feelings of others in your group
- Do not panic
  - Step back and try to objectively observe
  - Show confidence and do not over react
- Be open to suggestions
  - This must be balanced with getting tasks done quickly
- Commend participants for their efforts
  - Keep your group informed of the progress of efforts

FOLLOW-UP
Debrief serious incidents with staff, participants, supervisors, families, consider professional assistance

with this. Remember people are going to have many different feelings about what just happened. Some participants and staff may feel guilty, depressed, angry, sad, confused, scared etc.

The Ten Commandments of Wilderness First Aid Emergency Management
- I. Do not become a victim
- II. Your safety and the safety of your group come first.
- III. Do remain calm and use thy brain.
- IV. Do use what thou hast and improvise what thou hast not.
- V. Always remember the ABC's, if you don't know your ABC's, see Commandment IX
- VI. Do not leave thy patient alone.
- VII. Do write it down, for if it wasn't written, it wasn't done.
- VIII. Do not take it all on thine own head, but delegate it, for thou art not alone.
- IX. Do get trained and stay current.
- X. Do plan ahead, keep thine eyes open and sweat the details for an ounce of prevention is worth a pound of cure. (AMC Mountain Leadership)

Problem # One
On a weekend backcountry ski trip in New Hampshire, you have completed your first day, when in camp someone falls and hurts their leg. They can not walk on it, what do you do? How do you coordinate the other leader and six participants? What will be your plan? The day time temperature was 30 degrees F and night temp is expected to be in the teens. Write out your plan.

Weather
In a training manual written by the AMC Leadership Training Committee they present the following information.

Weather is an important factor in any outdoor activity. Being aware of the weather forecast and preparing your group for it will help make your trip more enjoyable and safe. Before going on a trip, listen to the local television or radio forecasts. You can find excellent forecasts for your destination using the internet.

As we all know, forecasts are not entirely accurate, especially in the mountains. You and your group must always be prepared for the worst possible conditions that may occur at a given time of year. You can stay one step ahead of the weather by paying attention to what is going on around you and applying some basic principles of meteorology. You can easily master these basic principles, but, like all rules, they are not always accurate. The more you know about the weather, the better off you will be and the more fun you are likely to have.

Rule #1: Mountains Often Cause Their Own Weather
When wind hits a mountainside, it meets a barrier. The mountain funnels the wind into valleys or forces it over the mountain or ridge top. If the wind goes over the mountain, its speed increases; the air cools, and moisture may begin to condense.

This brings us to rule #2.

Rule #2: The Higher You Go, The Cooler and Damper It Gets. (Usually)
The adiabatic lapse rate states that for every 1,000 foot elevation gain air will cool by 3 to 5 degrees Fahrenheit. The exact lapse rate depends on many things. As you climb, prepare for cooler temperatures.

THE NOBLE GIFT

As air cools, it can hold less water vapor. It will feel damper and you may climb into a cloud. Rule #1 showed that when wind hits a mountainside, the mountain forces it up and over. As the air goes up, it cools off and moisture in it may condense, forming a fog or a cloud, or increasing the size of existing clouds. As the moist, hot air cools, it condenses and forms water droplets on cooler surfaces. If the mountains cause the air to cool enough and if the air contains enough moisture, it will condense, causing rain or snow if the right conditions exist. Because of the exposure to high winds, cooler temperatures and lightning, move your group off peaks and ridges at the first sign of bad weather.

One exception to Rule #2 sometimes occurs; it's called a temperature inversion.

An inversion usually happens on a clear, still night because cool air sinks down into valleys. During a temperature inversion, if you stay higher on a mountain, you can experience temperatures up to 20 degrees Fahrenheit warmer than in the valley.

Rule #3: A Falling Barometer Can Spell Trouble

I bring an altitude, barometer, compass watch with me! This seems very high tech, but very useful in gauging the weather and it is really cool. It is also very important in the mountains when arriving clouds, can be hidden and that extra hour to get off the mountain can help your safety margin quite a bit.

A change in barometric pressure over several hours usually indicates a change in the weather. Of course, knowing this isn't going to do you much good in the field unless you bring your own barometer. Generally high, steady barometric pressure indicates good weather. Falling barometric pressure indicates that bad weather is coming, and rising barometric pressure indicates improving conditions. A good watch like mine is somewhat expensive, however they can prove highly valuable as well as fun to learn and use.

Rule #4: Fronts Bring Bad Weather

A front is the dividing line between two air masses, one of which pushes the other out of its way. Fronts are often associated with bad weather and high winds. When a cold front moves in, cold air forces out warmer air. Similarly, when a warm front moves in, warm air forces out cold air. Cold fronts move relatively quickly -up to 35 mph- and often cause rapid and dramatic storms.

They may not last as long as the warm front, but they pack a real punch in many cases. Thunder and lightning are not uncommon and those towering thunderheads (cumulonimbus clouds) are most often associated with the cold front. Warm fronts, on the other hand, tend to last longer and are not usually as dramatic. They lead to long drizzly or rainy days). Warm fronts give more advanced warning, with high, thin clouds, than cold fronts and take longer to clear out.

Rule #5: Forecasting Means Noticing Weather Changes Throughout the Day

To stay one step ahead of the weather, keep an eye on the clouds and what they are dong. Are those fluffy cumulus clouds you saw in the morning getting larger and growing significantly by 1 or 2 PM? If so, they may well produce showers. Are the thin wispy cirrus clouds that seemed so high earlier, bunching together and thickening? Is the cloud ceiling lowering during the day? If the answer is yes to any of these questions, something is up and it is probably not going to lead to lots of sunshine.

Let's take it one step further. Consider the direction or change in the direction of the wind. The weather in the Northeast is mainly continental. The predominant wind direction is westerly (from the West). Westerly winds generally give us fine weather, though plenty of storms come on this wind, too. A southerly wind could spell trouble as warm moist air may be moving north. A northerly wind, or a change to a northeasterly wind, indicates that bad weather is a strong possibility. The northeast is famous for its

Nor'easters (low pressure storms centered just off the coast which deposit large amounts of snow or rain).

To make this part of forecasting simpler, a cloud identification and wind direction chart has been devised. This handy tool is easy to understand and can be purchased at numerous places and most outdoor shops, including the Appalachian Mountain Club in Boston or at Pinkham Notch.

Source adapted from AMC Boston Chapter Fall Leadership Training Committee

Problem # 2

While hiking up a 4000 footer in the Adirondacks, your group is strong and ready. It was going to be in the low 50 degrees F. When you parked your car, your altimeter said you were at approximately at 900 feet. What will the actual temperature be at the summit? The wind is going to be gusting between 20 MPH and 30 MPH. What will the wind chill factor be at the summit?

Summary

The weather can change radically in a moderately short time period. You must always be prepared! Remember the Boy Scout motto "Be Prepared," it has huge implications to all outdoor leaders. Ample warm clothing, rain gear and wind protection are a must at any time of the year. Wind protection will help save you from the cooling effects of wind chill (See Chart Below) and the effects of hypothermia.

To take full advantage of your forecasting ability, stay aware of the ever-changing surroundings. Continual awareness and changes in the clouds combined with wind direction can give you the edge you may need. If you have an Altimeter, Barometer, Compass watch like the Suunto Vector, you can check all facets of weather forecasting right from your wrist. If the weather looks like something might be changing, let the group know. This way they can be ready to follow whatever directions or plans will need to be made. The need to turn back early is always an option, remember "Nature will never accept your excuse." If it is going to beat you down it is going to beat you down! By paying attention to your environment, you gain the advantage of time and planning before the beating commences!

Expertise in forecasting takes time and practice. Get a weather book study the formations of the clouds and what they mean, use your compass to determine wind direction changes, do this even on nice days and keep your eye on the conditions. Besides being fun, this is an age old skill you and those you lead will be safer because of your experience.

Wind (mph) \ Temperature (°F)	Calm	40	35	30	25	20	15	10	5	0	-5	-10	-15	-20	-25	-30	-35	-40	-45
5		36	31	25	19	13	7	1	-5	-11	-16	-22	-28	-34	-40	-46	-52	-57	-63
10		34	27	21	15	9	3	-4	-10	-16	-22	-28	-35	-41	-47	-53	-59	-66	-72
15		32	25	19	13	6	0	-7	-13	-19	-26	-32	-39	-45	-51	-58	-64	-71	-77
20		30	24	17	11	4	-2	-9	-15	-22	-29	-35	-42	-48	-55	-61	-68	-74	-81
25		29	23	16	9	3	-4	-11	-17	-24	-31	-37	-44	-51	-58	-64	-71	-78	-84
30		28	22	15	8	1	-5	-12	-19	-26	-33	-39	-46	-53	-60	-67	-73	-80	-87
35		28	21	14	7	0	-7	-14	-21	-27	-34	-41	-48	-55	-62	-69	-76	-82	-89
40		27	20	13	6	-1	-8	-15	-22	-29	-36	-43	-50	-57	-64	-71	-78	-84	-91
45		26	19	12	5	-2	-9	-16	-23	-30	-37	-44	-51	-58	-65	-72	-79	-86	-93
50		26	19	12	4	-3	-10	-17	-24	-31	-38	-45	-52	-60	-67	-74	-81	-88	-95
55		25	18	11	4	-3	-11	-18	-25	-32	-39	-46	-54	-61	-68	-75	-82	-89	-97
60		25	17	10	3	-4	-11	-19	-26	-33	-40	-48	-55	-62	-69	-76	-84	-91	-98

Frostbite Times: 30 minutes | 10 minutes | 5 minutes

Wind Chill (°F) = 35.74 + 0.6215T − 35.75($V^{0.16}$) + 0.4275T($V^{0.16}$)

Where, T = Air Temperature (°F) V = Wind Speed (mph) *Effective 11/01/01*

National Weather Service 2001

Lightning Guidelines:

Prior Planning

Examine Route—Determine if there are areas of high risk (see the next section). Plan for bail out points is there are parts of the route that will be exposed to higher than normal lightning danger.

Weather Report—Obtain one if possible and consider modifying your plan if the forecast calls for thunderstorms.

Daily Pattern—Certain mountainous areas have very regular patterns of summer thunderstorms. Know the pattern and plan accordingly to be in a safer area at the time of the likely storms. Lightning related to frontal systems is less predictable.

I remember watching one mountain in Colorado for four days before I climbed it. Every day right after one o'clock, there would be a major storm. I did my time control plan while I was acclimatizing and figured out I would have to leave my campsite by 3am to be off the Mountain by the afternoon storm. The plan worked perfectly. When I got down, I looked up the mountain and it was getting nailed! Lightning and six inches of snow in August!

Location during a Lightning Storm
- Avoid—Peaks, ridges and other high points, open bodies of water, shallow caves and the drainage bottoms (wet or dry).
- Other Potentially Dangerous Areas—Wet or lichen covered rock, cracks or crevices in rock, wet ropes and tree roots can all serve as conductors.
- Head For—Wooded areas with trees of generally equal height. Position yourself equidistant between trees of approximately equal height. Avoid the tallest trees. Valleys (but not drainage bottoms) and low on slopes are better than most locations higher up. If you are out on the water, head for shore.
- If caught in the Open—Utilize likely strike points as a means of protection. Locate a tree, pinnacle or other point that is five or more time your height. Estimate the height of the object and position yourself approximately 50% of that distance from the base of the object. Avoid being the highest point in your vicinity.

As a Storm Approaches
- Monitor—Keep a diligent eye on the approach of weather systems. Learn to identify the cumulonimbus clouds that are likely to produce lightning discharges.
- Flash to Crash—When you see lightning begin counting off the seconds until you hear thunder. The light reaches you almost immediately; however the sound travels more slowly. The sound of thunder takes approximately 5 seconds to travel 1 mile—dividing your second count by 5 gives the approximate distance of the storm in miles.
- Head to Safer Areas—Generally it is advisable to head for safer areas if you feel that a thunderstorm may be approaching. If your route takes you into an exposed area, this is likely the time to alter your plan.

"Lightning Drill"
- Two to Three Miles Away—At this distance (based on your second count) a group should enter into a "lightning drill." Three miles (15 seconds) is the standard for US Outward Bound Schools, which have had several deaths caused by lightning.
- Ideal "Drill"—This consists of squatting on insulating material (if available), heels touching, knees apart and hands off the ground. You should be in this position when the storm is at its closest. The insulating material might be a sleeping pad, a pack or a coiled climbing rope.
- Sitting—The duration of the storm may make if difficult to squat the whole time, thus individuals may choose to sit when the storm is not immediately on top of them.
- Spread Out—Groups should spread out to reduce the likelihood of more than one person being affected by a strike. Everyone should be within audio or visual contact of other group members.
- Location, Location—Lightning drills should be conducted in safer areas of terrain, as outlined above. When caught in a highly exposed area, it is usually advisable to continue travel to a safer area, if one is nearby, rather than enter into a lightning drill. Think! If you are on a peak or a ridge, get down off of it before doing the drill.
- Hypothermia—This is a real concern during lightning drills. Make sure everyone has raingear and, if necessary, insulating layers. Snacks and water should be available.
- Falling Objects—Be aware of dead trees or branches close to your location that might get blown down, hail could also be a concern.
- Holding Tight—If the group is in a tent or under a tarp in an ideal location, it may be advisable to remain dry and sheltered.
- Metal—Avoid any contact with metal, which can cause serious burns if it is exposed to an electrical current.

First Aid
- Pulse & Breathing—If a patient has no pulse provide CPR (chest compressions and rescue breathing). For the patient with a pulse who is not breathing, provide rescue breathing. Spontaneous resuscitation is more likely after a lightning strike than with other causes of loss of circulation or respiration. ***Wilderness protocols to terminate efforts after half an hour do not apply in this situation.***
- Burns & Trauma—Both are common in lightning victims. Evaluate and treat accordingly.
- Evacuate—Carefully decide on a safe and expedient evacuation plan.

Behind the Guidelines

Lightning is a real hazard for the outdoor traveler. The highest concentrations of lightning injuries occur high in mountainous areas and on large bodies of water. A majority of the 200-300 lightning fatalities in the US each year are people who were engaged in recreational activities—golf more than anything else. On the positive side, most of those affected by lightning are not killed, and many are not seriously injured.

Knowledge of lightning and prudent decision making eliminate much of the risk of lightning. It is useful to plan for possible lightning in advance and to practice re-analyzing your situation once out in the field. The differential between the speed of light and the slower speed of sound make it possible to learn the approximate distance of any given storm. Use the distance of the storm and observations on its movement to create a plan of action. The highest object in a given area is the most likely to be struck by lightning, thus many of the guidelines above are an attempt to keep people from being that high point. The lightning drill is important in that the insulating material may help protect a person in the event or lightning splash or ground transfer. The squatting position allows current to flow through the lower body without running through the heart. Many lightning strikes have affected more than one person, thus it is critically important to spread out to avoid this situation. It is important to remember that most lightning victims are not exposed to a direct strike. A person can come into contact with lightning four different ways:

1. Direct Hit
2. Ground Transfer—Electrical energy, dissipating outward from the object it hits, flows through the ground and potentially those nearby.
3. "Splash"—Lightning hits another object and splashes onto objects or people nearby.
4. Direct Transmission—Lightning hits an object the person is in contact with and current is transferred.

Those who do not suffer the effects of a direct strike are far more likely to recover. Lightning knocks many victims into unconsciousness or may otherwise affect their level or consciousness. Victims may also suffer paralysis of extremities, ruptured eardrums, and, of course, burns. Treat these conditions as outlined above, but keep in mind that the electrical current which caused the heart to stop or breathing to stop may not have permanently damaged the organs. Unless it is dangerous or you are completely exhausted, do not stop CPR or rescue breathing on a lightning victim

A commonly repeated story from the North Carolina Outward Bound School illustrates the benefits of rescue breathing and being prepared. This particular course was caught on a ridge in a storm and both instructors were knocked unconscious by ground transfer lightning. Luckily the instructors, who were not breathing, had just taught their students rescue breathing and CPR (as is required on US Outward Bound courses). The students performed rescue breathing on their instructors and both spontaneously began breathing within a short period of time. (Kosseff -AMC Mountain Leadership Guide)

General First Aid Procedures

Hypothermia
- Hypothermia is the number one cause of accidents and deaths in the backcountry.
- Hypothermia is the lowering of one's internal body temperature.

We are warm-blooded animals and we require a constant body temperature to insure our survival. Doing this in our day-to-day life is usually pretty easy: if we are cold, we turn up the heat; if we get wet, we go to the closet and change our clothes. These luxuries do not exist in the backcountry. The lowering of normal body temperature from 98.6 degrees to 97 or 96 degrees can make a backpacker confused or disoriented; further lowering of body temperature to 95 or 94 degrees can be fatal. Initial identification and prompt action are the keys to preventing hypothermia from taking another victim. Remember, hypothermia occurs in all four seasons; it is 100% preventable and 100% treatable if recognized in time. Prevention of hypothermia involves preventing heat loss, encouraging heat production and detecting the emerging problem early.

Heat loss occurs in the following ways;
1. Conduction
2. Convection
3. Radiation
4. Evaporation
5. Respiration

Preventing heat loss can be done in a variety of ways:
- **Controlling convection**–wear wind and rain gear to prevent wind currents from transporting the heat away from you.
- **Controlling evaporation**–sweating leads to a wet body and a wet body is a cold body. It is important to maintain a warm, dry body by not over-sweating. To control evaporation reduce the amount of insulation or ventilate your insulation and/or wind and rain barrier.
- **Controlling radiation**–prevent your body from radiating its heat to the surrounding air. Insulate the total body, especially the head, with the proper fibers. We lose a large quantity of heat from our head.
- **Controlling conduction**–eliminate the transfer of your body heat to heat sucking objects around you. Avoid sitting or sleeping on cold, wet ground unless you are on an insulating pad.
- **Control respiration**- by breathing in cold air the victim is being chilled internally. So attempt to warm air by breathing through a scarf or bandana.

Heat production can be encouraged in the following ways
- Eat a mix of foods high in calories
- Drink warm beverages high in calories
- Keep moving if possible
- Change into dry clothing

Symptoms of hypothermia are not always apparent, even to the most experienced backpacker. Symptoms such as irritability, lack of concentration and clumsiness are inherent in all hikers, particularly late in the day. At this point, hypothermia can be treated with a handful of GORP, some warm, high-calorie fluids and an extra layer of clothing. Symptoms of moderate to severe hypothermia come quickly, sometimes in less than 30 minutes, and will include uncontrollable shivering, slurred speech, and loss of fine motor coordination eventually advancing to physical collapse, unresponsiveness, cessation of shivering, unconsciousness and decreased pulse and respiration. At this point treatment requires stopping the group and managing the victim.

First Aid for hypothermia means preventing hypothermia. If you and your group are dry, well hydrated, well fed, and physically active, you will not need to provide First Aid. However, hypothermia is insidious and is often referred to as the silent killer.

First Aid would include the following
- Eat a mix of foods high in calories
- Drink warm beverages high in calories
- Change into dry clothing
- Keep moving if possible

THE NOBLE GIFT

Physical activity involved in continued hiking will often generate enough heat to re-warm mild to moderate hypothermia. However, to engage in physical activity requires calories and hydration. Don't expect a hungry and dehydrated hiker to be willing to keep moving. Generally hypothermic victims oppose this suggestion, wanting to sit and rest a while. Resist this temptation and move the group forward. Even if the group is wet, at least they will be warm. Anyone who spends time in the backcountry will, at some point, personally experience hypothermia. Every backcountry leader needs to become familiar with its symptoms and basic treatments. Remember: well-fed, well-hydrated, well- dressed groups will not fall prey to hypothermia. *(Silver, AMC Mountain Leadership Manual)*

Problem # 3
While hiking today the sun went behind the clouds. It is now in the 50's. You have an easy stream crossing, but a young man slips and falls; he spends about 1 one minute trying to get out of the mountain stream. He is very cold! What do you do? Organize your thoughts and your group. What should you have done differently?

HYPERTHERMIA—Heat Exhaustion- Heat Stroke

Hyperthermia is the opposite of hypothermia. Next to oxygen, water is most important in sustaining life. We are approximately 30% fluid by weight. A loss of a small percent of body fluids, such as 2% to 3%, will decrease the working effectiveness of our musculo-skeletal system by 20% to 30%. The average backpacker needs to consume approximately four quarts of fluid each day for optimal performance. Four quarts is a minimum; some backpackers may require as much as eight. The suggested consumption regime is one quart with breakfast, two quarts during the day and one to two quarts in the evening. In the summer, the hot temperatures encourage us to drink and the risks of dehydration are much more apparent to us. However, dehydration is an equally serious problem during the cold winter months. Dehydration, along with the intense heat of the summer sun, leads to hyperthermia. Staying hydrated helps hikers maintain their regular body temperature during the physical exertion of a backpacking trip. A well-hydrated hiker also generates lucid thought, an important criteria for decision-making in the backcountry. We have all experienced the hyperthermic condition when we got the flu and our temperature went up. Can you imagine trying to hike while you have a fever? Basically, this is what happens to individuals who become dehydrated.

Three conditions, working in conjunction with dehydration, that lead to hyperthermia are:
- Heat Exposure–Internally from strenuous exercise and externally from air temperature
- Heat Loss ability–Perspiration and increased blood flow to the skin
- Environmental Conditions–Air temperatures greater than 90 degrees drastically reduces the body's ability to shed heat through radiation. Normally, 65% of heat loss occurs through radiation. Relative humidity above 75% drastically reduces the body's ability to release heat through perspiration. Normally 20% of heat loss occurs due to sweating

Prevention
- Drinking water–The best prevention for dehydration is constantly drinking water throughout the day. Water is the recommended source of fluid. It is the easiest for the body to absorb.
- Rest–A short rest is advisable so that the body can absorb the water
- Shade–If shade is available, use it. This includes sun visors.

If preventive measures are not taken, then more serious problems can result. These can lead to death if not cared for immediately.

Advanced Dehydration/Heat Exhaustion

Excessive sweating is an early sign of dehydration. More advanced dehydration is often called heat exhaustion.

Symptoms
- Weak, thirsty, headache, nausea, vomiting, cramps, disorientation
- Excessive sweating
- Reddening of skin on face and extremities
- Skin is cool and clammy to the touch

First Aid
- Water—Start with small amounts, a mouthful at a time, and working up to larger amounts over a period of several hours. This is to prevent vomiting which often happens when a severely dehydrated individual takes large amounts of fluid in a short time
- Rest—A long rest is advisable; you will probably not cover much ground with an advanced dehydration condition
- Shade—If shade is available, use it; if not, construct some shade using a tent fly or other available material
- Radiation—The body cannot tolerate high temperatures for a long period of time; rapid cooling off of the severely dehydrated individual must be accomplished quickly. Often these victims are unconscious and are unable to take fluids orally. These victims should have water poured on their bodies or be placed in a stream if available. This will rapidly decrease the victim's body temperature. Once they are conscious, begin treating with small amounts of fluid. Be cautious not to bring the persons temperature to a hypothermic stage by over cooling.

Today many electrolyte replacement fluids are available. But before using these products on hikes, try them in a more controlled environment such as during a workout in the gym or a run in your neighborhood. Don't assume these products will decrease the amount of fluid you will need.

Severe Dehydration/Heat Stroke

A life threatening situation that appears in two forms:
> **Classic heat stroke** (perspiration ceases due to dehydration) or
> **Exertion heat stroke** (air is too hot and humid for hiker's heat loss mechanisms to work effectively).

Symptoms
- Rapid pulse and ventilations, confusion, seizures
- Sweating profusely—exertional
- Reddening of skin on face and extremities
- Skin is hot and dry to the touch—classical
- Rapid loss of consciousness

First Aid
Same treatment as for Advanced Dehydration/Heat Exhaustion (see above)

THE NOBLE GIFT

The Miseries
There is always going to be small little injuries, bumps, scrapes, scratches and bruises. Blisters and bites is another area I call "the miseries" we should pay close attention to the general first aid procedures to treat these smaller wounds by remembering **I'm NOT HELPLESS**.

Cuts & Punctures:
You can treat most cuts and punctures yourself. But you will need to get medical treatment if you are bleeding a lot, or if you are hurt very badly. Blood gets thicker after bleeding for a few minutes. Apply direct pressure over the wound, if bandaging gets soaked apply new bandaging on top of the blood soaked material, this should help slow down the bleeding. You may have to apply pressure for 10 minutes for a bad cut. If not being controlled, elevate the wound above the heart, apply pressure to the supplying arteries for leg and arm injuries. Sometimes a cut needs stitches. Your first aid kit should contain some type of wound closure system, steri strips work very well, as do butterfly closures. Depending on the length of your trip you should consider having antibiotic medications, perhaps even a broad based prescription with directions from your physician for administration.

I'm NOT HELPLESS (T.S. Cook 2004)
Questions to ask about wounds.

Infection–Have I taken steps to prevent and control?

Not–stopped the bleeding after 20 minutes of applied pressure, even if it is a small cut?

Open–deep, or does it go down to the muscle or bone?

Tenderness–at or around the wound, pain that gets worse instead of better. A sick feeling? A day or two after the injury is there a Fever of 101 degrees Fahrenheit or higher with redness and or swelling?

Head–or face cuts, lacerations, bruises? May mean more serious injury i.e. concussion, fracture, internal bleeding.

Edges–Do the edges of the cut skin hang open? This may mean you will have to close the wound, and watch for infection.

Length–Is the cut an inch long or on a body part that bends such as an elbow, knee or finger?

Pressure–Is the cut still bleeding a lot after 10 minutes of pressure being applied? Directly to the wound and to the supplying arteries, (pressure point) ?

Loss–Has the person lost a lot of blood? (1/2 cup for an adult, less for a child)

Elevate–Have I elevated the wound above the heart?

Spurting–blood flow from the wound? This may mean an artery has been cut. If bleeding still persists, after Direct Pressure, Elevation, and Pressure Point, a tourniquet between the injury and the heart may be required. This method should only be used in extreme situations, once applied do not remove, write information on the limb what time put on, remember this is a question of Life or Limb? The person is going to loose the limb! Learn about advanced first aid techniques in your First Responder course!

Shock–Is the person in shock? Am I treating for it? Have I been aware of any of the symptoms?

By using the acronym **I'm NOT HELPLESS** remember the steps of wound care.

Care for minor cuts:
- Clean around the wound with soap and water. (It's okay if some gets into the cut, but it may hurt.)
- Press on the cut to stop the bleeding. Do this for up to 10 minutes if you need to. Use a sterile bandage or a clean cloth. Use a clean gloved hand if you don't have a bandage or cloth.
- Lift the part of the body with the cut higher than the person's heart. This slows down blood flow to that spot.
- To relieve initial pain or throbbing, hold an ice bag on the bandaged wound for 15 to 20 minutes.
- Put anti biotic on the cut when it is clean and dry. Use a sterile cloth or cotton swab. Try Triple Antibiotic, Polysporin, Neosporin
- Put one or more Band-Aids on the cut.
- Leave the bandage on for 24 hours. Change the bandage every day or two. Change it more often if you need to
- Take aspirin, acetaminophen, ibuprofen or naproxen sodium for pain. Don't take aspirin every day unless doctor tells you to. Aspirin can keep blood from clotting if you take it for a long time.

Note: Do not give aspirin or any medication containing salicylates to anyone 19 years of age or younger, unless directed by a physician, due to its association with Reye's syndrome, a potentially fatal condition.

Procedures for Punctures
- You need to determine the tetanus shot is within in the last 10 years (or whatever your health car specialist recommends). If not you will need to get the person to a doctor. It is a good idea on long trips to check your record and make sure everyone is protected,
- Let the wound bleed to clean itself out.
- Take out anything that caused the puncture if possible. If not possible leave it in and bandage around it. Use clean tweezers. (Dip the tweezers in alcohol for five minutes to clean them. Or you can hold a lit match to the ends.) *Don't pull anything out of a puncture wound, if the object goes all the way through the body part, is very deep or if blood gushes from it or if it has been bleeding a lot. Bandage around the object and seek emergency care.*
- Wash the wound with warm water and soap.
- Apply antibiotic. Cover it with a bandage if it is big or still bleeds a little.
- Soak the wound in warm, soapy water two to three times a day.

Fractures
A fracture is classified as either a simple (closed) or compound (open).
Signs (are things you can see) that a fracture is present include:
    1. The area may or may not be deformed, swollen or discolored.
    2. The victim is unable to place weight on the area without experiencing pain.
    3. A grating sensation or sound may be present during any motion of the injured area.
Symptoms (things the victim tells you) may include;
    1. I heard something snap.
    2. I feel grating, popping or grinding.
    3. I feel pain at the affected area.
Treatment is as follows:
    1. If in doubt, treat the injury as a fracture.

2. Splint the joints above and below the fracture.
3. If the fracture penetrated (or may) the skin, it could be necessary to apply traction to straighten the deformity.
4. Be sure to pad your splinting material.
5. Check the ties frequently to be sure they do not hinder circulation.
6. Cover all open wounds with a clean dressing before splinting.

Dislocation

A dislocation happens when the ligaments near a joint tear, allowing the movement of the bone from its socket. It is unwise to treat a dislocation unless you are a trained professional as permanent damage may occur. Seek additional training on dislocation reduction. The affected extremity should be supported using a sling or other device and pain controlled with aspirin or other suitable drugs.

Sprains

These are the worst! They also can be very common. By wearing good and appropriate footwear, this can be prevented for the most part. Teaching people about the likelihood of this type of injury and how to prevent it, goes a long way. I always tell people "for every step into the woods we take, you will have to take that step in pain if you are careless.s"

Treat sprains by applying cold to the area for the first 24 hours then once the swelling has subsided, let the sprain sit for a day. Apply heat the following day to aid in the healing process. The sprain should be splinted and rendered immobile until the pain has completely disappeared.

Muscle Cramps

Muscle cramps occur when the muscle accumulates excessive lactic acid or a loss of salt through perspiration. Dehydration and overexertion can aggravate cramping. Treatment includes resting, fluids, deep breathing and stretching. Restore the salt balance immediately.

Burns

Burns are most commonly followed by shock. Administer a pain reliever immediately; apply gauze covered in Vaseline to the affected area and bandage. The patient should consume more water than usual.

Snow blindness

Symptoms of snow blindness include scratchy or burning eyes, excessive tearing, sensitivity to light, headache, halos around light and temporary loss of vision. Bandage the victim's eyes and use cold compresses and a painkiller to control the pain. Vision will generally be restored after 18 hours without the help of a doctor. Always wear snow goggles or sunglasses when traveling on snow or on water to prevent snow blindness.

Blisters

Blisters are the painful, common, result of ill-fitting footwear. At the first sign of discomfort, (what we teach as the hot spot technique), remove boots, socks and place a piece of moleskin over the affected area. Replace socks with two layers of sock a thin wicking / Friction barrier and a heavier cushioning layer. If it is absolutely necessary, open a blister by first washing the area thoroughly then inserting a sterilized needle into the side of the blister. Apply disinfectant and a bandage.

Note: You can prevent some blisters from forming by proper foot and footwear care, and also by taking action at the first sign of discomfort.

Headaches

The leading cause of a headache is dehydration. If someone complains of a headache have them drink lots of water. This is something that should be taught to all participants. Headaches can be experienced in the mountains due to inadequate eye protection. Aspirin may be used to alleviate the pain, but one should find the source of headache to prevent further pain.

Snakebites

Snake bites are not overly common in North America. Different species of venomous rattlesnakes, copperheads and water moccasins can be found in their habitats. When planning a trip, know what snakes can be found in that habitat, and how to avoid them. If you come across a snake slowly ease back. A snake bite rarely causes death; victims may be left untreated for up to eight hours.

After a bite occurs:
1. Keep the person calm, reassuring them that bites can be effectively treated. Restrict movement, and keep the affected area just below heart level to reduce the flow of venom.
2. Remove any rings or constricting items because the affected area may swell. Create a loose splint to help restrict movement of the area.
3. If the area of the bite begins to swell and change color, the snake was probably poisonous.
4. Monitor the person's vital signs—temperature, pulse, rate of breathing, blood pressure. If there are signs of shock (such as paleness), lay the victim flat, raise the feet about a foot, and cover the victim with a blanket.
5. Get medical help immediately. Start planning your evacuation of the victim.

Bee stings, allergies, food reactions.

Bee stings are common and harmless unless you are allergic. Remove the stinger then apply disinfectant and cold water to reduce the swelling. When doing a medical pre trip screening, look closely at allergies and reactions. People who have food allergies, will need to be consulted before the trip so the menu can be planned accordingly. Make sure anybody with a reaction of any sort brings their own medicine (Epipen, Benedryl, etc.). Also be sure that medication goes with the participant on all parts of a trip. It can not be left behind on the trip to the stream. Any delay in treatment could be deadly. Consult with your Doctor and get a prescription for a program epi-pen, (if your state allows this—if not write a letter to your Representative). Receive training in anaphylaxis care.

Allergic reactions in the wilderness can become life threatening—Be Prepared!

Silver, J. AMC Mountain Leadership Manual "General First Aid Procedures"

Summary

No matter how good of a leader you are, these skills are going to get tested. For example, like one day on a caving trip one of our participants had an asthma attack, pulled out her inhaler and immediately stopped breathing! One quarter of a mile into the cave system, my quick thinking staff person recognized an obstructed airway and did an obstructed airway maneuver on the girl. Out flies a woodchip! The offending chip must have been in her pocket, and because she did not have the cover on her inhaler, this woodchip got into the opening and then straight to the back of her throat. If my staff had not reacted quickly and appropriately, this could have been a very different story!

Start your training now and play the "what if" game all the time. It will keep you on your toes and out of court!

CHAPTER 12

FACILITATION SKILLS

Experiential Facilitation
"Experiential Education, often called Wilderness Adventure Education, is not intended to replace classroom learning. It is instead, an alternative approach that can be "intelligently and successfully used by any teacher in all subject areas."

Freeberg

'Teaching, in my estimation, is a vastly overrated function….. I see the facilitation of learning as the aim of education' (Rogers, 1969). Rogers, C. (1969) *Freedom to Learn: A View Of What Education Might Become.* Columbus, Ohio: C. E. Merrill.

Next to the right to life itself, the most essential of all rights is that of being in charge of our lives. Or put a little differently, the right to decide for ourselves how we interact with the world around us and our relationship to it. We each have the right and responsibility to explore our universe and our personal environment. To think about the experiences and relationships gained from these activities and to apply our conclusions to our personal lives adding new meaning and depths of understanding.

We are not the same people we were a few short years ago. We are not exposed to the same living conditions as those who preceded us. Many, many changes have taken place since our parents were children—all of which affect our behavior and our perceptions. Even as we acknowledge these societal changes, we must also hasten to respond to the resultant (and prospective) changes within our educational process. (Buell, 1983)

One philosophy of education, put forth by well known educator, John Holt, says that schools do an injustice to the learning process. While I do not wholeheartedly champion this position, I do believe that students, especially adolescents, are restricted by the structure of the classic classroom approach and therefore limited from progress beyond the learning of certain basic facts. Certainly, the self discipline of learning in the traditional manner is important and we recognize the need to acquire good study techniques and habits. In addition, we cannot diminish the value of good observing and reporting skills in the process of seeking a working knowledge of the fundamental facts underlying our understanding. We need to know about the universe and how it works. Yet today's educational structure often produces an undefined role or direction for the adolescent student who seeks a personal environmental security accompanied by a sense of belonging, love, respect and prestige.(Source unknown)

Some characteristics related to these needs and problems encountered in our personal roles as members of a so called mass society are identified in Dennis Poplin's important study of American communities:

1. <u>a sense of alienation</u>, a feeling of being cut off from meaningful group affiliations.

2. <u>morale fragmentation</u> in which members pursue divergent goals and feel no sense of oneness with other people.

3. <u>disengagement,</u> a feeling by members that they have no need to participate in the collective activities of various groups

4. <u>segmentation,</u> a view held by members in which they regard each other as means to ends and give little or no intrinsic worth or significance to individuals.

The implications of these characteristics, manifested in today's society are frightening. (Buell, L-Unpublished Doctoral Dissertation 1983)

I have no desire to present a gloomy or discouraging view of our future only to view the present picture honestly with an eye toward improvement and correction. The way I see it, the real power of education comes from experience. Experiential Education is poised to make the connection between education, recreation, leadership, therapy and learnership.

The path toward a better future for today's young people, the environment and society lies in our facilitators. Our Leaders! This is truly your Noble cause!

What does it mean to facilitate? Can we educate to appreciate our vital natural world? Will our grandchildren praise or scorn us? Where will the direction for our future come from? Our Leaders! Can our Education system be the key? Not when we have to beg for funds so we can do our job! When will "our leaders" see the potential investment in the future of young minds instead of a war machine? You are asking has he lost it. No, but I am searching for the solution to a large problem, and I feel you are the answer. So, what do you need to know to facilitate in a dynamic changing classroom? The answer is simple the 12 core competencies. As well as some dynamic facilitating skills. Remember we don't want to teach just the mind. There is so much more to learning.

James Neill wrote the following article entitled; "Characteristics of effective Outdoor Education Instructors" and in it summarizes quite well the personal qualities of an effective facilitator. Some research has been done in the area of instructor effectiveness and their personal qualities. Hendy (1975) found that Outward Bound instructors typically had a clear self-concept, were bright, tender-minded, very imaginative and creative. In addition, some instructors were rated by participants as superior to other instructors, with one of the distinguishing factors being enthusiasm.

"Enthusiasm was a very noticeable quality of the superior instructors as was forthrightness. In view of the short time period instructors have with their students, the ability to dispense with trivia, peel away the facades and get down to business is desirable in an instructor. Furthermore, teacher effectiveness studies have shown that students trust and like such teachers and in the Outward Bound situation when students perceive themselves to be at risk, all they have to begin with is trust in their instructor and in their peers. It isn't until later that they trust themselves…Also noteworthy are the high scores by the superior instructors on being imaginative and experimenting." (Hendy, 1975)

On the subject of personality, let us remember if we do not like what we are doing we are in the wrong field. Quality facilitators love working with people and there is a warmth to their spirit that can

THE NOBLE GIFT

be felt by the participants. Research evidence has suggested that teacher warmth tends to be associated with student creativity. Teachers who like their pupils tend to have pupils who like one another. Emotional security is highest in students whose teachers are warm, understanding and business-like (Richards, 1977). Gage suggested that:

> "Warmth may be understood in relation to conditioning theory as the teachers' overall tendency to emit positive reinforcements. Hence, pupils who have warm teachers are less inhibited about making responses, because whatever they do is likely to be met with positive reinforcing behavior on the part of the teacher.
>
> In another sense, however, the value of teacher warmth may be understood in terms of the theory of cognitive balance, which predicts that we will tend to like someone whom we recognize as like us." (Gage, 1970)

Warmth is important for teachers, but essential for instructors, because outdoor education places participants in unfamiliar situations without many usual anchors for emotional security. Instructor warmth can help participants to find the new experiences stimulating and rewarding, as opposed to overwhelming and threatening.

In addition, outdoor education tends to operate without an extensive syllabi or detailed lesson plans. Personal development is often placed as the priority, and a basic framework provided, but the instructor has a large amount of flexibility in terms of how information and activities are presented and how they interact with the participants. With the priority on personal development through experiential learning, instructor warmth is important for the process of inspiring participants towards feeling comfortable taking initiative for themselves and for supporting participants' sense of rewards from their own achievements. (Neill)

Using your "Noble Gift"

With your "noble gift" people will feel the spark of your passion, personality and concern. They will join with you, (not just following) on a journey that will take them to places unexplored. Soon they open a very creative mindset. You as a facilitator help open those doors. Is there a greater reward for our efforts? Taking people to new worlds is exciting. Last night I taught a Scuba class and shared with the participants an alien world. They came back energized about their potential to explore that world. Pleased with their performance, they will never look at water the same way! The world outdoors is a place where models and routines are left behind. It is exhilarating to change the way we dress, feel, think and behave. Going outdoors can also be a journey of discoveries where people find things out about themselves, each other and the natural world.

Most people when going on a simple walk in the woods miss most of what the woods are saying to them. Remember you're personal Core Competencies—Silence—This opens your spirit, mind and body to the learnings from nature. On any given walk allow your participants the opportunity to listen to nature calling to them. The woods are always screaming to me, "Listen to my story—Look at me—I'll be your friend." On an adventure trip you may be leading, ask your participants to listen to themselves and respect what they are hearing/feeling. Ask them to be a detective or a co discoverer with you. Your job is not over yet, you now have a golden teachable moment. Ask for permission to take them on a stroll outside their normal comfort zone! It is possible that very little will happen. But, on another day you might ask someone to take a walk around their comfort zone and ask them to look through a door (a place yet unexplored—like Scuba). When they look through, they see themselves in a whole different light.

Remember Colin, the high school freshman in Chapter 11. You rocked his world, in a way that only experiential education can. Growth may not be perceived, or if noticed may not be enjoyed. I have never enjoyed being cold, wet, hungry or bug-bitten. But when I look back on my trips those are among my favorites! Even if your client gets pleasure from each experience, they may not have much 'educational' value, as defined by "the system." But, who defines what is learning and what is worthwhile? I can learn more from watching an ant colony at work for an hour, than I can in a day of classroom learning. Then when I open up the "ant learning" and relate it to my world, is my education not valued? The path toward co-discovery can wane if the visitors are not in the frame of mind or perhaps they do not have the confidence to become a detective. They may have forgotten how to have fun, let go, or worse they could have forgotten about "magic." Magic is the thing that keeps us believing in our super heroes! Magic is the feeling you get, when you believe so strongly in something, you can not fail. Magic is the unexplainable fascination/need we have to be in the out of doors and with other living beings. If you have a participant that has been programmed to learn in a certain manner (conformed to societies wish to train people to learn in only one style), if they have become habituated to being customers, spoon-fed learners, they will remain insecure about how to become a detective with you. I once had a college sophomore in one of my classes and she said, "This is the first time I have ever gone outside for one of my classes" I thought, how sad.

When you add talented facilitation to the total environment (people, nature, spirit and magic) now you have a "teaching tool" that ignites the spark and creates a dynamic combination at your disposal. You have tapped into Experiential Education. You may not always know the outcome, but be willing to explore all the possibilities. This is education at its finest.

You (as a facilitator) first need a reasonably clear picture of what it is that you want to facilitate. A meeting? An activity? Group development? Personal development? Self-directed learning? A learning climate? A learning outcome? Learning skills? Self-esteem? Support? An adventurous attitude? A self-reliant expedition? A commitment to sustainability? Curiosity about nature? Spiritual awareness? Independence? Interdependence? Almost any experience or change valued by participants? (Barret, J. & Greenaway, R. 1995)

Once you have set SMART goals for your program and activity, you now need to PREPARE. Now you are ready to facilitate. It will be useful to think about any other variable that would effect you being able to accomplish your goals. Barret, J. & Greenaway, R identify these as the personal attributes of participants, their individually different experiences, the group dynamics, the nature of the activities, and the influence of the natural environment. In experiential education settings there are so many influences around, that it makes sense to ensure that they are identified, appreciated and engaged. The value of doing so, and of doing so in a facilitative way, also happens to be well supported by research studies reviewed in 'Why Adventure?' (Barret & Greenaway, 1995).

There is a huge variety of facilitation styles to be used when teaching in the experiential classroom. This assortment of possible techniques can be puzzling. Despite much overlap in practice, facilitation is commonly understood to be less directive than teaching. If we look at Leadership styles, we would ideally be going in back and forth between appropriate leadership styles and effective facilitative styles. With these tools and techniques in your hip pocket you are truly a "practitioner of the noble gift." Now you begin to teach people how to begin building their own castle.

"A useful 'rule of thumb' distinction between facilitation and teaching is that in facilitation, the goal is usually for people to learn something that nobody knows at the beginning, whereas in teaching the goal is usually for people to learn what the teacher already knows." (Barret & Greenway 1995)

THE NOBLE GIFT

The following description of facilitation style is reprinted & adapted with permission from Roger Greenaway the author of (1995) *Why Adventure? The Role and Value of Outdoor Adventure in Young People's Personal and Social Development.* In most forms of experiential education it is likely that both kinds of goals exist—so you may want to move between facilitating and teaching. But even when you have the knowledge or skill that others are trying to learn, it does not automatically follow that you abandon facilitation. There are many aspects of experiential education (camp cooking, map reading, weather forecasting, first aid, and many environmental education topics) that are unlikely to be discovered without some assistance. But with imagination, even these very teachable skills and topics can be learned by experiential methods and appropriate facilitation. For example, Joseph Cornell is an outstanding example of an environmental educator for whom direct experience is central to his philosophy and methods. In his foreword to "Sharing Nature With Children," Cornell writes:

"Each of the games creates a situation or an experience, in which nature is the teacher. Each game is a mouthpiece for nature—sometimes speaking in the language of the scientist, sometimes in that of the artist or mystic." (Cornell, 1979:8).

In 'Sharing the Joy of Nature' Cornell describes the four stage sequence that he uses to facilitate what he describes as 'Learning with a Natural Flow'. This interestingly corresponds with the Circle of Group Growth from chapter 3.

1. **Awaken Enthusiasm**–East–Illumination
2. **Focus Attention**–South–Innocence and Trust
3. **Direct Experience**–West–Introspection
4. **Share Inspiration**–North–Wisdom

Cornell explains:
I call the fourth stage 'sharing inspiration', because sharing strengthens and clarifies our own deep experiences. Sharing is also one of your Core personal Competencies. After a successful Flow Learning session, each person feels a subtle, enjoyable awareness of oneness with nature, each other and an increased empathy with all of life (Cornell, 1989).

This is the challenge for all experiential educators: to make students' own experiences central to the whole process—especially if we happen to believe that 'all genuine knowledge originates in direct experience' (Mao Tse Tung). Experiential education is not just about changing the scenery. It is an opportunity for much deeper change—which facilitation can help or hinder. The type of leadership style you use can have a direct effect on your outcome, so choose wisely. Then by using cues the environment, the participants, and from your goals you are liberated to add a facilitative style.

Varieties of Facilitation
'Facilitation' is often described as the art of making things easy for others, but if you make things too easy you risk returning to the spoon-feeding tradition in which learners passively digest whatever the educator wants them to. In essence, facilitation is an enabling role in which the focus is usually on what the learner is doing and experiencing rather than on what the educator is doing. Some of the facilitation styles that are used by outdoor educators are described next.

Non-directive facilitation
In his essay 'Adventure Education' David Charlton provides an example of this approach:

'The facilitator recognizes the various signals given by the students indicating when and which way they want to go. The facilitator then creates the opportunity that enables them to go that way' (Charlton, c.1980).

Even if you do not adopt a non-directive stance all of the time, there are situations where it can be an effective strategy—for example, where you believe that students can work things out for themselves and will find it more rewarding to do so. An impartial stance can also help to encourage discussion or defuse conflict or help students become more independent and responsible. But there are some issues on which you should not attempt to be neutral. These are your non-negotiable values—which you should be clear about to yourself and to others (Heron, 1999:33-4).

Appreciative facilitation

Appreciative facilitation emphasizes what works well and pays attention to success and achievement. At its simplest, it involves catching students at their best moments and providing positive feedback about what they did or said. Alternatively you can invite positive comments from participants for each other following a group exercise. Or just ask, 'What is working well?'. Cheri Torres brings together her enthusiasm for appreciative facilitation and mobile ropes courses in 'The Appreciative Facilitator' (Torres, 2001). Her handbook includes summaries of key research supporting appreciative facilitation, such as the 'Pygmalion Effect' ('As the teacher believes the student to be, so the student becomes') and how watching videos of your own successful performances leads to much greater improvements than watching videos of your mistakes. Appreciative facilitation draws on ideas and principles from Appreciative Inquiry (an approach to organization development) and Solution Focused Brief Therapy ('Be careful what you attend to. What you focus on expands.'). Appreciative facilitation fits well with outdoor education, both as a source of techniques and as a philosophy.

Activity facilitation

This approach emphasizes the facilitator's role during a group activity. Sometimes the facilitator may simply be enabling a group to achieve a task in the time available. But where the purpose of the activity is to generate experiences from which people will learn, the facilitator may want to intervene during the activity in order to influence what is experienced. This will typically involve changing the rules in some way—with or without consultation with the group. The Facilitator's Toolkit (Thiagarajan & Thiagarajan, 1999) is mostly about activity facilitation. The context is indoor training for adults, but much of this 'toolkit' can readily be adapted for outdoor education. Outdoor educators have less control over the many variables that influence what is experienced, but there are always plenty of ways in which 'activity facilitation' can enhance the quality of the experience. In 'Learning Through First Hand Experience Out of Doors', Pat Keighley describes many ways in which activities in the outdoors can be designed and adapted to provide experience-based elements of the National Curriculum in Physical Education, Science, Geography, Maths and English (Keighley, 1998).

Group facilitation

'Group Facilitation' can apply to any group situations–from the running of effective meetings (and keeping to the agenda) through to sensitivity group training (where there is no agenda). Like it or not, the group dynamics in experiential education can have greater impact than 'the outdoors'. If the development of group skills is not a priority it may still be necessary to use group facilitation skills to redirect attention to 'the outdoors'. If the primary aim is social development or team building, group facilitation is clearly a must. But whatever your main purpose, you will at the very least want to ensure that the group climate is a highly favorable climate for learning and development. 'The Zen of Groups' (Hunter, Bailey & Taylor, 1992) is a good introduction to the basics of facilitating group development. More advanced (and drawing on much of his experience working with groups in the outdoors) is Martin Ringer's 'Group Action' (Ringer, 2001) which provides a psychodynamic perspective on group facilitation in experiential learning and adventure therapy.

Adventure programming

This approach to facilitation includes such techniques as 'Frontloading', 'Isomorphic Framing', and 'Paradoxical Symptom Prescriptions' (Priest & Gass, 1997:190-221). This language implies a directive style of facilitation that leaves little to chance. Their emphasis on 'presenting' metaphors in advance of the activity puts the facilitator in the role of storyteller before participants have had the experiences to fit the story. This is an interesting mixture of drama and adventure in which participants are effectively improvising within the frame provided by the facilitator's script. It is a style of facilitation that has been comprehensively challenged by Johan Hovelynck who is concerned that 'adventure education is increasingly adopting the didactic teaching methods that it set out to be an alternative for' (Hovelynck, 2001). Priest and Gass appreciate the 'drawbacks' of framing. This is the last of six drawbacks that they identify:

> By narrowing the focus of a frame to a predetermined metaphoric message, you are dictating what will be learned in the activity. Even if you are on target with the frame, by prescribing the way the experience will be interpreted, other metaphors may not be available for the group to interpret (Priest & Gass, 1997:215).

Your group sits on the logs looking at you as the story unfolds; You live in the village " Ican." Nestled in a remote valley Ican is an ideal place, people believe in their abilities, in each other and their role within the village.

On the mountain, in a castle lives an inventor, who incidentally does not like the village of Ican. His name is "Nevercan Ever," he has developed a shrinking potion and put it into your towns water supply! Everybody drank the water and hence the shrinking potion. You are all getting smaller, throughout the day the challenges will get bigger and bigger, as you get smaller and smaller.

Your village has elected your team to sneak into Nevercan Evers castle and to retrieve the antidote. You will have sneak past giant spiders and tilting alarmed floors. You will have to balance, crawl, climb and support each others efforts. It will not be easy, the goal will be to get as many group members as possible on top of his laboratory counter, to bring back as much antidote as you can carry.

Don't expect to agree on everything. Do agree to work together and to be safe. The future of "Ican" village is in your hands.

At the end of an amazing day, you process the learning and the experiences. You ask, what was the antidote? A quiet group member speaks up, "Confidence and respect." You ask why she feels that to be true? Laurens' reply is the goal you wanted to achieve when you started the day; "because with confidence and respect, we kids can really save the world." You sit stunned, because that out of the mouth of a twelve year old has come a statement, more profound than you have heard in a long time! You remind the group that they live in the village of "Ican," and from this day forward they need to believe in the special power they now have inside them. You close with a quote from a new 12 year old friend named Lauren "that if they can change the course of the future, they need to believe in their own magic powers." They all agree they will rise to each challenge they will face.

While saying goodbye Lauren, the 12 year old comes over to you and thanks you for a great day. You both say at the same time "Thanks for helping me out today." You say "I guess great minds think alike." Lauren who barely spoke a word during the first few activities replies "no they don't, they think for themselves." Stunned, again you agree, and off she goes. On this day you truly feel you have learned more from a 12 year old than she could have possibly learned from you. This is OK. Remember, we as leaders need to continue to grow, and the population of "Ican" has grown by 10 today. Tomorrow it will grow some more. T. S. Cook

Even when there is pressure to achieve particular outcomes, it by no means follows that 'predetermined' and 'prescribed' interpretations will be the most effective facilitation strategy. If interpretation precedes experience, the 'experience' is little more than an illustration in the facilitator's story. This is 'confirming through experience' rather than 'learning from experience'.

Choosing a Facilitation Style
As we have seen Barret & Greenaway have identified five styles of facilitation found in experiential education as outlined above. They continue to point out that they all have their advantages and disadvantages. In practice, facilitators often have a 'home' style that corresponds most closely to their values, and pick and mix ideas from other sources. If this sounds too haphazard, you will find excellent guidance in John Heron's 'The Complete Facilitator's Handbook' about switching between different styles according to what is most facilitative for learners at the time. Heron's matrix of the dimensions and modes of facilitation can be used to help you decide when to take charge, when to negotiate and when to stand back. It can also be used as a self-review tool (Heron, 1999:342-3).

Does research provide any guidance about choosing a facilitation style? Sivasailam Thiagarajan (Thiagi) spent 15 years in field research in what he admits was 'a futile attempt' to discover the secrets of 'effective facilitators' (who were rated highly by their peers and participants). Thiagi reported:

I did not find consistent, common behaviors among these facilitators. Further, even the same facilitator appeared to use different behaviors with different groups, even when conducting the same activity. To make matters worse, the same facilitator sometimes used different behaviors with the same group within the same activity at different times (Thiagarajan & Thiagarajan, 1999:48).

Inconsistency appears to be what effective facilitators have in common! Thiagi eventually concluded that effective facilitators are: flexible, adaptive, proactive, responsive and resilient. Stuart Wickes came to similar conclusions when he carried out a study of effective facilitation in outdoor management development. Wickes' study highlighted (amongst other factors) the importance of personal commitment, the ability to work with 'feelings and intuition' and the ability to work with 'clarity of intention' (Wickes, 2000:40).

Such findings are consistent with this guidance from Dale Hunter and colleagues for group facilitators:
Be yourself. As a facilitator, you will be most effective when you are being your natural self and allowing your own personality to be expressed. People get permission to be themselves from the way a facilitator behaves—that is, through modeling. If you are stiff and formal, the group tends to be like that. If you are relaxed and self-expressed, the group tends to be like that too (Hunter et al., 1992:54).

Search hard enough and you can probably find research supporting your own preferred facilitation style. Whatever that may be, the research reported above suggests that you should not be a slave to just one style. Such advice is particularly relevant in the unpredictable arena of outdoor education. You need freedom for maneuver, room for judgment, flexibility to respond and to make the most of unexpected events and experiences. The challenge is to develop a facilitation style or combination of styles that works for you and your students and that makes good use of the many facilitative influences that are found in outdoor education settings.

Facilitating Reflection

'Quality action and quality reflection on that action are of fundamental and equal to facilitate reflection on experience. This process is referred to variously as 'reviewing' or 'debriefing' or 'processing'. Much of the advice in this area centers on the art of questioning. Clifford Knapp's 'Lasting Lessons' is an excellent resource for helping experiential educators develop their questioning skills (Knapp, 1992). But there are traps awaiting the unwary. After the stimulation of the activity, reviewing sessions can be an anti-climax. In 'Islands of Healing', Schoel warns:

Without the sense of action to the Debrief, it is often a lifeless, futile exercise …The experience can come alive in the Debrief. The experience can be relived. The discussion is not a static, safe, merely cognitive exercise. It has feeling, anger, frustration, accomplishment and fun (Schoel, Prouty & Radcliffe, 1988:166).

What students experience during a review is at least as important as the experience that they are reviewing. It is not enough to expect that the stimulation of the activity will keep students alert and involved during a dull review in which the facilitator runs through a series of questions. Review sessions are an ideal opportunity for enabling students to be more active learners. Experiential learning is based on learners being active, curious and creative (Kolb, 1984). We should at least seek out learners' own questions. When reviewing in the outdoors there is no shortage of opportunities for active reviewing. The outdoors provides:

- a breath of fresh air and change of scene that can inspire a refreshingly new approach to learning
- an abundance of visual aids, some of which are 'the real thing' rather than substitutes for it
- a naturally stimulating environment for learning that is more 'brain-friendly' (and arouses more 'intelligences') than the most well equipped indoor classrooms
- space that is useful for more physical reviewing such as action replays, human sculpture, human graphs, or human scales
- privacy for solo reflection
- freedom from fixed or cumbersome furniture—you can move quickly between large group, small group, paired and individual reviewing activities
- opportunities for walking and talking—for paired discussions or for interviewing each other
- sand or soft earth for drawing anything such as a graph for showing ups and downs, a journey towards a goal, a force field, a flow chart, or a learning model
- natural objects and materials that can be collected and arranged as collages or sculptures or maps of a journey
- natural objects that can be arranged and moved to represent the changing group dynamics
- viewpoints from where participants indicate places that evoke thoughts or feelings associated with the experience being reviewed
- opportunities for reflective exercises such as guided reflections or making personal gifts from natural materials (Greenaway, 1995)
- opportunities for reflective drama inspired by the location or by environmental themes such as life cycles, the food chain, the web of life
- A 'Canterbury Tales' journey where each review topic happens at a different location.

- the opportunity to 'walk through' what happened or perform an action replay
- the opportunity to have a second go, and compare the differences between 'take one' and 'take two'
- 'teachable moments' or 'learning opportunities' which are best caught there and then as they happen.

Once you discover that you can abandon indoor teaching aids and exploit resources and opportunities in the outdoors for reviewing, you will become tuned in to spotting good reviewing locations and making the most of them. By making reviewing active, mobile and outdoors, the reviews themselves can be at least as memorable as the outdoor experiences being reviewed. This makes the learning as memorable as the experience in which it is grounded. (Reprinted and adapted with permission Greenaway, R. (2004) "Facilitation and Reviewing in Outdoor Education")

CHAPTER 13

CONCLUSION OR THE BEGINNING?

My Waukabiashi men have had an extraordinary day! We've hiked, swam in the stream, had a cook-out and played capture the flag—Native American style! One kid has been sitting out most of the day. He is different than the other kids; he is smaller and a lot frailer. The group adapts for Paul, the members sincerely like him and his contributions to the group. This is not always the case, his parents have told me. "He hates going to school because the kids there make fun of him." They really appreciate the way our group works together and respects each other for their abilities. I tell the parents, "We are just teaching the kids to be caring and respectful."

The next day we start off in the field with Reggie's "EMP" Energy Management Plan. Several non-competitive games to channel the kid's energy into working on the totem pole after swim lessons. Paul does not feel like playing, so he sits over on the edge of the lower field, at my suggestion looking for a four leaf clover. During a water break, I go over to Paul and ask how's he doing? He seems pleased; I have joined him for a bit. What happens next rocks my world forever! If ever there was a doubt, as to why I was put on this earth, it would be clear in a month. This next minute and events in September would solidify my desire to make a difference in people's lives!

"Paul" I say, "What are you looking at? "Did you find any four leaf clovers?" The reply was simple and to the point, "No" he says, "but you see that bumble bee?" I look and see the bumble bee, I've seen them before I thought, "Yes." He goes on "You know the bumble bee should not be able to fly, its wings are too small, and its body is too big." I think for a minute, and almost get sucked back into the ensuing game. But I'm curious. Paul continues "But you know what Scott- it doesn't know that, so it flies anyway."

I sat with Paul for the next game looking for clovers and he tells me when he grows up he wants to be an entomologist. I said "that's interesting." He found a clover and he gave it to me. I still have it in my box "of little things that mean a lot to me."

Paul died the following September from a tumor in his brain. At the service I found out he knew he was going to die, and yet found the courage to dream about growing up!!!! I suddenly felt very small, and then I remembered the- bumble bee. I remembered the summer he had as a Waukabiashi, and I felt very tall. It was Paul's spirit and what I learned from him that was lifting me up. His mother came over to me and said, "Paul was so proud of his accomplishments this summer, he wanted you to know, that he is a hairy chested man!" "What does that mean?" I simply said "that's a part of our group cheer."

It wasn't until now that I realized how much our program meant to Paul and his family and why. He had been able to find acceptance, confidence and a place were he could dream. We should all be so lucky!

I now realize how much I was to learn about life and where my education would really come from! Thanks Paul, your spirit lives in me and guides me daily.

I don't know who you are or what you are going to do with the information in this book. You've made it this far, we must be doing something right! Like Paul, you have an opportunity! An opportunity to dream and to make a difference in peoples lives. In the process, you may feel like you are too small too really make a difference. That's OK! The Bumble Bee continued to make our world just a little more beautiful by carrying out its daunting task. The flowers it helped remain a testament to its tenacity.

With the information given you in these pages, there lays in you the potential to make this world a better place. With the power of experiential education and your skills as an Outdoor Leader you will rise to greet each new challenge and accomplish your goals.

From the beginning of this book, we have built our leadership castle one block at a time. Now it's your turn to show the world what you've got! Remember yours is a "Noble Gift."

The foundation on which your castle sits:
1. Respect
2. Circle
3. Sharing
4. Silence

The walls of your castle are built from your CORE Competencies, quarried with hard work and placed thoughtfully where they will show your purpose and potential;
1. Organizational skills
2. Technical skills
3. Environmental philosophy
4. Safety sense & Risk management
5. Instructional strategies
6. Group Development
7. Decision-making.
8. Problem-solving
9. Effective communication
10. Experience-based judgment skills
11. Leadership ethics
12. Sharing values

Your castle was built so all that travel past can see the thought that went into its construction. You have added the inner workings, the true guts of your castle, your leadership styles. These are the doors that let you out into the community and let people in to your castle.
1. Telling
2. Selling
3. Testing
4. Consulting
5. Joining

THE NOBLE GIFT

When consulting a different engineer you also explored the different leadership styles;
- Authoritarian or autocratic
- Participative or democratic
- Delegate or Free Reign

You have invested hours in your education as a leader, your leadership skills are getting better, people recognize your competency. You understand the stages that groups will go through during your time together. Once again you've explored two different theories; these are the windows that let you see what you are doing.

The circle theory (Cook 2004):
1. lumination—East
2. The Big Winds—East to South
3. Innocence & Trust—South
4. Gentle Breezes—Toward the West
5. Introspection—West
6. Harvest Winds, Toward the North
7. Wisdom—North
8. Dawn Winds- Toward the East

The second theory (Tuckmans);
1. Stage 1: Forming
2. Stage 2: Storming
3. Stage 3: Norming
4. Stage 4: Performing
5. Stage 5: Adjourning

We have looked specifically at how people will behave while on our trips (Wagstaff);
1. Individual to individual:
2. Individual to group:
3. Group to individual:
4. Group to group:
5. Individual and group to multiple users:
6. Individual and Group to administrative agencies:
7. Individual and group to the local populace:

We have even gotten the rules of trip leadership (Tomb)
1. Get the hell out of bed.
2. Do not be cheerful before breakfast.
3. Do not complain.
4. Learn to cook at least one thing right.
5. Either A) Shampoo, or B) Do not remove your hat for any reason.
6. Do not ask if anybody's seen your stuff.
7. Never ask where you are.

8. Always carry more than your fair share.
9. Do not get sunburned.
10. Do not get killed.

The individuals we work with will react differently to different situations but we are prepared because we know about participant roles (AMC Leadership Guide 2005)
1. The AGREER.
2. The OPPOSER/CRITICIZER.
3. The SILENT OBSERVER
4. The NON-LISTENER.
5. The CLOWN
6. The DOMINATOR
7. The INTERRUPTER
8. The FOLLOWER
9. The BYSTANDER

You have also learned about Erikson's Eight Stages of Development
1. Learning Basic Trust Versus Basic Mistrust (Hope)
2. Learning Autonomy Versus Shame (Will)
3. Learning Initiative Versus Guilt (Purpose)
4. Industry Versus Inferiority (Competence)
5. Learning Identity Versus Identity Diffusion (Fidelity)
6. Learning Intimacy Versus Isolation (Love)
7. Learning Generativity Versus Self-Absorption (Care)
8. Integrity Versus Despair (Wisdom)

With applied leadership we learned how people learn and behavior patterns;
1. Learnership (Cook)
2. EXTRAVERSION (Scholl)
3. INTROVERSION
4. SENSING
5. INTUITION
6. THINKING
7. FEELING
8. JUDGING
9. PERCEIVING

1. Reflecting, (Kolb)
2. Doing
3. Interacting
4. Absorbing
5. The Doer; (Foster)
6. The Thinker

7. The Watcher/ Seer
8. The Feeler
9. The Struggler
10. The Achiever

We learned what the issues are related to the ethics of leadership
1. Informed Consent <u>Hunt (1990)</u>
2. Deception
3. Secrecy
4. Captive Populations
5. Sexual Issues:
6. Environmental Concerns: <u>Yerkes & Haras, 1997</u>)
7. Individual versus Group Benefit:
8. Students' Rights
9. Social Implications
10. Paternalism

We've set SMART goals (Nikitina)
1. S = Specific
2. M = Measurable
3. A = Attainable
4. R = Realistic
5. T = Timely

Even taken steps to set goals
1. Goal-awareness (Unestahl)
2. Goal-inventory
3. Goal-analysis.
4. Goal-selection.
5. Goal-formulation
6. Multiple goals

Following the steps GO PREPARE we are ready to meet our group.
1. GO = Goals and Objectives (Martin, B., Cashel, C., Wagstaff, M., Brenig, M)
2. P = Participants
3. R = Resources
4. E = Equipment
5. P = Plan
6. A = Access
7. R = Rationing
8. E = Emergency Plan
9. LOGSTICS

We packed our bags and we have the ten essentials (<u>Mountaineers</u> 1930) and proper gear lists;

1. Matches
2. Fire Starter
3. Map
4. Compass
5. Flashlight, Extra Batteries and Bulb
6. Extra Food
7. Extra Clothing
8. Sunglasses.
9. First Aid Kit
10. Pocket Knife
11. Shelter

A practical look at Risk management and how accidents occur. Despite it all, we have to take steps to protect our castle from lawsuits and we need to know how to avoid and prevent accidents.

The Outdoors as a Risk Activity (Rick Curtis)
1. *Theory of Accidents - How Accidents Occur*
2. Environmental Hazards
3. Human Factor Hazards
4. *Record Keeping*
5. *Pre-trip Planning*
6. *Implementing Program Change*
7. *Safety = Judgment*

We have learned about what to do if something goes wrong and somebody gets hurt. There is a lot more work to do with hard skills here.

I'm NOT HELPLESS (T.S. Cook 2006) <u>Steps to control wounds</u>

Infection
Not stopping bleeding
Open
Tenderness
Head
Edges.
Length
Pressure,
Loss
Elevate
Spurting
Shock

THE NOBLE GIFT

Facilitation skills have allowed us to adapt out skills so we can be even more effective
1. Awaken Enthusiasm (Cornell)—East—Illumination (Cook)
2. Focus Attention—South—Innocence and Trust
3. Direct Experience—West—Introspection
4. Share Inspiration—North—Wisdom

We have also learned (Barret & Greenaway) the following facilitative styles
1. Non-directive facilitation
2. Appreciative facilitation
3. Activity facilitation
4. Group facilitation
5. Adventure programming

A good friend of mine Tom Foster once said in this field (outdoor leadership) you need to be a "jack of all trades and the master of a few." The first chapter of this book is about learning who you are and what you want to accomplish. I called it "finding your passion." Now in the last chapter I am imploring you to use your skills and reach out to those who need you. Share your "Noble Gift."

As a species we need to look at our effect on other people, the environment, "The Full **Circle**." We need to understand our role as an individual and as a leader. We should search for ways to "**Share** our Gift" with others, in the hopes of creating a citizenry that is prepared to meet the challenges of the future. We must acquire the confidence to "Consider **Silence**" by listening to what is truly going on around us and within us. We lead with purity of purpose. On your journey "Teach **Respect**" for all things.

If we can take a look backward to gain some insight that would be good right now. Native Americans when making a decision would consider the effect of that decision on the "seventh generation." That my friend is leadership! When we consider our actions as a part of the whole circle, perhaps we can look forward knowing the difference we have made will be appreciated by the seventh generation.

In the Native American Circle the "Medicine Wheel" connects all things. "The Leadership Wheel" is your way of knowing you are connected and grounded in your efforts to lead, towards that brighter future.

APPENDICES

Westfield State College
Office of Outdoor Leadership
Health and Medical Record

_____
Last Name   First Name   Middle   Birth date

_____( )_____
Home Address (Number & Street)   City or Town   State   Zip Code   Home Phone #

_____( )_____
Emergency Contact Name   Emergency Phone #

Do You Have Health Insurance   No   Yes

_____( )_____
Health Insurance Company   Address   Phone #

_____
Name of Insured   Policy Number

NOTICE

The Office of Outdoor Leadership integrates both classroom style teaching and physical activity into the instructional curriculum. Each participant is encouraged to choose their level of active participation in the programs offered by this Office. The ability of each participant to manage his or her emotional and physical well-being, and for the group to support the individual decisions that are made by each participant is essential for the success of our programs.

To assist you in assessing your ability to succeed safely in our programs, and to enable us to assist you in case of an emergency, please complete this Health and Medical Record. Please note that Westfield State College does not administer medications (unless to children), except in emergencies, and we accept no responsibility for determining an individual's fitness to participate in the Outdoor Leadership programs. **Any questions you may have about your ability to participate should be directed to your physician.** The information you are providing in this Health and Medical Record will be treated confidentially. It

TAYLOR SCOTT COOK, PH.D.

will not be released to anyone without your permission, except in an emergency situation where you are unable to otherwise communicate your wishes.

1. Please rate your current level of physical activity

Activity	Times Per Week	Times Per Week	Times Per Week
Walking	☐ 1-2	☐ 3-5	☐ 5+
Jogging	☐ 1-2	☐ 3-5	☐ 5+
Cycling	☐ 1-2	☐ 3-5	☐ 5+
Aerobics	☐ 1-2	☐ 3-5	☐ 5+
General Sports	☐ 1-2	☐ 3-5	☐ 5+
Swimming Ability	☐ Beginner	☐ Intermediate	☐ Advanced

Do you currently experience any **Allergies**? No   Yes*   Do you carry personal **medications**? No   Yes

Have you ever experienced an **Anaphylaxis Reaction?** q No q Yes

*Allergy	Reaction	Treatment

Do you currently experience **Diabetes**? No   Yes*   Do you carry personal **medications**? No   Yes

*Type of Diabetes	Reaction	Treatment

Do you currently experience **Asthma**? No   Yes*   Do you carry personal **medications**? No   Yes

*Type of Asthma	Reaction	Treatment

Do you currently experience **Seizures**? No   Yes*   Do you carry personal **medications**? No   Yes

*Type of Seizures	Reaction	Treatment

Do you currently have **Cardiac Symptoms**? No   Yes*   Do you carry personal **medication**? No   Yes

*Cardiac Symptoms	Reaction	Treatment

THE NOBLE GIFT

Pre-existing condition information C = **Current** (within last 12 months) P = Past N= N/A

Have you ever had	C	P	N	Have you ever had	C	P	N
Complete/partial hearing loss				History of heart disease (in family)			
Head injury				Palpitations (heart)			
Heat related illness				Heart murmur			
Orthopedic injury				Chest pains with or w/o exercise			
Ever dizzy or faint during exercise?				Bleeding disorder			
Shortness of breath with or w/o exercise				Stroke			
Ever told not to participate in sports?				High Blood Pressure			

Additional comments or information if checked a current or past condition.

_____

_____

_____

_____

2. Please list any additional illnesses or medical conditions for which you are currently being treated.

Condition   Year Diagnosed   Treatment

Condition   Year Diagnosed   Treatment

3. Please list any operations or hospitalizations you have had in the past year.

Reason   Hospital   Doctor   Date

Reason   Hospital   Doctor   Date

4. Please list additional medications you are now taking.

Name of Medication   Dose   How Often

Name of Medication   Dose   How Often

TAYLOR SCOTT COOK, PH.D.

5. *Physician Consultation*

If you responded affirmatively to any of our requests for medical information, we urge you to contact your physician to discuss your ability to participate in the Outdoor Leadership programs. If you or your physician requires additional information regarding these activities, please contact us.

I have consulted with my physician about my participation in the Outdoor Leadership program?   No   Yes

If you answered yes to the previous question, please provide the physician's recommendation:
- ☐ Advised to participate
- ☐ Advised not to participate
- ☐ Advised to use caution while participating in certain activities

Physician's signature maybe required for certain conditions or activities.
_____

Physician's signature   Printed Name   Date
_____

Physician's Approval to participant
_____

Physician's Disapproval to participant
_____

Physician's Advised to use caution while participating in certain activities
_____

Any other concerns or fears
_____
_____
_____

The foregoing information is true and correct to the best of my knowledge.

Date: _____ Student Signature: _____

THE NOBLE GIFT

Wilderness Experiences Unlimited & Westfield Water Sports.

Accident, Incident and Crisis Report Form
Complete within 48 hours and then give to: Director in charge of program. Use additional paper wherever needed. Important Phone Numbers;
Facility managers 413-562-7431, 413-568-8764, 787-2090,
Store Manager 781-7260, 531-9102
Camp Program Director 827-9054

PERSON REPORTING_____
DATE_____
PHONE NUMBER
(DAY)(____)_____(EVENING)(____)_____
Name of person Injured: _____
Describe what happened:
_____
_____
_____
_____

List any equipment involved:
_____
_____
_____

Where did this occur (include the name of the camp, event, facility etc):
_____
_____

Describe the exact location(use diagram if appropriate):
_____
_____

What time:_____ A.M. ___ or P.M.___

Describe any medical or first aid treatment given, and who gave it"
_____
_____
_____

List in order the actions taken to deal with the Accident/Incident/Crisis:
1._____
2._____
3._____
4._____
   List those involved:
   Name   Age   Sex   Address Phone
   1._____ ____ ____ _____

TAYLOR SCOTT COOK, PH.D.

2._____ ____ ____ _____
3._____ ____ ____ _____
4._____ ____ ____ _____

If any involved are minors complete the following:

Child's Name   Parent/Guardian   Name Address Phone (include area code)

1._____ _____ _____
2._____ _____ _____
3._____ _____ _____
4._____ _____ _____

List the names of Witness: (write down statements made)

Name   Age Sex   Address Phone

1._____ ____ ____ _____
2._____ ____ ____ _____
3._____ ____ ____ _____
4._____ ____ ____ _____

Record parent reactions when notified:

_____

_____

List others involved and their jurisdiction, name and contact phone number:

Law Enforcement:

_____

Fire Department:

_____

Medical Aid (Event First Aider, Rescue Squad, Etc.):

_____

Hospital:_____

Other: _____

List the name of the WEU & WWS representative contacted and the time contacted:

_____

_____

Describe any contact made with the media regarding this situation. If known, list their name and media affiliation:

_____

_____

Was an Insurance claim form given to anyone? List name and address:

_____

Signature_____ Date_____

_____ Check here if additional pages are attached. _____How many attached

THE NOBLE GIFT

Pro-forma: Analysis of activities for risk and safety management

Activity and venue

List safety issues, risks, hazards

- _____
- _____
- _____
- _____
- _____

Can a satisfactory plan be developed to keep participants safe?

YES
Develop safety
Management plan

NO
Avoid activity

Consider/include:

- ☐ Nature of the venue—special characteristics of this location, specific checks for immediate hazards, weather, and venue check prior to excursion

Notes:_____
_____
_____

- ☐ The activity and level of the activity, its appropriateness for the age, maturity, physical stature, ability level and readiness of the students; the suitability for this location for this group

Notes:_____
_____
_____

- ☐ Staff qualifications and/or experience specific to the activity, the nature of the group and the venue to be used

Notes:_____
_____
_____

- ☐ Participant preparation, including skill development, fitness development and advance briefing

Notes:_____
_____
_____

☐ Equipment safety—maintenance procedures and checks (including personal equipment, special equipment for specific activities, transport, equipment for emergencies)

Notes: _____
_____
_____

☐ Protective clothing

Notes: _____
_____
_____

☐ Organizational arrangements for conducting the activity, including staff—student ratios, location, roles of staff and use of safety measures

Notes: _____
_____
_____

☐ Group management arrangements, including additional activities if waiting time is long

Notes: _____
_____
_____

☐ Alternatives to the activity plan in case of weather changes, injuries or other circumstances

Notes: _____
_____
_____

☐ Procedures to be implemented in emergencies, a communication plan.

Notes: _____
_____
_____

Note: This pro-forma provides one suggested way of documenting an analysis of activities for risk and safety management purposes. Original source (R. Curtis)

THE NOBLE GIFT

Leadership Lessons The Nature of Geese

In a flock of geese, every single bird within the group knows exactly where it is headed and is ready and able to take over the leadership position at any given moment. The goose in the front of the formation leads for a while, but as it tires it will drop back and another goose will take its place in front. Leadership and responsibility are shared by all.

To meet the demands and changes impacting them, many organizations are creating environments where employees at all levels have the ability, willingness, and opportunity to exercise leadership.

Ralph Stayer finally realized that he required a dramatic shift in his leadership style when his company was losing business. He saw that the people in his organization did not work as well as they could, and he was the cause of that. He realized that what he needed was a group of responsible, interdependent workers who would take initiative and responsibility. To do that, he knew he had to transfer more ownership and responsibility to his workers.

Fact	Lesson
1. As each goose flaps its wings, it creates an "uplift" for the birds that follow. By flying in a "V" formation, the whole flock adds 71% greater flying range than if each bird flew alone.	People who share a common direction and sense of community can get where they're going more quickly and easily because they are traveling on the thrust of each other.
2. When a goose falls out of formation, it suddenly feels the drag and resistance of flying alone. It quickly moves back into formation to take advantage of the lifting power of the bird immediately in front of it.	If we have as much sense as a goose, we stay in formation with those headed where we want to go. We are willing to accept their help and give our help to others.
3. When the lead bird tires, it rotates back into the formation to take advantage of the lifting power of the bird immediately in front of it.	It pays to take turns doing the hard tasks and sharing leadership. As with geese, people are interdependent on each other's skills, capabilities, and unique arrangements of gifts, talents, or resources.
4. The geese flying in formation honk to encourage those up front to keep up their speed.	We need to make sure our "honking" is encouraging. In groups where there is encouragement, the production is much greater. The power of encouragement (to stand by one's heart or core values and to encourage the heart and core values of others) is the quality of "honking" that we seek.
5. When a goose gets sick, wounded, or shot down, two geese drop out of formation and follow it down to help and protect it. They stay until it dies or is able to fly again. Then, they launch out with another formation or catch up with the flock.	If we have as much sense as geese, we will stand by each other in difficult times as well as when we are soaring.

Leadership Lessons from Geese

What does the geese metaphor tell us about possibilities for human leadership? Below are five facts about the behavior of geese in flight. In the space to the right of each fact, write down what you think the fact implies for human organizational behavior.

Transcribed from a speech by Angeles Arrien, based on the work of Milton Olson and given at the 1991 Organization Development Network conference. Created in 1998 by Don Clark.

Leadership secrets from foreign penguins
Penguins show how leadership by example works
by David Leonhardt

There's a brand new fitness program at the San Francisco Zoo—a program that sort of just took off on its own without any goals or leadership from the zookeeper. This fitness program is for the birds, but it carries a **leadership lesson** for all of us.

The birds are penguins. Penguins are supposed to swim. In fact, 46 penguins at the San Francisco zoo have been taking regular dips in the pool to cool off and keep their feathers sleek. Ah, ain't life grand. Lie around, eat, swim, rest, eat, swim, relax, eat, swim.

Until six "bodybuilder" penguins moved in from Ohio. The newcomers jumped into the pool and swam. And swam. And swam. In fact, those six penguins kept swimming laps all day long. Day after day. They must have been using a very effective antiperspirant.

The newcomers would start early in the morning and keep swimming in circles until they would "stagger" out of the pool at dusk. What is most amazing, though, is that the six penguins have convinced the other 46 to join them. Hitherto "society" penguins are now swimming the whole day through like commoners.

What is the secret to the Ohio penguins' success? I don't speak "penguin" very well, but I think I overheard the following conversation:

"C'mon, what are you, a penguin or a rock?"

"Why, I'm a penguin, of course."

"You don't look like a penguin. All you do is sit around like a rock."

"That's not true. I swim…sometimes."

"Ha! A true penguin swims all day long. Pepperoni!" SPLASH!!

"Hey. I'm a real penguin, too."

"Who you shouting at, Percy?"

"That swimmer with too much adrenaline in his feathers. He says I'm not a real penguin because I don't eggplant enough."

"Oh, yeah? We'll show him, won't we, Percy?"

"You bet! Uh, how?"

"By out-swimming the showoff penguins." SPLASH!!"

"Oh, oh. I guess I better get swimming right creamy teacups." SPLASH!!

Foreign penguins show their leadership and their penguinhood

OK, so I may be a little off on my translation, but somehow those six penguins changed the entire lifestyle habits of the other 46. The zookeeper is reported by the wire service to have said, "We've completely lost control." The wire story quotes an aquatic biologist as saying she would be more surprised if the six had taught the other 46 how to jump through hoops—something few penguins do in the wild with any success.

The point is not that the 46 penguins have learned to swim, which they had always been doing as a leisurely pastime, but that they are now in full aquatic stampede mode…and that they were convinced by the other six to change their entire lifestyle. How did the six penguins do it?

Well, I was suspicious about penguins that come from Ohio. Everyone knows that penguins come from Antarctica. Last I could recall, Ohio was nowhere near Antarctica. Sure, it's cold in Ohio this time

THE NOBLE GIFT

of year, but not THAT cold. My atlas confirmed that Ohio is indeed still in the United States, not in Antarctica, meaning that these penguins were foreigners, perhaps victims of persecution—refugees from their homeland.

So these foreign penguins have come in and motivated the local penguins to live up to their full…ah…penguinhood. What an accomplishment! What success! And what great leadership lessons we can learn from this.

Lesson number one: don't be afraid to try new things and accept outside influences.

Lesson number two: be a penguin not a rock (unless, of course, you are a rock).

And lesson number three: don't give up. If six penguins can whip 46 homebodies into shape, imagine how you could kick-start your own fitness program (or any other goal you set your mind to.)

But don't count on learning success from penguins.

Team Building Quotes

We are most effective as a team when we compliment each other without embarrassment and disagree without fear.
—Unknown

Wearing the same shirts doesn't make a team.
—Buchholz and Roth

A team is more than a collection of people. It is a process of give and take.
—Barbara Glacel & Emile Robert Jr.

The basic building block of good teambuilding is for a leader to promote the feeling that every human being is unique and adds value.
—Unknown

Talent wins games, but teamwork and intelligence wins championships.
—Michael Jordan

None of us is as smart as all of us.
—Ken Blanchard

When a team outgrows individual performance and learns team confidence, excellence becomes a reality.
—Joe Paterno

A group becomes a team when each member is sure enough of himself and his contribution to praise the skill of the others.
—Norman S Hidle

*Coming together is a beginning.
Keeping together is progress.
Working together is success.*
—Henry Ford

Michael, if you can't pass, you can't play.
—Coach Dean Smith to Michael Jordan in his freshman year

We must all hang together, or assuredly, we shall all hang separately.
—Benjamin Franklin

The ratio of We's to I's is the best indicator of the development of a team.
—Lewis B. Ergen

A championship team is a team of champions.
—Unknown

Teamwork: Simply stated, it is less me and more we.
—Unknown

Teamwork is the fuel that allows common people to attain uncommon results.
—Unknown

THE NOBLE GIFT

Teams share the burden and divide the grief.
—Doug Smith

Never doubt that a small group of thoughtful, committed people can change the world. Indeed, it is the only thing that ever has.
—Margaret Mead

Teamwork doesn't tolerate the inconvenience of distance.
—Unknown

No one can whistle a symphony. It takes an orchestra to play it.
—H.E. Luccock

There is not I in Teamwork.
—Unknown

Wild ducks make a lot of noise, but they also have the sense to benefit from occasionally flying in formation.
—Unknown

It is amazing how much you can accomplish when it doesn't matter who gets the credit.
—Unknown

Teamwork divides the task and doubles the success.
—Unknown

Overcoming barriers to performance is how groups become teams.
—Unknown

Teamplayer: Once who unites others toward a shared destiny through sharing information and ideas, empowering others and developing trust.
—Dennis Kinlaw

Big Dog's Leadership Quotes

Managers are people who do things right, while leaders are people who do the right thing.
—Warren Bennis, Ph.D. "On Becoming a Leader"

If it's a good idea, go ahead and do it. It is much easier to apologize than it is to get permission.
—Admiral Grace Hopper

The most important quality in a leader is that of being acknowledged as such.
—Andre Maurois

You gain strength, courage and confidence by every experience in which you really stop to look fear in the face. You must do the thing you think you cannot do.
—Eleanor Roosevelt

Leadership in today's world requires far more than a large stock of gunboats and a hard fist at the conference table.
—Hubert H. Humphrey

All of the great leaders have had one characteristic in common: it was the willingness to confront unequivocally the major anxiety of their people in their time. This, and not much else, is the essence of leadership.
—John Kenneth Galbraith, U.S. economist "The Age of Uncertainty"

The real leader has no need to lead — he is content to point the way.
—Henry Miller

It's amazing how many cares disappear when you decide not to be something, but to be someone.
—Coco Chanel

Most of the ladies and gentlemen who mourn the passing of the nation's leaders wouldn't know a leader if they saw one. If they had the bad luck to come across a leader, they would find out that he might demand something from them, and this impertinence would put an abrupt and indignant end to their wish for his return.
—Lewis H. Lapham

Leadership consists not in degrees of technique but in traits of character; it requires moral rather than athletic or intellectual effort, and it imposes on both leader and follower alike the burdens of self-restraint.
—Lewis H. Lapham

I am a leader by default, only because nature does not allow a vacuum.
—Bishop Desmond Tutu

If one is lucky, a solitary fantasy can totally transform one million realities.
—Maya Angelou

People ask the difference between a leader and a boss... The leader works in the open, and the boss in covert. The leader leads, and the boss drives.
—Theodore Roosevelt

The final test of a leader is that he leaves behind him in other men the conviction and the will to carry on... The genius of a good leader is to leave behind him a situation which common sense, without the grace of genius, can deal with successfully.
—Walter Lippmann

There is no such thing as a perfect leader either in the past or present, in China or elsewhere. If there is one, he is only pretending, like a pig inserting scallions into its nose in an effort to look like an elephant.
—Liu Shao-ch'i

There's no such thing as a race and barely such a thing as an ethnic group. If we were dogs, we'd be the same breed... Trouble doesn't come from Slopes, Kikes, Niggers, Spics or White Capitalist Pigs; it comes from the heart.
—P. J. O'Rourke (b. 1947), U.S. journalist. Holidays in Hell, Introduction (1988).

Our flag is red, white and blue, but our nation is a rainbow-red, yellow, brown, black and white-and we're all precious in God's sight.
—Jesse Jackson (b. 1941), U.S. clergyman, civil rights leader. Speech, 16 July 1984.

If you obey all the rules, you miss all the fun.
—Katharine Hepburn

E pluribus unum. (Out of many, one.)
—Motto for the Seal of the United States. Adopted 20 June 1782, recommended by John Adams

Benjamin Franklin and Thomas Jefferson, 10 Aug. 1776, and proposed by Swiss artist Pierre Eugene du Simitière. It had originally appeared on the title page of the Gentleman's Journal (Jan. 1692).
If we cannot end now our differences, at least we can help make the world safe for diversity.
—John F. Kennedy (1917-63), U.S. Democratic politician, president. Speech, 10 June 1963, American

THE NOBLE GIFT

University, Washington, D.C., on Russo-American relations.

In organizations, real power and energy is generated through relationships. The patterns of relationships and the capacities to form them are more important than tasks, functions, roles, and positions.
—Margaret Wheatly *Leadership and the New Science*

Whoever is careless with the truth in small matters cannot be trusted with the important matters.
—Albert Einstein

Life is change. Growth is optional. Choose wisely.
—Karen Kaiser Clark

The quality of leadership, more than any other single factor, determines the success or failure of an organization.
—Fred Fiedler & Martin Chemers *Improving Leadership Effectiveness*

Don't be afraid to take a big step when one is indicated. You can't cross a chasm in two small steps.
—David Loyd George

There is no contest between the company that buys the grudging compliance of its work force and the company that enjoys the enterprising participation of its employees
—Ricardo Sempler

Excellence is not an accomplishment. It is a spirit, a never-ending process.
—Lawrence M. Miller

You will do foolish things, but do them with enthusiasm.
—Colette

The first responsibility of a leader is to define reality. The last is to say thank you.
—Max DePree

When what you are doing isn't working, you tend to do more of the same and with greater intensity.
—Dr. Bill Maynard & Tom Champoux *Heart, Soul and Spirit*

Every organization must be prepared to abandon everything it does to survive in the future.
—Peter Drucker

A friend of mine characterizes leaders simply like this: "Leaders don't inflict pain. They bear pain."
—Max DePree

Ah well! I am their leader, I really ought to follow them!
—Alexandre Auguste Ledru-Rollin

Dictators ride to and fro upon tigers which they dare not dismount. And the tigers are getting hungry.
—Winston Churchill

A new leader has to be able to change an organization that is dreamless, soulless and visionless…someone's got to make a wake up call.
—Warren Bennis

I used to think that running an organization was equivalent to conducting a symphony orchestra. But I don't think that's quite it; it's more like jazz. There is more improvisation.
—Warren Bennis

When the effective leader is finished with his work, the people say it happened naturally.
—Lao Tse

Most of what we call management consists of making it difficult for people to get their jobs done
—Peter Drucker

I start with the premise that the function of leadership is to produce more leaders, not more followers
—Ralph Nader

Never tell people how to do things. Tell them what to do and they will surprise you with their ingenuity
—George Patton

*To lead people, walk beside them…
As for the best leaders, the people do not notice their existence.
The next best, the people honor and praise.
The next, the people fear;
and the next, the people hate…
When the best leader's work is done the people say,
"We did it ourselves!"*
—Lao-tsu

Unless commitment is made, there are only promises and hopes… but no plans.
—Peter Drucker

Hell, there are no rules here—we're trying to accomplish something.
—Thomas A. Edison

Good plans shape good decisions. That's why good planning helps to make elusive dreams come true.
—Lester R. Bittel The Nine Master Keys of Management

Never mistake knowledge for wisdom. One helps you make a living; the other helps you make a life.
—Sandra Carey

Understanding human needs is half the job of meeting them.
—Adlai Stevenson

Leadership is understanding people and involving them to help you do a job. That takes all of the good characteristics, like integrity, dedication of purpose, selflessness, knowledge, skill, implacability, as well as determination not to accept failure.
—Admiral Arleigh A. Burke

Lead and inspire people. Don't try to manage and manipulate people. Inventories can be managed but people must be led.
—Ross Perot

We must become the change we want to see.
—Mahatma Gandhi

Drowning in data, yet starved of information
—Ruth Stanat in The Intelligent Organization

THE NOBLE GIFT

A competent leader can get efficient service from poor troops, while on the contrary an incapable leader can demoralize the best of troops.
—General of the Armies John J. Pershing

The quality of a person's life is in direct proportion to their commitment to excellence, regardless of their chosen field of endeavor.
—Vincent T. Lombardi

Where there is no vision, the people perish.
—Proverbs 29:18

I have lived some thirty years on this planet, and I yet to hear the first syllable of valuable or even earnest advice from my seniors.
—Henry David Thoreau

Kind words can be short and easy to speak, but their echoes are truly endless.
—Mother Theresa

An empowered organization is one in which individuals have the knowledge, skill, desire, and opportunity to personally succeed in a way that leads to collective organizational success.
—Stephen R. Covey, Principle-centered Leadership

Nearly all men can stand adversity, but if you want to test a man's character, give him power.
—Abraham Lincoln

One can never consent to creep when one feels an impulse to soar.
—Helen Keller

It is important that an aim never be defined in terms of activity or methods. It must always relate directly to how life is better for everyone… The aim of the system must be clear to everyone in the system. The aim must include plans for the future. The aim is a value judgment.
—W. Edwards Deming

The very essence of leadership is its purpose. And the purpose of leadership is to accomplish a task. That is what leadership does—and what it does is more important than what it is or how it works.
—Colonel Dandridge M. Malone

We know not where our dreams will take us, but we can probably see quite clearly where we'll go without them.
—Marilyn Grey

It is not a question of how well each process works, the question is how well they all work together.
—Lloyd Dobens and Clare Crawford-Mason *Thinking About Quality*

Do not follow where the path may lead. Go instead where there is no path and leave a trail.
—Muriel Strode

The leader has to be practical and a realist, yet must talk the language of the visionary and the idealist.
—Eric Hoffer

In war, three quarters turns on personal character and relations; the balance of manpower and materials counts only for the remaining quarter.
—Napoleon I

To manage a system effectively, you might focus on the interactions of the parts rather than their behavior taken separately.
—Russell L. Ackoff

The significant problems we face cannot be solved at the same level of thinking we were at when we created them.
—Albert Einstein

The final test of a leader is that he leaves behind him in other men the conviction and will to carry on.
—Walter J. Lippmann

Leadership should be born out of the understanding of the needs of those who would be affected by it.
—Marian Anderson

You may have afresh start any moment you choose, for this thing that we call 'failure' is not the falling down, but the staying down.
—Mary Pickford

People are more easily led than driven.
—David Harold Fink

Leadership has a harder job to do than just choose sides. It must bring sides together.
—Jesse Jackson

What is character but the determination of incident what is incident but the illustration of character?
—Henery James

The trouble is, if you don't risk anything, you risk even more.
—Erica Jong

No man will make a great leader who wants to do it all himself, or to get all the credit for doing it.
—Andrew Carnegie

The first responsibility of a leader is to define reality.
—Max DePree *The Art of Leadership*

Processes don't do work, people do.
—John Seely Brown

Leadership is practiced not so much in words as in attitude and in actions.
—Harold Geneen

The task of the leader is to get his people from where they are to where they have not been.
—Henry Kissinger

The quality of a leader is reflected in the standards they set for themselves.
—Ray Kroc, Founder of McDonald's

Jingshen is the Mandarin word for spirit and vivacity. It is an important word for those who would lead, because above all things, spirit and vivacity set effective organizations apart from those that will decline and die.
—James L. Hayes *Memos for Management: Leadership*

THE NOBLE GIFT

Uncertainty will always be part of the taking charge process.
—Harold Geneen

Genius is one percent inspiration and ninety-nine percent perspiration.
—Thomas Alva Edison

You can use all the quantitative data you can get, but you still have to distrust it and use your own intelligence and judgment.
—Alvin Toffler

Remember that it is far better to follow well than to lead indifferently.
—John G. Vance

The only real training for leadership is leadership.
—Anthony Jay

Quality has to be caused, not controlled.
—Philip Crosby *Reflections on Quality*

Probably my best quality as a coach is that I ask a lot of challenging questions and let the person come up with the answer.
—Phil Dixon

Don't be afraid of the space between your dreams and reality. If you can dream it you can make it so.
—Belva Davis

The future is taking shape now in our own beliefs and in the courage of our leaders. Ideas and leadership—not natural or social 'forces'—are the prime movers in human affairs.
—George Roche, *A World Without Heroes*

The art of leading, in operations large or small, is the art of dealing with humanity, of working diligently on behalf of men, of being sympathetic with them, but equally, of insisting that they make a square facing toward their own problems.
—S. L. A. Marshall *Men Against Fire*

And when we think we lead, we are most led.
—Lord Byron

Never hire or promote in your own image. It is foolish to replicate your strength and idiotic to replicate your weakness. It is essential to employ, trust, and reward those whose perspective, ability, and judgment are radically different from yours. It is also rare, for it requires uncommon humility, tolerance, and wisdom.
—Dee W. Hock, *Fast Company*

All serious daring starts from within.
—Eudora Welty

… As we, the leaders, deal with tomorrow, our task is not to try to make perfect plans. …Our task is to create organizations that are sufficiently flexible and versatile that they can take our imperfect plans and make them work in execution. That is the essential character of the learning organization.
—Gordon R. Sullivan & Michael V. Harper

In matters of style, swim with the current;
In matters of principle, stand like a rock.
—T. Jefferson

TAYLOR SCOTT COOK, PH.D.

If you think you can do a thing or that you cannot do a thing, in either case you are right.
—Henry Ford

When nothing is sure, everything is possible.
—Margaret Drabble

Think of managing change as an adventure. It tests your skills and abilities. It brings forth talent that may have been dormant. Change is also a training ground for leadership. When we think of leaders, we remember times of change, innovation and conflict. Leadership is often about shaping a new way of life. To do that, you must advance change, take risks and accept responsibility for making change happen.
—Charles E. Rice, CEO of Barnett Bank

Give us the tools, and we will finish the job.
—Winston Churchill

*Not everything that is faced can be changed.
But nothing can be changed until it is faced.*
—James Baldwin

The world is round and the place which may seem like the end, may also be only the beginning.
—Ivy Baker Priest

Copyright 1997 by Donald Clark
Created May 11, 1997. Updated March 1, 2000
http://www.nwlink.com/~donclark/leader/leadqot.html

Trends, Change & Future in Outdoor Education
By James Neill

Predictions: for Outdoor Education, Theory, & Research in 2003 & the Decade Ahead

1. Increasing disconnection between what academics interested in OE want to spend their time doing and what people and organizations in the field want from academics. Basically, academics want to study process, people in the field want evaluation outcomes.

2. Increasingly quiet library book service because the new generation of content is emerging in web-form. Basically, websites such as Active Reviewing, OutdoorEd.com, and the Outdoor Education Research & Evaluation Center are collectively serving hundreds of hits for research info each day, seemingly reducing traffic on listservs.

3. No significant changes in the quality or quantity of research and knowledge generation in traditional publication forms. Basically, it appears that there are no current major initiatives in building substantial new research programs or generation of new theory, etc. that are likely to bear significant fruition in the coming year. If I could pick one exception, it would be Keith Russell's work on Adventure Therapy research at the Wilderness Research Center, Uni of Idaho. Don't get me wrong—there is other good work around—but there is little work that is appearing as part of a long-term knowledge-building strategy. One study proves nothing —a series of cumulative studies can.

4. Increase in 'research at the fringes.' OE methodology remains compelling and needed; it will continue to attract increasing attention from alternative-thinking psychologists, social workers, educators, etc. and this will continue to foster a bubbling of 'research at the fringes'. Whilst tantalizing and interesting, such research is never going to go deep within OE to build a new platform of knowledge.

5. Domination of US-based research will begin to wane. In the beginning decades of OE since World War II, the UK generated the little research and theory-building that was conducted, then the US dominated in terms of programming, theory-building and research from the 1960s-1990s. This domination may have peaked. Little new seems to be emerging from the US, and there is too much focus on safety, liability, risk management, etc. issues. On the other hand there are positive signs of knowledge-building growth from the UK and Europe. A good example is the strong emergence of the refocused Journal of Adventure Education & Outdoor Leadership. In the longer-term, future decades could see the significant emergence of OE knowledge-building from Asia. The situation in Australia / New Zealand seems to be, like the US, somewhat stable or in possible decline.

6. Adventure Therapy —the one to watch. I have always felt optimism and excitement that within the practice and theory of adventure therapy, gems of knowledge can be discovered and polished which will shed new light on the way in which OE operates. With the upcoming 3rd International Adventure Therapy conference being held in North America, and the ongoing challenges of people coping with Western society, adventure therapy may emerge during the coming decade as a significant hothouse for the development of OE-related theory.

7. Graduate Training will be sought. As organizations mature and become increasingly sophisticated, they will have an increasing need to have managerial and director-level staff who have received post-graduate training. At the same time, universities are increasingly under the pump to bring in dollars, but most of this comes from undergraduate education. Thus, there will be a widening gap in the current decade between the needs and provision of graduate training in outdoor education.

8. The big and small OE organizations are endangered. The big organizations such as Scouts and Guides, Outward Bound, Project Adventure, and NOLS all faced a very tough decade in the 1990s. The big movers now are the medium-sized, specialist organizations. Small operators are going to continue to suffer greatly with all the increasing administrative challenges of running programs. But it is the very success of the big organizations which has spawned this new generation, and they will not become extinct because they have some sound ideas —they will simply continue to adapt and fractionate.

9. The possible connections between outdoor education and other fields will become more apparent. In the global, multiple age, a key strength to survival and evolution is investing in connections. Thus, connections between OE and other fields will emerge as increasingly important in the coming decade.

10. The role and purpose of nature in outdoor education will become more apparent. As society becomes more disconnected from natural environments, the primary importance of human experience in nature becomes more highly valued and studied. Whilst the US-dominance of outdoor education during the 1960's-1990's lead to adventure programming approaches which place little emphasis on human relationship with nature, it is predicted that the role of nature will emerge during the next decade as being more critical in OE theory and research.

CREDITS AND SOURCES

REFERENCES

Carlson, R. E. (1980). Innovations for the future: Where have we come from and where are we going? *The Bradford Papers 1980.* http://www.indiana.edu/~outdoor/bponline/bp1980/bp80carl.doc

Priest, S., & Gass, M. (2001). *The future of adventure programming.* Adventure Safety International.

Southern Connecticut State University (n. d.) *Future role of recreation and leisure studies.* http://www.southernct.edu/departments/recreationandleisure/future.htm

Watters, R. (1997). Changing Times in Outdoor Education: An Essay. *In Proceedings of the 1997 International Conference on Outdoor Recreation and Education,* Rob Jones and Brian Wilkinson (ed.) Association of Outdoor Recreation and Education, Boulder, 1998, pp. 228-230.

WORKS CITED

Chapter 1

Goldenberg, Marni. "Outdoor and Risk Educational Practices" University of Minnesota-unpublished Doctoral Dissertation. 23 Oct. 2005 <http://www.rbff.org/educational/BPE9.pdf.>

Cited in the work of Goldenberg;

Buell, L. 1983. "Outdoor Leadership Competency: A Manual for Self-Assessment and Staff Evaluation." Greenfield, MA: Environmental Awareness Publication.

Goldenberg, Marni. "Outdoor and Risk Educational Practices" University of Minnesota—unpublished Doctoral Dissertation. 24 Feb. 2006 <http://www.rbff.org/educational/BPE9.pdf>

Hattie, J., H. Marsh, J. Neill, and G. Richards. "Adventure education and Outward Bound: Out-of class experiences that make a lasting difference." Review of Educational Research, 67 (1), 43-87. 1997

Mendence, D. 1979. "An integrated-interdisciplinary model in outdoor education for higher education." Unpublished dissertation, University of Northern Colorado, Greeley, Colorado 1979

Priest, S. "<u>Outdoor Leadership Training in Higher Education</u>." Journal of Experiential Education, 11 (1), 42-47. 1998

Shiner, J."<u>Developing Professional Leadership in Outdoor Recreation</u>." Unpublished doctoral dissertation, State University of New York, Syracuse, NewYork..1970

Swiderski, M. "<u>Outdoor leadership competencies identified by Outdoor Leaders in Five Eastern Regions.</u>" Unpublished doctoral dissertation, University of Oregon, Eugene, Oregon 1981

Chapter 2

Bennis, Warren. and Nanus, Burt. "<u>Leaders: The Strategies for Taking Charge</u>" 1997. Dec. 12, 2005 <http://www.nwlink.com/~donclark/leader/leadchg.html>

Cohen, William. "30 Vital Leadership Actions.." 2003. Dec. 12,2005 <http://www.stuffofheroes.com/30_vital_leadership_actions.htm—>

Chapter 3

Cook, T. Scott. "<u>The Winds of Change—Circle Theory</u>": Working with Groups, 2005. Unpublished Thesis.

Tomb, Howard. "**Expedition Behavior**" -The Finer Points. April 17, 2006. <http://www.radford.edu/~recparks/faculty/behavior.htm—>

Tuckman, B. "Developmental Sequence in Small Groups." Psychological Bulletin, 63 (1965): 384-399.

Tuckman, B. & Jensen, M. (1977) "Stages of Small Group Development. Group and Organizational Studies." 2, 419-427

Drury, J & Bonner B.—(1992), *The Backcountry Classroom*—Wilderness Education Association, <u>Expedition Behavior</u>, Page 51-53

Chapter 4

"Appalachian Mountain Club Mountain "Leadership Guide Student Manual 2005." <u>Leaders and Groups</u>" Feb. 06 <http://www.outdoors.org/pdf/upload edu-mlshandbook-2005.pdf Page 3>

"Appalachian Mountain Club <u>Outdoor Leader Handbook</u>." 2005, Feb. 12, 2006 <http://www.amcsem.org/pdf/amcleadershiphandbook.pdf> page 5

THE NOBLE GIFT

"Appalachian Mountain Club Mountain Leadership School Student Manual." <u>Screening Participants</u> 2004 <http://www.outdoors.org/pdf/upload/ edu-mlshandbook-2005.pdf> Page 28

Child Development Institute, "<u>Stages of Social-Emotional Development</u>." March10, 2006 <http://www.childdevelopmentinfo.com/development/erickson.shtml>

Messina,J, & Messina ,C.—"<u>Overcoming Fears</u>" 2001, 12 Oct. 2006 <<u>www.tampabay.rr.com</u>/overcomingfears>
Wikipedia dictionary 2006—"<u>Definition of Fear</u>"—<www.wikipedia.com>

Chapter 5

Cook, T. Scott . "<u>Wilderness Outdoor Leadership Fundamentals : Learnership</u>" 2004: Unpublished Training Manual.

Foster, T. "<u>Outdoor Center of New England, ACA Instructor Trainer Clinic</u>" 1991

Kolb, D. A. "<u>Experiential Learning: Experience as the source of learning and Development</u>." New Jersey: Prentice Hall 1984

Larson, K.—"<u>**LIFESTYLE** Mindsets: Understanding Yourself Better</u>" <http://www.virginactive.co.za/get_healthy/lifestyle_mindsets.htm>

Scholl, R. "<u>How People Learn</u>" 2001 Source unknown

Chapter 6

Cook, T. Scott. Wilderness Experiences Unlimited 2004—. "<u>Wilderness Outdoor Leadership Fundamentals —Mission Statement</u> ." Unpublished Training Manual

Neil, J.—"Outdoor Education, Ethics, & Moral Development" www.wilderdom.com

References cited in work of James Neil

Bureau of Land Management (2002). *Outdoor ethics and Leave No Trace.*

DeZeeuw, J. (2002). Masters thesis, University of New Hampshire, Durham, NH.

Gass, M. & Garvey, D. (2001). Poster presented to the Coalition for the Outdoors Research Symposium.

Garvey, D. (*). PhD thesis.

Giampietro, P. (2001). Masters thesis, University of New Hampshire, Durham,

Hunt, J. S. (1990). *Ethical issues in experiential education* (2nd ed.). Boulder, CO: The Association for Experiential Education.

Yerkes, R. & Haras, K. (1997). *Outdoor education and environmental responsibility*. ERIC Digest.

New York State Outdoor Guides Association, "Mission Statement & Ethics." 2003 <http://www.nysoga.com/codeofethics.html> 12 Oct. 2005

Officers Training Manual; "Ethical Reasoning" 2002. 12 Oct. 2005 <https://atiam.train.army.mil/soldierPortal/atia/adlsc/view/public/4788-1/fm/22-100/ch4.htm>

Chapter 7

Nikitina, Arina. "Goal Setting Guide." 2004. 7 Nov. 2005 <http://www.goal-setting-guide.com/goal-writing.html>

Rushall, B. S. "Introduction to goal-setting skills *Mental skills training*" *for sports*< http://www.rohan.sdsu.edu/dept/coachsci/csa/vol22/rushall3.htm > 1995. Spring Valley, CA: Sports Science Associates. 10 Nov. 2005

Chapter 8

Martin, C. Cashel, M. Wagstaff and M. Breunig, 2006., et al. *Outdoor Leadership: Theory & Practice*. Pages 143—145 Reprinted with permission from Human Kinetics: (Champaign. IL). Works Cited in original work of; Cashel, C., Martin, B., Wagstaff, M., Brenig, M. (2006)

Drury, J. & Holmlund, E. *The camper's guide: To outdoor pursuits*. Sagamore Publishing: Champaign, IL. 1997

Ford, P., & Blanchard, J. *Leadership and Administration of Outdoor Pursuits* (2nd ed.). Venture Publishing. 1993

Harvey, M. *The National Outdoor Leadership School's Wilderness Guide*. Simon & Schuster: NY, NY. 1999

Pearson, C.. *NOLS cookery*. Stackpole Books: Mechanicsburg, PA. 1997

Priest, S. & Gass, M. A. Effective Leadership in Adventure Programming Human Kinetics: Champaign, IL. 1997

Leave No Trace —Center for Outdoor Ethics: "Informational Brochure" 2004. 15 March 2006 <http://www.lnt.org/programs/lnt7/index.html>

Wilderness Education Association. "WEA NSP Curriculum 15 March 2006 <http://www.weainfo.org/nsp.html>

Outward Bound—"Women of Courage Participant Information Package"
15 March 2006 <http://www.outwardbound.com/pdf/woc_pre-course.pdf>
<http://www.outwardbound.com/pdf/woc_medical.pdf>

AMC Outdoor Leader Handbook "Screening Participants."page 28, 2005 16 March 2006-05-10 <http://www.outdoors.org/pdf/upload/edu-mlshandbook-2005.pdf>

Chapter 9
Priddy, A. and Watters R, "Coffee Can Car Survival Kit":
2004. 23 April 2006<http://www.isu.edu/outdoor/survival.htm>

Watters R. "The Ten Essentials." 2005. 23 April 2006.
<http://www.isu.edu/outdoor/ten.htm>
Cited in work of Watters—"The Mountaineers Article" 1930-
<www.mountaineers.org>

Watters R. "Outdoor Packing Lists" 2005. 23 April 2006.
<http://www.isu.edu/outdoor/packlist.htm>

Watters R. "Outdoor Packing Lists"1998. 23 April 2006.
<http://www.isu.edu/outdoor/packlist.htm> Contributors: Byrd,M.
Eperlding, Matt.

Watters R. River, "Rafting and Kayaking trips." 2004. 23 April 2006.
<http://www.isu.edu/outdoor/packlist.htm>
Cited in the work of Watters, R.; The Whitewater River Book: A Guide to Techniques, Camping and Safety

Watters R. "Ski Camping: A Guide to the Delights of Backcountry Skiing."2004.
23 April 2006 <http://www.isu.edu/outdoor/ski.htm>

Chapter 10
Barnard, R. "Risk Management Manual: Federation of Ontario Naturalists" March 2001
Works Cited in Barnard, R.—"Risk Management Manual"
Bjarnason et al.—"Organizing Events, Avoiding Risk and Promoting Safety"
Borden and Elliot.—"Duties and Liabilities of Directors"
Bromwich—."Insuring Business Risks in Canada"
C.A. Magazine. "Effective Governance."
Rocall and Gertsch-."Leadership Basics: A Guide to Leading Groups of Volunteers." Federation of Ontario Naturalists.
Sierra Club USA—"Sexual Abuse Risk Management Issues."
Underwriter's Manual. St. Paul Canada—"Risk Management Manual" Insurance Institute of Ontario.

Curtis R, "Outdoor Safety Management" 2002. 28 April 2006 <http://www.outdoorsafety.org/articles/Article2.asp?ArticleID=121&TextFilename=2000/2000-121-1.asp>

Curtis R. & Cline P. 2002 "Risk Management for Organizations: Keeping the Ship Afloat" 2002. 29 April 2006 <http://www.outdoored.com/articles/article.aspx?ArticleID=136>

Chapter 11

Blackwood R.—"Emergency First Aid in the Wilderness, begins with your own personal first aid kit" 17 Feb. 2006 <http://www.outdoorclub.org/Firstaid.html>

Silver, J.—'AMC Mountain Leadership Manual -First Aid and Accident Scene Management" 1998 17 Feb .2006 <http://www.outdoors.org/pdf/upload/edu-mlshandbook—2005.pdf>

Silver, J. -AMC Mountain Leadership Manual—"Weather and Forecasting" 1998 18 Feb. 2006 <http://www.outdoors.org/pdf/upload/edu-mlshandbook-2005.pdf >page 66

National Weather Service—"Wind Chill Chart" 2001. 16 March 2006 <http://www.weather.gov/om/windchill/>

Kosseff A-, AMC Mountain Leadership guide "Lightning Guidelines" 1998 16 March 2006 <http://www.outdoors.org/pdf/upload/edu-mlshandbook-2005.pdf > Page 69

Silver, J.AMC Mountain Leadership Manual "General First Aid Procedures" 1998 17 March 2006. <http://www.outdoors.org/pdf/upload/edu-mlshandbook-2005.pdf> Page 70

Cook, T. Scott—Wilderness Experiences Unlimited—"Staff training manual—Wound Management" 2004

Chapter 12

Rogers, C. "*Freedom to Learn: A View Of What Education Might Become.*" Columbus, Ohio: 1969 C. E. Merrill.

Buell, L, Unpublished Doctoral Dissertation "Competency Based Outdoor Leadership"1969

Neill,J. "Characteristics of effective Outdoor Education Instructors" 22 March 2006 <http://www.wilderdom.com/facilitation/CharacteristicsInstructors.htm>

Greenaway, R. "Facilitation and Reviewing in Outdoor Education" in Barnes, P. and Sharp, R. (Eds) The RHP Companion to Outdoor Education Russell House Publishing 2004

Cited in Original Material by; Greenaway, R. "Facilitation and Reviewing in Outdoor Education" in Barnes, P. and Sharp, R. (Eds) The RHP Companion to Outdoor Education Russell House Publishing 2004

Greenaway R.. "Why Adventure? The Role and Value of Outdoor Adventure in Young People's Personal and Social Development." 1995

Barret, J. & Greenaway, R. "Why Adventure? The Role and Value of Outdoor Adventure in Young People's Personal and Social Development. Coventry": Foundation for Outdoor Adventure. 1995
Charlton D. "Adventure Education." (essay) North Wales: CELMI. 1990

Cornell, J. "Sharing Nature with Children Beyond didactics: a reconnaissance of experiential learning." Exley/Amanda Publications 1979.

Cornell, J. "Sharing the Joy of Nature." Dawn Publications. 1989

Greenaway, R. "Playback: A Guide to Reviewing Activities." Windsor: The Duke of Edinburgh's Award. 1993

Heron, J. "The Complete Facilitator's Handbook." London: Kogan 1999.

Hovelynck J. "Australian Journal of Outdoor Education, 6, (1), 4-12. 2001

Hunter, D., et al "The Zen of Groups: The Handbook for People Meeting with a Purpose." Auckland: Tandem Press. 1992

Keighley, P. "Learning Through First Hand Experience Out of Doors: the contribution which outdoor education can make to children's learning as part of the National Curriculum." Sheffield: National Association for Outdoor Education. 1998

Knapp, C. "Lasting Lessons: A Teacher's Guide to Reflecting on Experience." Charleston, ERIC/CRESS. 1992

Kolb, D.A. "Experiential Learning: Experience as the Source of Development." New Jersey: Prentice-Hall. 1984

Mortlock, C." Beyond Adventure." Milnthorpe: Cicerone Press. 2001

Priest, S., & Gass, M. "*Effective Leadership in Adventure Programming*" Champaign: Human Kinetics. 1997

Ringer, M. (2002) "Group Action: The Dynamics of Groups in Therapeutic, Educational and Corporate Settings." London and Philadelphia: Jessica Kingsley 2002

Chapter 13
As referenced in Chapters 1–12

Appendices
Wilderness Accident Report formats from www.wilderdom.com/reports Clark, D. "Team Building & Leadership quotes" 1997. 27 Nov. 2005 <http://www.nwlink.com/~donclark/leader/leadqot.html>

Leonhardt, D. "Leadership secrets from foreign penguins" 2 Jan. 2006 http://www.themanager.org/HR/Leadership_secrets.htm

Unknown "Leadership Lessons The Nature of Geese," 2 Jan. 2006 <http://www.guidedones.com/issues/snippets/geese10.htm>

Neill, J "Trends, Change & Future in Outdoor Education Predictions: for Outdoor Education, Theory, & Research in 2003 & the Decade Ahead" 2003. 22 19 Jan. 2006 <www.wilderdom.com>

Works cited in article by Neill J. 2003

Carlson, R. E. (1980). "Innovations for the future: Where have we come from and where are we going?" *The Bradford Papers 1980*. 12 Dec. 2005 Http: www.isu/Indiana.edu/~outdoor/bponline/bp1980/bp80carl.doc>
Priest, S., & Gass, M. "*The future of adventure programming.*" Adventure Safety International. 2001

Southern Connecticut State University (n. d.) "*Future role of recreation and leisure studies.*" 2004 28 April 2007 <http://www.southernct.edu/departments/recreationandleisure/future.htm>

Watters, R. "Changing Times in Outdoor Education: An Essay. *In Proceedings of the 1997 International Conference on Outdoor Recreation and Education*," Rob Jones and Brian Wilkinson —Association of Outdoor Recreation and Education, 1997

Every task needs a worthy conclusion! T.S.Cook
Life is change. Growth is optional. Choose wisely.
—Karen Kaiser Clark

PHOTO CREDITS

Cover—Ryan Crocket—Author, and Skip Armstrong on Rio Picaure in Costa Rica
Preface—Ryan Crocket Lower Picaure River
Introduction Ryan Crocket—Upper Upper Picaure
Chapter One Ryan Crocket
Chapter One T. Scott Cook—Kayak Class being led by Matt Preye—Deerfield MA.
Chapter 2 Photo Ryan Crockett
Chapter 4 Photo Ryan Crockett
Chapter 10 Photo T. Scott Cook